A Special Issue of
Cognition and Emotion

The Cognitive Psychology of Depression

Edited by
Ian H. Gotlib
Department of Psychology, Stanford University, USA

Co-Editors
Howard S. Kurtzman and Mary C. Blehar
National Institute of Mental Health, USA

Routledge
Taylor & Francis Group
LONDON AND NEW YORK

First published 1997 by Psychology Press Ltd

Published 2018 by Routledge
2 Park Square, Milton Park, Abingdon, Oxon OX14 4RN
52 Vanderbilt Avenue, New York, NY 10017

First issued in paperback 2018

Routledge is an imprint of the Taylor & Francis Group, an informa business

ISSN 0269-9931
ISBN 13: 978-1-138-87733-7 (pbk)
ISBN 13: 978-0-86377-973-2 (hbk)

Index by Christine Boylan

Contents

*This book is also a special issue of the journal Cognition and Emotion which forms issues 5 and 6 of Volume 11 (1997). The page numbers used here are taken from the journal and so begin with p.497

COGNITION AND EMOTION, 1997, *11* (5/6), 497–500

The Cognitive Psychology of Depression: Introduction to the Special Issue

Ian H. Gotlib

Stanford University, USA

Howard S. Kurtzman and Mary C. Blehar

National Institute of Mental Health, USA

Of all the psychiatric disorders, depression is by far the most common. Each year, more than 100 million people world-wide develop clinically recognisable depression. During the course of a lifetime, it is estimated that anywhere between 8 and 18% of the general population will experience at least one clinically significant episode of depression (Kessler, McGonagle, Swartz, Blazer, & Nelson, 1993; Weissman, Bruce, Leaf, Florio, & Holzer, 1991), and that approximately twice as many women than men will be affected by this disorder (Blehar & Oren, 1995; Weissman et al. 1991). The costs of depression are significant. In terms of economic costs, for example, Rice and Miller (1995) estimate that affective disorders places a burden of over 30 billion dollars per year in the American economy, accounting for about 21% of costs for all mental illness. Depression also has a significant personal cost. Some estimates of suicide attempts for those with severest recurrent mood disorders range as high as 15% (Hirschfeld & Davidson, 1988). From a somewhat different perspective, Rice and Miller (1995) estimate that 60% of suicides are due to mood disorders. In fact, the mortality risk from all causes appears to be considerably elevated in depressed individuals (e.g. Murphy, Monson, Olivier, Sobol, & Leighton, 1987). Finally, depression is a recurrent disorder, with up to 75% of depressed patients experiencing more than one episode over the course of their lives (Belsher & Costello, 1988; Keller, 1985).

Requests for reprints should be sent to Ian Gotlib, Department of Psychology, Bldg. 420, Jordan Hall, Stanford University, Stanford, CA 94305, USA; email: gotlib@pysch. stanford.edu.

Neither this paper nor any other in this issue of Cognition and Emotion reflects the official policies or positions of the National Institute of Mental Health or of any other component of the United States Government.

The heterogeneity of the affective disorders makes it unlikely that a single set of factors can adequately explain the full range of phenomena associated with depression. Mood disorders epitomise complex psychobiological adaptations; consequently, investigators examining depression have pursued both biological and psychological approaches to understanding the aetiology, maintenance, and treatment of this disorder. Over the last two decades there has been a swell of research designed to examine cognitive factors in depression. The impetus for this line of research comes from theories that have implicated cognitive functioning in the aetiology and maintenance of depression (e.g. Beck 1967, 1976; Bower, 1981, 1992; Teasdale, 1988). Increasingly, this research has drawn both theoretically and methodologically from mainstream cognitive psychology, including work in social cognition and cognitive neuropsychology.

In an effort to examine the current state of research and theory in this area, the National Institute of Mental Health held a workshop on "The cognitive psychology of depression" in Bethesda, Maryland, in September 1995. Fourteen leading basic and clinical researchers participated, presenting and discussing their most recent work (see Kurtzman & Blehar, 1996 for a summary of the workshop). This Special Issue of *Cognition and Emotion* is a direct result of that workshop. Each of the nine articles in this issue is authored or co-authored by a participant at the conference (although not all participants contributed a paper to this issue).

Reflecting the breadth of work in this area, the papers address diverse aspects of the relation between cognition and depression. They examine attention, memory, and schematic processing, as well as transient mood effects and underlying brain activity. Moreover, they examine a diverse set of samples, including children and young and middle-aged adults, encompassing a range of severity of depressive symptoms.

The first three papers in this issue involve an empirical examination of attentional and/or memory functioning in depressed individuals. In the first paper, Segal and Gemar use a modified version of the emotion Stroop task to examine the cognitive organisation of self-relevant material in depressed patients before and after their participation in a course of cognitive behaviour therapy. Gilboa and Gotlib also utilise a modified version of the emotion Stroop task to assess negative biases in attention and memory in currently nondepressed individuals who had a history of depression. Alloy and Abramson and their colleagues examine negative biases in the processing of self-referential information in college students who were identified as cognitively vulnerable to depression. Hertel then discusses depression-related problems in attentional control for neutral information and how they may be related to the bias toward negative self-relevant information.

The next two papers highlight the role of mood in the production of cognitive biases in depressed individuals. Miranda and Gross present a detailed and critical discussion of what has come to be referred to as the mood-state dependent hypothesis (i.e. that cognitive vulnerability factors for depression are present but remain inaccessible until they are activated by negative mood), and suggest a number of directions for future research. Eich, Macaulay, and Lam extend the study of mood dependent memory to a sample of patients with rapid-cycling bipolar disorder, addressing questions concerning the generalisability to serious depression of findings obtained with nonclinical samples.

Garber and Robinson extend the study of cognitive vulnerability for depression to children of unipolar depressed mothers. They examine a wide range of cognitive constructs in these children and relate the children's functioning to the chronicity of depression in their mothers. Heller and Nitschke broaden the study of cognitive functioning in depression by providing explicit links among cognitive deficits and biases, sad mood, and specific regional brain activity. Finally, Gotlib, Kurtzman, and Blehar offer a closing commentary concerning both issues raised by this group of papers, and issues faced by researchers in the area of cognition and depression more generally.

REFERENCES

Beck, A.T. (1967). *Depression*. New York: Hoeber Medical.

Beck, A.T. (1976). *Cognitive therapy and the emotional disorders*. New York: International Universities Press.

Belsher, G., & Costello, C.G. (1988). Relapse after recovery from unipolar depression: A critical review. *Psychological Bulletin, 104*, 84–96.

Blehar, M.C., & Oren, D.A. (1995). Women's increased vulnerability to mood disorders: Integrating psychobiology and epidemiology. *Depression, 3*, 3–12.

Bower, G.H. (1981). Mood and memory. *American Psychologist, 36*, 129–148.

Bower, G.H. (1992). How might emotions affect learning? In S.A. Christianson (Ed.), *Handbook of emotion and memory* (pp. 3–31). Hillsdale, NJ: Lawrence Erlbaum Associates Inc.

Hirschfeld, R.M.A., & Davidson, L. (1988). Risk factors for suicide. In A.J. Frances and R.E. Hales (Eds.), *Review in psychiatry* (pp. 307–333). Washington, DC: American Psychiatric Press.

Keller, M.B. (1985). Chronic and recurrent affective disorders: Incidence, course and influencing factors. In D. Kemali & G. Recagni (Eds.), *Chronic treatments in neuropsychiatry*. New York: Raven.

Kessler, R.C., McGonagle, K.A., Swartz, M., Blazer, D.G., & Nelson, C.B. (1993). Sex and depression in the National Comorbidity Survey. I: Lifetime prevalence, chronicity and recurrence. *Journal of Affective Disorders, 29*, 85–96.

Kurtzman, H.S., & Blehar, M.C. (1996). New research on cognition and depression. *Psychotherapy and Rehabilitation Research Bulletin* (NIMH), *5*, 11–13.

Murphy, J.M., Monson, R.R., Olivier, D.C., Sobol, A.M., & Leighton, A.H. (1987). Affective disorders and mortality. *Archives of General Psychiatry, 44,* 473–480.

Rice, D.P., & Miller, L.S. (1995). The economic burden of affective disorders. *British Journal of Psychiatry, 166,* 34–42.

Teasdale, J.D. (1988). Cognitive vulnerability to persistent depression. *Cognition and Emotion, 2,* 247–274.

Weissman, M.M., Bruce, M.L., Leaf, P.J., Florio, L.P., & Holzer, C., III (1991). Affective disorders. In L.N. Robins & D.A. Regier (Eds.), *Psychiatric disorders in America* (pp. 53–80). New York: Free Press.

COGNITION AND EMOTION, 1997, *11* (5/6), 501–516

Changes in Cognitive Organisation for Negative Self-referent Material Following Cognitive Behaviour Therapy for Depression: A Primed Stroop Study

Zindel V. Segal and Michael Gemar

Clarke Institute of Psychiatry and University of Toronto, Canada

Cognitive organisation of self-relevant material was examined in 55 depressed patients before and after cognitive behaviour therapy (CBT) for depression. The paradigm used was a version of the Stroop task modified to permit the to-be-colour-named self-relevant target adjectives to be primed by emotional phrases which varied according to their degree of self-description. Analyses indicated that those patients who were less depressed at post-treatment showed less colour-naming interference for self-descriptive negative targets primed by self-descriptive negative phrases (when compared with nonself-descriptive primes). In contrast, patients who were still highly depressed after treatment showed higher levels of negative interference, as has been found in nontreated depressed patients. These findings support the hypothesis that negative information about the self is highly interconnected in the cognitive system of depressed patients and suggests possible changes to the organisation or accessibility of cognitive structures; changes which may result from successful treatment for depression.

INTRODUCTION

Cognitive models of depression focus not only on the content of depressed patients' thoughts but also on the manner in which information is processed and the types of cognitive organisations that might support depressive symptoms. The specific nature of the organisation of cognitive content

Request for reprints should be sent to Zindel Segal or Michael Gemar, Clarke Institute of Psychiatry, 250 College Street, Toronto, Ontario M5T-1R8, Canada.

This research was supported by a grant awarded to the first author from the John D. and Catherine T. MacArthur Foundation, Program on Conscious and Unconscious Mental Processes. The authors would like to thank Susan Andersen, Peter Salovey, and Len Horowitz for their valuable input to this work.

can be conceptualised in a number of different ways. Perhaps the most dominant view is that of Beck (1967), who has described how the thinking of depressed patients reflects a negative bias towards the self, the future, and the world. According to this clinical cognitive theory, this bias is the product of a recently activated cognitive structure or schema containing depressive self-attributes. Alternative accounts have used proceduralist or connectionist models of representation that place less emphasis on stable local representations than does the schema approach (Hertel & Milan, 1994; Teasdale & Barnard, 1993). Central to all of these accounts, however, is the importance of interconnected cognitive content in the patterns of thinking often seen in depression. These cognitive features are seen as arising not simply from negative mood *per se*, or from a generally greater accessibility of negatively valenced cognitive concepts. Rather, the individual's experience with specific negative material determines the way in which this information is interrelated and interacts, and it is this interconnectedness among specific negative material which contributes to the disturbances of mood and thought that characterise depression.

One measure that has been frequently employed to assess cognitive-processing in emotional disorders is the Stroop colour-naming task, especially a modification of this task that allows for the use of emotionally laden stimuli. On this task, depressed patients generally take longer to name the presentation colour of negative words than positive or neutral words (Gotlib & McCann, 1984; Williams & Nulty, 1986), whereas non-depressed controls show no difference in colour-naming speed as a function of the valence of the word. The greater interference shown by depressed patients for negative material is thought to result from extended processing of the semantic content of stimuli, perhaps because this material is more accessible for the subject, and therefore harder to suppress in favour of rapid colour-naming (Williams, Mathews, & MacLeod, 1996).

Although the Emotional Stroop paradigm can indicate the extent of semantic-processing of valenced material, this particular methodology is unable to examine the more detailed question of whether material is organised in some fashion. To look at this question, some form of priming methodology can be used to advantage, by examining the effect that prior presentation of material has on the processing of later-presented items. Segal, Gemar, Truchon, Guirguis, and Horowitz (1995) further modified the Emotional Stroop paradigm to incorporate such a priming design in which the colour-naming of a target word, relevant to the individual's view of self, was preceded by a prime word thought to be related or unrelated to the subject's self-concept. By previously activating one element in the depressive cognitive system, other interconnected and related elements of the organisation may also become activated, thus influencing performance on these related elements. In this way, the degree of interconnection between elements in the self-representation can be studied. Within a primed Stroop paradigm, if a prime is related to a target item presented in colour, the prime's influence should be demonstrated by an increase in the time it takes to name the target's colour, because the target's semantic content, activated by the prime, should interfere. Using this approach, Segal et al. (1995) found that depressed patients showed increased interference for negative self-referent material when it was primed by similar negative information than when it was primed by negative information that was not self-descriptive. These results indicate that negative self-attributes are more highly organised in the self-concept of depressed patients than attributes that are negative but not particularly descriptive of the self.

These findings are consistent with accounts of depression that emphasise the importance of cognitive organisation in the maintenance of the disorder. Because cognitive behaviour therapy (CBT) is thought to alter the negative nature of such organisations (Beck, 1967), successful treatment of this nature should reduce the strong associations between negative elements in an individual's cognitive system, and thus affect the amount of interference noted on such tasks as the primed Stroop task.

Several studies have examined changes in performance on the unprimed emotional Stroop colour-naming task associated with a variety of treatments for a number of clinical disorders. Mathews, Mogg, Kentish, and Eysenck (1995) reported that treatment significantly reduced selective interference effects for threatening words in anxious patients. Mattia, Heimberg, and Hope (1993) found similar results for social phobic patients who had responded to either CBT group treatment or phenelzine. In the eating disorders, Cooper and Fairburn (1994) have shown that selective processing of food and weight information was reduced following either behaviour therapy, cognitive behaviour therapy, or interpersonal therapy.

One of the first studies to examine the question of effect of treatment in the area of depression was reported by Gotlib and Cane (1987), who found that interference for negatively valenced target words was reduced following discharge from hospital where patients had received a variety of different treatments for depression. Their study is especially relevant in the current context because they included a priming manipulation, but found no effect of priming on Stroop performance.

Similar changes toward normal performance after treatment have been found using other measures and paradigms. In one instance, Pace and Dixon (1993) tested depressed college students before and after cognitive therapy for depression and found that self-referent judgements and recall were reduced following successful treatment, but neither the Stroop task nor measures of cognitive organisation were included in their study.

At present, there are no studies in which Stroop interference scores in depressed patients have been examined following a purely psychological intervention designed to reduce depression. Furthermore, only Gotlib and Cane (1987) addressed the question of changes in the way self-information is organised after successful treatment, but using a mixed treatment group (i.e. psychotherapy and/or pharmacotherapy) which may not be optimal to detect such changes. The current research, a follow-up to that carried out by Segal et al. (1995), is designed to address these issues.

In the present research, we used the group of depressed patients studied by Segal et al. (1995). This group showed selective processing on the primed Emotional Stroop task for negative self-referent adjectives. These individuals were given CBT, and then retested on the primed Emotional Stroop task. According to the cognitive model of depression (Beck, 1967), successful treatment should be accompanied by modification or reduction of depressive knowledge structures. This account argues that the accessibility of, or processing of, negative self-referent material should diminish in order for the clinical symptoms to change. We would predict that reduction in level of depression with CBT should lead to a reduction in interference for negative self-referent adjectives primed by self-descriptive material. As far as we are aware, this is the first study to examine post-treatment differences in cognitive organisation (and Stroop responding) following CBT for depression.

METHOD

Subjects

Fifty-five depressed subjects were tested in the present research, with the gender distribution being 39 women and 16 men. All subjects were between the ages of 18 and 65 years (mean age = 34.5, SD = 10.4), met a minimum eighth-grade education requirement or were able to complete the assessment measures unassisted, and their primary language was English (the mean score on the Hartford–Shipley measure of verbal IQ was 107.8, SD = 11.4). All patients were drawn from the clinical services of the Clarke Institute of Psychiatry, Toronto, Ontario. The selection criteria for subjects were: (1) a primary diagnosis of Major Depressive Disorder, MDD [established using the Schedule for Affective Disorders and Schizophrenia-Lifetime criteria (Endicott & Spitzer, 1978) to derive Research Diagnostic Criteria, RDC (Spitzer, Endicott, & Robins, 1978) for MDD]; and (2) a Beck Depression Inventory (BDI) score of 17 or more at time of initial testing. Exclusion criteria included the following: (1) an RDC current diagnosis of Bipolar Affective Disorder or Substance Abuse Disorder; and (2) a trial of ECT within the past six months. All subjects were patients who agreed to treatment and completed the six-month treatment protocol. Of these individuals, 30 had earlier participated in the Segal et al. (1995) study. The treatment consisted of 20 weekly sessions of CBT as outlined in the treatment manual developed by Beck, Rush, Shaw, and Emery (1979).

Stimulus Materials

The stimulus generation procedure used here follows that developed by Segal et al. (1995). The stimuli used in the colour-naming test were 120 trait adjectives, half of which were positive in content (e.g. trustworthy, sincere) and half of which were negative (quarrelsome, selfish), and 48 short phrases also divided in half by positive (able to feel close, I can take criticism) and negative (hard to trust others, I often feel judged) content. All of the positive and 53 of the negative adjectives were taken from Anderson (1968) with the remaining 7 negative adjectives derived from clinical descriptions of depressed persons. Care was taken not to include descriptions that were also affect labels (e.g. blue, lonely). The phrases were constructed to represent the main theme in each of the 12 subscales of the 127-item Inventory of Interpersonal Problems (IIP; Horowitz, Rosenberg, Baer, Ureno, & Villasensor, 1988). This measure assesses behaviours that subjects execute with ease, with difficulty, or compulsively (e.g. intimacy, aggression, assertion).

Generation and Construction of Prime/Target Stimuli Pairs

Given the importance of ensuring that stimulus materials maximally reflect subjects' idiosyncratic views of self, an idiographic approach was taken in the selection and construction of prime and target stimulus pairs on the initial testing occasion prior to treatment.

Prime Selection.   Subjects' primes were chosen on the basis of their IIP subscale scores. The IIP was modified in order to identify interpersonal behaviours that subjects did or did not find problematic. Ratings for each IIP item were made on a 9-point scale ranging from −4 (very difficult) to +4 (very easy), with a midpoint of 0. The three subscales with the highest mean scores (item ratings of +4 or +3) were used to choose the positive prime phrases for each subject. These phrases described nonproblematic interpersonal interactions. For example, self-descriptive positive primes for a subject with a positive score on the Sociable Subscale were "I can make friends" or "I meet others easily". Self-descriptive negative primes were chosen on the basis of the three subscales with the most negative scores (item ratings of −4 or −3) and were reflective of interpersonal difficulties. For example, negative primes for a subject with a negative score on the Hypersensitive subscale were "I often feel judged" or "I am too easily hurt". Nondescriptive, or neutral, primes were chosen from three of the subscales lying between these two poles. For the positive valence, the positive phrases for these neutrally rated subscales were used as the primes, and for the negative valence the negative versions of the primes for these same subscales were used.

Target Selection. The 12 self-descriptive adjectives of each valence used as targets for each subject were chosen through two procedures: a card sort task, and an adjective rating task. In the initial task, sets of 30 cards with one adjective on each were sorted by subjects, with two card sets containing the positive targets and two sets containing the negative targets, making 60 positive and 60 negative adjectives altogether. The sorts alternated between valences (e.g. positive, negative, positive, negative). The order and valence of sorts were counterbalanced across all subjects. For each sort, participants were asked to identify all of the 30 adjectives in the given set that were *extremely* self-descriptive, up to a maximum of 15 adjectives. This procedure, therefore, yielded a maximum of 30 positive and 30 negative chosen items. The resulting items served as the initial pool of targets for the particular subject.

After the sorting, subjects also rated each of the entire set of 50 descriptors in each valence on a 7-point rating scale, ranging from +3 (exremely self-descriptive) to −3 (extremely nonself-descriptive), with a midpoint of 0. Ratings were done immediately after the sorting of all adjective sets was completed, with the adjectives in each valence presented on separate rating sheets, in the same valence order as that for the card sort. For each valence, the 12 adjectives chosen in the card sort which received the highest positive ratings (usually +2 or +3) were considered to be self-descriptive targets, whereas the 12 adjectives not chosen on the card sort which received a rating of a −1, 0, or +1 were considered nonself-descriptive targets, or netural targets. Following standard procedures (Markus, 1977), the term "neutral", as used here, refers to information that is not relevant to a person's sense of identity.

Construction of Prime/Target Pairs. Prime/target pairs of the same valence were constructed to satisfy four experimental conditions in which the degree of self-description or relatedness to the subject of the prime and target varied: SS (self-descriptive prime/self-descriptive target); SN (self-descriptive prime/nonself-descriptive target); NS (nonself-descriptive prime/self-descriptive target); NN (nonself-descriptive prime/nonself-descriptive target). For each valence separately, subjects were shown a two-column list of their 6 descriptive primes and 12 targets and instructed to match each prime in one column with one target in the other column. Instructions to subjects for the positive material were as follows: "This is a list of statements and characteristics which you have chosen as reflecting your view of yourself in situations when you feel good about yourself. Please try and match the items on the left with those on the right in terms of how they best fit together in your experience." For negative prime/target pairs the phrase "when you are harsh or judging yourself" replaced the phrase "when you feel good about yourself". This procedure therefore yielded 6 prime-target matches, which served in the SS condition, with the 6 unmatched targets serving as the self-descriptive targets for the NS condition.

For each subject, the material for each Stroop condition in each valence was assembled as follows: The 6 prime/target personal matches made by each individual served in the SS condition (self-descriptive primes/self-descriptive targets). For the SN condition (self-descriptive primes/nonself-descriptive targets), the 6 primes used in the matching task were paired with a randomly chosen 6 of the 12 neutral target items. For the NS condition (nonself-descriptive primes/self-descriptive targets) the 6 targets not matched to primes in the matching task served as the self-descriptive targets, with the IIP subscales that were neutral for that subject providing the 6 unrelated primes of the appropriate valence. The NN condition (nonself-descriptive primes/nonself-descriptive targets) was created by pairing the nonself-descriptive primes used in condition NS with the 6 nonself-descriptive targets remaining from the 12 nonself-descriptive target items. In the SN, NS, and NN conditions, the primes and targets were matched randomly.

Procedure

At the first pre-treatment testing session, subjects generated the prime-target stimulus pairs as described earlier. At the second pre-treatment testing session, the primed emotional Stroop task was administered. All stimulus pair conditions, blocked on valence but otherwise ordered randomly, were presented using an IBM-compatible 386SX personal computer, and a 12-inch VGA colour monitor, running on software developed specifically for this task, which enabled the presentation of the stimuli and the recording of response latency and accuracy. In the primed Emotional Stroop colour-naming task paradigm, on each trial, a prime phrase appeared in black and white, which the subject was asked to read silently to him/herself, prior to the presentation of the target word in colour. The subject named the colour of the target, and response latencies were recorded via a voice key. After colour-naming the target, the subject repeated out loud the prime phrase to ensure that it had been read. Each pair was presented twice during the presentation sequence.

In the present research, subjects were retested on this task after the six-month CBT treatment. In addition to this task, subjects completed a Hamilton Rating Scale for Depression (HAM-D) and Beck Depression Inventory (BDI) on each occasion.

RESULTS

Effect of Treatment

As a group, subjects showed a significant reduction in symptomatology following treatment. The mean pre-/post-treatment reduction in Beck Depression Inventory scores was 12.1 [pre-therapy, 25.3; post-therapy, 13.2; $t(54) = 7.63$], whereas for the Hamilton Rating Scale for Depression it was 7.5 [pre-therapy, 16.5; post-therapy, 9.1; $t(54) = 8.44$]. The mean length of treatment (time between testing sessions) was 28.4 weeks.

Colour-naming Task

Colour-naming latency data was excluded from the analyses on those trials when response times were shorter than 100msec, with any responses longer than 2000msec lost as the presentation program cycled to the next presentation (these restrictions eliminated 2% of observations). In addition, mean response times were calculated by "trimming" the highest and lowest of the 12 responses for each subject in each condition to deal with possible outliers (Bush, Hess, & Wolford, 1993).

Means for all four prime-target pair conditions are presented in Table 1. The theoretical questions posed by the present study pertain to whether or not self-descriptive information in depressed subjects can be activated by the presentation of other self-descriptive information. Therefore, the conditions most relevant to answering this question are the primed and unprimed self-descriptive target conditions (SS and NS), where self-descriptive target words are colour-named following presentation of either self-descriptive or nonself-descriptive prime phrases.

The target adjectives to be colour-named in these pairs were initially chosen to be highly self-descriptive on the basis of patients' initial ratings. To ensure that the targets in each of these conditions of interest did not differ in rated self-descriptiveness, an initial examination of these ratings was performed. The mean self-descriptiveness ratings for the target adjectives in these conditions were very similar (for negative SS, 2.32; negative NS, 2.27; positive SS, 2.32; positive NS, 2.29), and an analysis of variance performed on these means failed to find a significant effect of pair valence

TABLE 1
Condition Means (msec), Standard Deviations in Parentheses

Condition	Negative		Positive	
	Pre-treatment	Post-treatment	Pre-treatment	Post-treatment
SS	867 (153)	823 (137)	837 (151)	807 (111)
NS	847 (145)	806 (123)	821 (153)	787 (120)
SN	843 (148)	797 (134)	820 (150)	798 (129)
NN	859 (165)	803 (140)	821 (146)	787 (125)

Note: SS, self-descriptive prime/self-descriptive target; NS, nonself-descriptive prime/self-descriptive target; SN, self-descriptive prime/nonself-descriptive target; NN, nonself-descriptive prime/nonself-descriptive target.

(positive or negative), prime type (self-descriptive or nonself-descriptive), or their interaction [all $Fs(1,54)$ = n.s.].

To provide a measure of colour-naming interference due to the presentation of negative self-descriptive versus negative nonself-descriptive material, an interference score was calculated separately for each subject. This score was obtained by subtracting the baseline condition of colour-naming time for self-descriptive targets when preceded by nonself-descriptive primes (NS condition) from the colour-naming time for the self-descriptive targets when preceded by self-descriptive primes (SS condition). Thus, any slowing of colour-naming in the SS condition relative to the NS condition would produce a positive interference score. This measure provides an index of the relative difference in difficulty in colour-naming, and thus the relative difference in semantic activation of the target item, between the two conditions (see Mathews et al., 1995 for a similar approach). In this manner, how much a self-relevant concept is activated or brought to mind by seeing an earlier self-relevant concept (as compared to seeing self-irrelevant material) can be determined. In their original study, Segal et al. (1995) reported that depressed patients showed increased Stroop interference only when negative target adjectives were preceded by self-referent negative primes. The present research follows up this work by examining whether this interference is affected by psychological treatment for depression.

Although most of the individuals in the current sample of depressed patients were also used by Segal et al. (1995), a number of additional depressed individuals were added for the present research, and some in the original research were not accepted for treatment or did not complete the course of therapy (of the present sample, 30 of the 55 patients had participated in the earlier group). [In the original Segal et al. (1995) sample of 58 depressed patients, 10 were not suitable for cognitive therapy, 3 declined therapy, 5 dropped out before completing the course of treatment, and 10 patients completed therapy but were unable for various reasons to participate in the second testing session.] In order to ensure that the changes in subject composition did not change the overall pattern of results noted originally by Segal et al. (1995) for their untreated sample, we checked whether, prior to treatment, the present group of depressed patients differed from the nondepressed controls, as reported in that earlier work. We did this by performing *t*-tests on the negative and positive interference scores for the current depressed sample and the original sample of controls tested in that study. As in the original research, our larger group of depressed subjects also evidenced higher negative interference scores than controls [Depressed mean = 19.8, SD = 70.2 vs. Control mean = -7.6, SD = 67.4, $t(97) = 1.97$, $P < .027$, one-tailed], suggesting that depressed subjects possess a more tightly interconnected and negative self-schema than do the controls. In contrast, the groups did not differ in terms of their interference scores for positive material [Depressed mean = 15.5, SD = 76.8 vs. Control mean = 17.7, SD = 32.1, $t(97) = 0.18$, n.s.].

The main relationship of interest to us was the association between negative interference scores and treatment response to CBT in depressed subjects. To examine this relation, we used a multiple regression approach, using post-treatment negative interference scores as the dependent measure, and examined the effect on this measure of post-treatment depression levels, as measured by HAM-D (HAM-D POST). Prior to entering post-treatment HAM-D into the regression model, we entered a number of variables into the model to control for various factors: age and time between testing sessions, entered together (to control for two of the obvious differences among subjects); pre-therapy levels of negative interference (to account for differences in individual pre-therapy levels of interference); post-treatment positive interference score (to capture general, valence-insensitive treatment effects on Stroop interference); and pre-therapy level of depression (HAM-D PRE). These variables were entered separately (except for age and delay, which were entered together), in the order just presented. Thus, in this equation, all obvious relevant sources of variation were entered, and therefore the analysis should indicate if, all else being equal, post-treatment negative interference scores are related to post-treatment levels of depression.

Regression statistics for the depressed patients are presented in Table 2. As can be seen from this table, only two of the variables entered showed significant relations with the dependent measure, as measured by change in R^2 with entry. One of these variables was positive interference scores at post-treatment [R^2 change = .090, $F(1,50) = 5.24$, $P < .05$], suggesting that

TABLE 2
Regression Statistics for Negative and Positive Material

Variable(s) Entered	R^2 Change	F Change (df)	P
Negative material			
Age and Testing Interval	.003	.08 (2,52)	n.s.
Negative Interference: Pre	.047	2.50 (1,51)	n.s.
Positive Interference: Post	.090	5.24 (1,50)	.026
Hamilton: Pre	.003	.17 (1,49)	n.s.
Hamilton: Post	.078	4.80 (1,48)	.033
Positive Material			
Age and Testing Interval	.013	.33 (2,52)	n.s.
Positive Interference: Pre	.213	13.99 (1,51)	.001
Negative Interference: Post	.019	1.26 (1,50)	n.s.
Hamilton: Pre	.012	.81 (1,49)	n.s.
Hamilton: Post	.002	.14 (1,48)	n.s.

the speeding up or slowing down of colour-naming interference with treatment was occurring for material of both valences.

However, more importantly, the results also showed that the critical relationship hypothesised between post-therapy negative interference and depression level was also significant. Negative interference scores following treatment were significantly predicted by post-treatment HAM-D scores [R^2 change = .078, $F(1,48)$ = 4.80, $P < .05$], even after all other variables were included in the regression equation. This result suggests that patients who are less depressed after treatment showed less of a priming effect on Stroop interference for negative self-relevant material than those who remained more depressed following CBT. This effect is not due to the mere passage of time or practice effects, because effects on Stroop interference for negative material were modulated by post-treatment mood—all subjects had the same amount of practice on the task, and delay between experimental sessions was entered in the regression equation prior to post-treatment HAM-D, but those who showed less depression at post-treatment still showed less of an effect on the Stroop task used.

A subsidiary regression was performed in similar fashion using post-treatment positive interference scores as the dependent measure, to rule out the possibility of the aforementioned effect being valence-independent. Again, a number of variables were entered in the regression: age and delay between testing sessions (entered together); pre-treatment positive interference scores; post-treatment negative interference scores; pre-treatment HAM-D; and post-treatment HAM-D. In this analysis, the only significant relationship found was for post-treatment positive interference scores to be related to pre-treatment positive interference scores [R^2 change = .213, $F(1,51)$ = 13.99, $P < .001$], suggesting that Stroop interference for positive material was highly correlated at pre- and post-treatment testing. Level of depression at either time of testing was unrelated to positive interference at post-treatment. Specifically, in contrast to the results for negative material, post-treatment positive interference scores were not affected by post-treatment levels of depression, when all other relevant variables were included in the regression.

Additional analyses were performed on the two nonself-relevant target conditions, SN and NN, to determine whether the relation between level of post-therapy depression and interference only holds for self-relevant targets. Because we hypothesised that it is the relationship among negative self-relevant material that would be affected by the therapeutic intervention, targets unrelated to self-concept should not show any change in priming effects with change in level of depression. To examine this question, in each valence we calculated interference scores for the pairs of nonself-relevant target conditions, SN and NN, in the same manner as the SS and NS conditions, and then performed regressions in the same manner as done for the self-relevant interference scores. For negative material, none of the variables entered produced a significant R^2 change, and for positive material, only the set of nuisance covariates produced a significant R^2 change. Specifically, in neither case did the final addition of post-treatment Hamilton score to the regression equation produce an increase in R^2 beyond the .05 level of significance.

These results suggest that reliable decreases in Stroop interference were obtained with self-relevant targets for some of the depressed patients and that these decreases were a function of the degree to which patients responded to treatment. The less an individual was depressed after the completion of therapy, the less he/she demonstrated a priming effect on Stroop interference for negative self-relevant material. This effect was, as predicted, limited only to material related to the individual's self-concept, as nonself-relevant targets of either valence did not show such a relation between interference and post-therapy depression level.

As an adjunct to the findings just described, we conducted similar analyses on a group of 27 nondepressed controls tested using the identical paradigm as for the depressed patients. Testing occurred over a 2- to 4-month interval (mean delay = 11.4 weeks, SD = 4.4), largely because subject availability was limited by the end of the school term. These subjects were significantly younger than the depressed patients ($\bar{X}$ = 24.3, SD = 4.8), but did not differ from them in terms of gender distribution or verbal IQ. As expected, at the initial session controls were significantly less depressed than patients as measured by both the BDI ($\bar{X}$ = 2.8, SD = 2.2) and the HAM-D ($\bar{X}$ = 1.9, SD = 2.5). We conducted regressions for this control sample in the same manner that we did for the depressed patients. Not surprisingly, in contrast to our main finding with depressed patients, level of depression at time of second testing had no effect on Stroop interference. Specifically, in the regressions no variable showed a statistically reliable relation to retest interference scores for either positive or negative material. Of course, due to floor effects the controls had little variation in their retest HAM-D scores, which mitigated against this variable being found to be significantly related to Stroop performance.

DISCUSSION

The primary purpose of the present study was to determine whether the effect of negative self-concept, as measured by Stroop interference effects for primed negative self-descriptive adjectives, would remain unchanged in depressed patients after they had been treated with CBT and had recovered. It was found that treatment had a specific effect on negative self-information, as measured by colour-naming, and seemed to be related to the degree of treatment response. Many of the patients were clearly improved following treatment and for those who did there was a concomitant decrease in their negative interference scores. There was no relationship between change in level of depression and positive interference scores, or between change in level of depression and interference scores for nonself-relevant targets in either valence. This decrease in negative interference scores for self-relevant material following successful treatment is not due to practice effects or mere passage of time, because although all patients received the same amount of practice at the task and testing delay was controlled for in the regression, the decrease is not uniform across all treated patients, but is related to the degree of treatment success. These findings indicate that the measure of cognitive organisation used here, a modification of the Stroop task in which a target to be colour-named is primed by material related or unrelated to it, is sensitive to change. The findings also add to previous work that points to the utility of the Stroop as an objective measure of cognitive bias in depressed patients.

Although one interpretation of these results is that the observed changes in selective interference following successful treatment are indeed due to an actual reorganisation of material in subjects' cognitive structures or schemata, there may be some question as to how this can come about as a result of 20 weekly sessions of CBT, and whether or not alternative explanations can account for the findings. Certainly, proponents of CBT would point to the fact that the therapy contains interventions that are intended to address dysfunctional assumptions and schema-driven appraisals (Kovacs & Beck, 1978), but it is still unclear how these effortful exercises could impact at a level of mental function that is largely out of the subjects' intentional control (MacLeod, 1991). Furthermore, cognitive changes with treatment are not specific to CBT, as changes in interference on a basic, unprimed Emotional Stroop task have been obtained with treatments as varied as interpersonal therapy (Cooper & Fairburn, 1994) and phenelzine (Mattia et al., 1993). More likely, patients in CBT learn "compensatory skills" (Barber & DeRubeis, 1989), which allow them to evaluate situations from a number of different vantage points, and in this way perhaps reduce the heightened accessibility of negative material in the cognitive system. As patients continue to improve, the mood-congruent effects of depressed mood on cognition will also be diminished and this will further reduce the accessibility of negative material, so that alternative information may come to mind more easily and be utilised in subsequent cognitive activity (Teasdale, 1983).

According to this view, an underlying cognitive structure is not altered through CBT, as much as its level of activation across situations is decreased. This implies that depressed patients' cognitive organisations may be an enduring characteristic associated with vulnerability to future depression, but that such cognitive structures are not active, and therefore do not evidence themselves, under normal mood. Because patients who responded to treatment showed an associated improvement in negative mood, the post-treatment data cannot address this question. Perhaps the presence of positive affect masks the selective processing effects that would emerge again under stress (Mathews et al., 1995). Further support for this comes from a review of studies in which recovered depressed patients were tested in normal versus induced sad mood conditions. Evidence of residual processing selectivity in this group of patients was consistently obtained, on a number of different cognitive tasks, when subjects were tested following a challenge or stressor of some sort (Segal & Ingram, 1994), and not as consistently when they were tested in euthymic mood. This result would suggest that some level of dysphoria is required for an underlying enduring cognitive bias in depression to become evident (Teasdale & Barnard, 1993). Interestingly, Hedlund and Rude (1995) report that following a self-focus manipulation intended to induce mild dysphoria, remitted depressed patients did not show increased interference for negative material on the unprimed Emotional Stroop task, while demonstrating large changes in measures of recall and sentence completion (in the direction of those found for currently depressed patients). This latter finding suggests that, in contrast to some other measures, Stroop performance (at least in the basic Emotional Stroop task) does indeed fundamentally alter with treatment, although it is unclear whether this result applies also to the use of the primed Stroop paradigm to examine cognitive organisation in depression.

It is important to note that, although the present research shows changes to cognitive organisation with CBT, these findings do not rule out the possibility that other psychological treatments or even pharmacological therapies would show similar results. As noted earlier, both interpersonal therapy and pharmacotherapy have been shown to change unprimed Stroop performance, and such therapies may also have effect on the measure used here as well. Currently, the present findings indicate only that performance on a measure of cognitive organisation normalises to the degree of treatment success. Whether this effect is general to all successful treatments, or specific to CBT, remains to be determined by future research.

In summary, the present findings add to the literature on changes in cognitive-processing of negative self-descriptive material by depressed patients following psychological treatment. The degree to which negative self-relevant material brings to mind other such material is related to the degree of depression remaining following treatment. Further work is needed to determine whether these changes truly represent reorganisation of an underlying cognitive structure, or whether treatment merely alters the accessibility of an otherwise unchanged negative self-representation. Determining whether recovered depressed patients reactivate these cognitive-processing patterns following a challenge or stressor would shed light on this issue. Similarly, additional research should be conducted to determine whether the changes noted are restricted to the effects of cognitive behaviour therapy, or if they are as likely to occur following alternative treatments for depression, even nonpsychological interventions such as pharmacotherapy.

REFERENCES

Anderson, N. (1968). Likableness ratings of 555 personality-trait adjectives. *Journal of Personality and Social Psychology, 9*, 272–279.

Barber, J.P., & DeRubeis, R.J. (1989). On second thought: Where the action is in cognitive therapy. *Cognitive Therapy and Research, 13*, 441–457.

Beck, A.T. (1967). *Depression: Clinical, experimental, and theoretical aspects.* New York: Harper & Row.

Beck, A.T., Rush, A.J., Shaw, B.F., & Emery, G. (1979). *Cognitive therapy of depression.* New York: Guilford Press.

Bush, L.K., Hess, U., & Wolford, G. (1993). Transformations for within-subject designs: A Monte Carlo investigation. *Psychological Bulletin, 113*, 566–579.

Cooper, M.J., & Fairburn, C.G. (1994). Changes in selective information processing with three psychological treatments for bulimia nervosa. *British Journal of Clinical Psychology, 33*, 353–356.

Endicott, J., & Spitzer, R. (1978). A diagnostic interview: The schedule for the affective disorders and schizophrenia. *Archives of General Psychiatry, 35*, 837–844.

Gotlib, I.H., & Cane, D.B. (1987). Construct accessibility and clinical depression: A longitudinal investigation. *Journal of Abnormal Psychology, 96*, 199–204.

Gotlib, I.H., & McCann, C.D. (1984). Construct accessibility and depression: An examination of cognitive and affective factors. *Journal of Personality and Social Psychology, 47*, 427–439.

Hedlund, S., & Rude, S. (1995). Evidence of latent depressive schemas in formerly depressed individuals. *Journal of Abnormal Psychology, 104,* 517–525.

Hertel, P.T., & Milan, S. (1994). Depressive deficits in recognition: Dissociation of recollection and familiarity. *Journal of Abnormal Psychology, 103,* 736–742.

Horowitz, L.M., Rosenberg, S.E., Baer, B.A., Ureno, G., & Villasenor, V.S. (1988). Inventory of interpersonal problems: Psychometric properties and clinical applications. *Journal of Consulting and Clinical Psychology, 56,* 885–892.

Kovacs, M., & Beck, A.T. (1978). Maladaptive cognitive structures in depression. *American Journal of Psychiatry, 135,* 525–533.

MacLeod, C.M. (1991). Half a century of research on the Stroop Effect: An integrative review. *Psychological Bulletin, 109,* 163–203.

Markus, H. (1977). Self-schemata and processing information about the self. *Journal of Personality and Social Psychology, 35,* 63–78.

Mathews, A., Mogg, K., Kentish, J., & Eysenck, M. (1995). Effect of psychological treatment on cognitive bias in generalized anxiety disorder. *Behaviour Research and Therapy, 33,* 293–303.

Mattia, J., Heimberg, R., & Hope, D. (1993). The revised Stroop colour naming task in social phobics. *Behaviour Research and Therapy, 31,* 305–313.

Pace, T.M., & Dixon, D.N. (1993). Changes in depressive self-schemata and depressive symptoms following cognitive therapy. *Journal of Counselling Psychology, 40,* 288–294.

Segal, Z.V., Gemar, M., Truchon, C., Guirguis, M., & Horowitz, L. (1995). A priming methodology for studying self-representation in major depressive disorder. *Journal of Abnormal Psychology, 104,* 205–213.

Segal, Z.V., & Ingram, R.E. (1994). Priming and construct activation in tests of cognitive vulnerability to unipolar depression. *Clinical Psychology Review, 14,* 663–695.

Spitzer, R.L., Endicott, J., & Robins, E. (1978). *Research diagnostic criteria for a selected group of functional disorders.* New York: Biometric Research Unit, New York Psychiatric Institute.

Teasdale, J.D. (1983). Negative thinking in depression: Cause, effect, or reciprocal relationship? *Advances in Behavior Research and Therapy, 5,* 3–25.

Teasdale, J.D., & Barnard, P.J. (1993). *Affect, cognition and change.* Hove, UK: Lawrence Erlbaum Associates Ltd.

Williams, J.M.G., Mathews, A., & MacLeod, C. (1996). The emotional Stroop task and psychopathology. *Psychological Bulletin, 120,* 3–24.

Williams, J.M.G., & Nulty, D.D. (1986). Construct accessibility, depression and the emotional Stroop task: Transient mood or stable structure. *Personality and Individual Differences, 7,* 485–491.

COGNITION AND EMOTION, 1997, *11* (5/6), 517–538

Cognitive Biases and Affect Persistence in Previously Dysphoric and Never-dysphoric Individuals

Eva Gilboa and Ian H. Gotlib

Northwestern University, USA

Persistence of affect and attentional and memory biases in dysphoria-prone and nonvulnerable individuals were investigated. In two experiments, never-dysphoric (ND) individuals and previously dysphoric (PD) individuals underwent a positive and a negative autobiographical mood-induction procedure (MIP). Following each MIP, individuals participated in an emotional Stroop task. Participants also rated their mood both immediately after, and five minutes after, each MIP. In addition, in Experiment 2, incidental memory for Stroop stimuli was assessed. PD participants reported more persistent negative affect following a negative MIP than did ND participants. Although PD and ND participants did not differ from each other with respect to their performance on the emotion Stroop task, PD participants demonstrated significantly better memory for negative stimuli than did ND participants. Thus, affect dysregulation and memory biases of PD participants outlasted the dysphoric episode. These findings suggest that memory biases and affect regulation style may play a causal role in susceptibility to depression.

INTRODUCTION

Results of a large number of studies suggest that depression (and depressed mood) is associated with biases in attention, memory, and judgement (see Gotlib, Gilboa, & Sommerfeld, in press; Mathews & MacLeod, 1994; and Williams, Watts, MacLeod, & Mathews, 1988 for reviews). In several studies, depressed individuals have been found either to attend more strongly to negative than to positive stimuli, or to fail to show the avoidance of negative stimuli demonstrated by nondepressed persons (e.g. Gotlib & McCann, 1984; McCabe & Gotlib, 1993, 1995; but see

Requests for reprints should be sent to Ian Gotlib, who is now at the Department of Psychology, Bldg. 420, Jordan Hall, Stanford University, Stanford, CA 94305, USA; e-mail: gotlib@psych.stanford.edu.

W. Gerrod Parrott served as the action editor for this article.

also Mogg, Bradley, Williams, & Mathews, 1993). In contrast to nonde-pressed individuals, depressed persons have also been found to exhibit superior memory for experimentally presented negative materials (e.g. Mathews & MacLeod, 1994; Matt, Vazquez, & Campbell, 1992) and to recall negative memories more quickly than positive memories (Williams, 1992). Finally, depressed persons have been found to make more negative judgements concerning both hypothetical and real-life events than do their nondepressed counterparts (e.g. Andersen, Spielman, & Bargh, 1992; Constans & Mathews, 1993).

Thus, there is considerable evidence suggesting that depressed persons are characterised by biased cognitive functioning. These findings support Beck's (1976) theory that depressed persons are characterised by negative schemata that bias the selection, encoding, categorisation, and evaluation of stimuli in the environment during a depressive episode. However, most cognitive theories of depression also postulate that such cognitive biases persist beyond the depressive episode in individuals who are vulnerable to depression (e.g. Beck, 1976; Teasdale, 1988; Teasdale & Barnard, 1993). Individuals with a history of depressive episodes have been found consis-tently to be at elevated risk for experiencing subsequent depression (e.g. Hammen, 1991; Keller, 1985). Therefore, these vulnerable individuals are expected to exhibit cognitive biases even after the depressive episode remits. Beck postulates further that, although negative schemata become latent following symptomatic recovery from depression, they can be reactivated in the face of schema-relevant stressful life events. Teasdale suggests that differences between vulnerable and nonvulnerable individuals are most likely to be apparent when these individuals experience dysphoric mood (Teasdale, 1988). Consistent with this formulation, Miranda, Per-sons, and Byers (1990) found that remitted depressives reported elevated levels of dysfunctional attitudes only when they were in a negative mood state. In contrast, nonvulnerable individuals did not show a mood-related elevation in dysfunctional attitudes. Thus, self-report data suggest that negative mood can serve to prime latent depressive schemata.

Other investigators have extended these results by examining the effects of negative mood on biases in information-processing. Findings of these studies, too, suggest that biases in attention, judgement, and memory processes can be observed in individuals who have previously been depressed but who are not currently symptomatic. Specifically, researchers have begun to examine attentional, judgement, and memory processes of formerly depressed and never-depressed individuals following a mood manipulation. These investigators have used information-processing tasks such as Stroop colour-naming, scrambled sentences, dichotic listening, self-referent encoding, and incidental recall. For example, Teasdale and Dent (1987) reported that, compared with never-depressed participants, remitted depressives exhibited a selective recall of negative trait words following a negative mood-induction procedure. Importantly, these two groups of participants did not differ when they were tested in a neutral mood. Hedlund and Rude (1995) similarly found that, compared with never-depressed controls, remitted depressives recalled a greater number of negative words and exhibited more negative interpretative biases following a self-focus manipulation. In a recent study examining attentional processes, Ingram, Bernet, and McLauglin (1994) found that, following a negative mood induction, remitted depressives exhibited enhanced attention to emotional stimuli (i.e. both positive and negative) on a dichotic listening task, compared with never-depressed controls. No processing differences were observed between the remitted and the never-depressed participants when they were tested in a neutral mood state. Using a different attentional measure, however, Hedlund and Rude failed to find significant differences between remitted depressives and never-depressed controls in their performance on a Stroop task following a self-focus manipulation (see Segal & Ingram, 1994, for a more detailed review of this literature).

In sum, recent evidence suggests that, at least under certain conditions, remitted depressives differ from never-depressed individuals on measures of information-processing. It is also apparent, however, that the association between depression vulnerability and biased information-processing is not well understood. In the light of the discrepancy between the findings reported by Ingram et al. (1994) and those reported by Hedlund and Rude (1995), it is important to examine both attentional and memory processes within a single study using identical materials for both tasks.

Teasdale's (1988) differential activation hypothesis suggests that vulnerable and nonvulnerable individuals differ not only with respect to their cognitive functioning following dysphoric affect, but also in the duration of their negative emotions. He argues that most individuals experience life events that produce mild dysphoria, and that differences between vulnerable and nonvulnerable individuals emerge *after* they begin to experience dysphoric mood. Nonvulnerable individuals engage in self-soothing functions that allow them to cope with their negative affect. In contrast, in vulnerable individuals negative moods persist and may spiral into clinical depression. Thus, Teasdale considers mood-regulation processes to be pivotal to depressive vulnerability. Because duration of emotional reaction is one of the defining features of depression, temporal aspects of emotional reactions might be an especially important marker of individuals' vulnerability to depression.

Other researchers have also emphasised variables associated with the persistence of dysphoric affect as important aetiological factors in the development of a depressive disorder. For example, Nolen-Hoeksema

(1987, 1991) proposed that individuals who respond to dysphoric moods with rumination are particularly vulnerable to persistent depression. Indeed, recent findings suggest that individuals with known vulnerability to depression report more ruminative tendencies than do less vulnerable individuals (e.g. Roberts, Gilboa, & Gotlib, in press). Specifically, Roberts and colleagues found elevated levels of rumination in remitted depressives, compared to never-depressed individuals, although these individuals did not differ on concurrent depressive symptomatology. This suggests that a ruminative response style and, by association, the duration of reactions to negative events, are important characteristics of *trait* vulnerability to episodes of persistent depression. In a similar manner, Gilboa and Revelle (1994) found that self-reported duration of negative emotions is associated with neuroticism. Based on the association of neuroticism and depression (e.g. Martin, 1985), Gilboa and Revelle argued that the protracted experience of negative emotions may represent an important vulnerability to experiencing a depressive disorder.

Considered collectively, these lines of research suggest that vulnerable individuals would experience a more protracted affective reaction to a negative event than would nonvulnerable individuals. However, this hypothesis has not yet been tested empirically. A direct test of this proposition is essential to the confirmation of Teasdale's differential activation hypothesis. Moreover, such a test could contribute to the understanding of the mechanisms leading to depression recurrence in vulnerable individuals.

The Present Experiments

The purpose of the present studies was to compare the differential impact of negative and positive mood-induction procedures on vulnerable and nonvulnerable individuals with respect both to their performance on cognitive (i.e. attentional and memory) tasks, and to the persistence of their resultant affect. We attempted to test three distinct, but related, hypotheses. First, extending Ingram et al.'s (1994) dichotic listening findings, we postulated that previously dysphoric individuals would exhibit greater attentional interference with negative stimuli following a negative mood-induction procedure (MIP) than would never-dysphoric individuals; we did not expect to observe this effect following a positive MIP. No specific predictions were made with respect to group differences in attentional interference with positive stimuli. Second, consistent with Teasdale and Dent's (1987) and Hedlund and Rude's (1995) findings, we predicted that previously dysphoric participants would exhibit enhanced memory for negative, relative to positive or neutral, stimuli. Third, following Teasdale's (1988) hypothesis, we predicted that previously dysphoric participants would experience more protracted dysphoric mood in response to a negative MIP than would never-dysphoric participants and further, that this protraction of affective response would be specific to negative (as opposed to positive) affect.

To test these hypotheses, we examined attentional and memory biases and affect persistence in previously dysphoric (PD) and never-dysphoric (ND) participants following authobiographical MIPs. In two experiments, PD and ND individuals participated in a positive and a negative MIP. Following each MIP these individuals participated in an emotion Stroop task. Participants also rated their mood both immediately after, and five minutes after, each MIP. Finally, incidental memory for Stroop stimuli was assessed in Experiment 2.

EXPERIMENT 1

Method

Participants and Design

A total of 66 undergraduate university students participated in this experiment in partial fulfilment of a course requirement. Mood induction (positive and negative) was a within-subject factor in the design, with the order of positive and negative induction conditions counterbalanced across participants. The participants were randomly assigned to one of two conditions: a positive followed by a negative mood-induction (PN) condition; and a negative followed by a positive mood-induction (NP) condition. To neutralise the participants' mood before the end of the experiment, all participants underwent a neutral MIP. Finally, participants completed the Beck Depression Inventory (BDI; Beck, Rush, Shaw, & Emery, 1979). The experimental session lasted about 45 minutes.

Participant Selection

Participants were recruited based on their responses during a group testing session at the beginning of an academic quarter. The Inventory to Diagnose Depression (IDD; Zimmerman, Coryell, Corenthal, & Wilson, 1986) was used to measure the overall severity of depressive symptomatology, as well as to determine whether participants met *Diagnostic and Statistical Manual—third edition* (DSMIII; APA, 1980) and *third edition—revised* (DSMIII-R; APA, 1987) symptom criteria for a major depressive disorder. The IDD correlates highly with other measures of depression, such as the Beck Depression Inventory ($r = .87$, Zimmerman et al., 1986) and the Diagnostic Interview Schedule ($k = .8$, Zimmerman & Coryell, 1988). The IDD-Lifetime version (IDD-L; Zimmerman & Coryell, 1987) was used to assess participants' worst lifetime depression. The IDD-L has good sensitivity (74%) and specificity (93%) (Zimmerman & Coryell, 1987). The IDD and the IDD-L were administered to the participants as part of a larger battery of questionnaires early in the quarter. Participants were recruited only if their responses to the IDD at the time of group testing met neither DSMIII nor DSMIII-R symptom criteria for a major depressive episode. Thus, all participants were currently nondepressed. Remitted dysphorics were defined as those whose worst lifetime depression, as assessed by the IDD-L, met either DSMIII or DSMIII-R symptom criteria. Never-dysphoric participants reported a worst lifetime experience of depression that failed to meet either DSMIII or DSMIII-R symptom criteria for major depressive disorder.

Materials and Apparatus

The stimulus list consisted of 40 words: 20 neutral words (e.g. "verbal", "tangible"), 10 negative emotion words (e.g. "rejected", "helpless"), and 10 positive emotion words (e.g. "joyful", "hopeful"). The positive and negative words were equated for frequency and emotionality based on John's (1988) ratings.

The stimuli and the instructions for participants were presented on an Apple Macintosh Quadra 660AV computer with a colour monitor. A custom-built voice-activated relay was used to record the participants' response latencies to the stimuli. The computer's audio system was used to play music segments to the participants.

Procedure

Participants were told that the experiment was designed to examine the effects of mood on simple cognitive-processing. The controlling software handled the mood-induction procedure and stimuli presentation. It also recorded participants' mood ratings and their reaction times (RTs) to the Stroop stimuli. The experiment consisted of four phases: introductory phase; two experimental phases; and neutralising phase.

Introductory Phase. First, participants were asked to recall, to rate the emotional intensity of, and to provide five "keywords" for an autobiographical experience during which they felt emotionally neutral. Next, participants were asked to concentrate on that experience until they felt themselves react as if they were actually there (instructions for this task were based on those used by Salovey, 1992). Following this re-experience, participants rated their current mood on six unipolar visual analogue scales and one bipolar scale. The six unipolar scales were "sad", "frustrated", "anxious", "happy", "content", and "optimistic". The scales were anchored with "not at all" (coded as an intensity rating of 0) and "extremely" (coded as an intensity rating of 100). The bipolar, overall, scale was anchored with "very positive" (coded as an intensity rating of +50) and "very negative" (coded as an intensity rating of −50). Next, instructions for the emotion Stroop task, which involved naming the colours of the displayed stimulus words, were given to the participants, followed by 20 practice trials. During these trials participants named the colours of neutral words (e.g. "one", "two").

Experimental Phases.   Each experimental phase consisted of three components: a 5-minute MIP, mood ratings, and the Stroop task. During the MIP participants recalled and relived an affective (either positive or negative) experience. The recall instructions for the affective experiences were similar to those used for the recall of the neutral experience. Next, participants were instructed to re-experience their sad/happy event (using "relive" instructions adapted from Salovey, 1992) while listening to music (an excerpt from Beethoven's string quartet op. 131 and an excerpt from Vivaldi's "Spring" violin concerto op. 12 were played for the negative and positive MIPs, respectively). Finally, before proceeding to the Stroop task, participants rated their mood on the seven visual analogue scales.

During the Stroop task participants were presented with 160 stimuli. The 40 stimulus words were presented four times, each time in a new random order. The order of presentation and the colour of stimuli were randomly determined for each participant, with the constraint that no two consecutive words were displayed in the same colour. Participants named the colour of each presented stimulus, and their colour-naming response terminated the display. A one-second interval separated consecutive trials. The task took about five minutes to complete. Following the completion of the Stroop task, participants again rated their mood.

At the end of the first experimental phase, participants were presented with a filler task in which they were asked to evaluate the computer program. This filler task was included to ensure that the effects of the first MIP dissipated before the beginning of the second MIP. After the completion of the filler task (which took about five minutes), participants proceeded to the second experimental phase. Except for the nature of the mood induced (positive in the NP condition, and negative in the PN condition), the structure of the second experimental phase was identical to the first. Again, after completing the MIP, participants rated their mood and performed the Stroop task.

Neutralising Phase. Finally, participants were instructed to relive a neutral experience in order to neutralise their mood. They then completed the BDI and were debriefed and thanked for their participation.

Results and Discussion

Current Depression Status

Four participants whose BDI scores were significantly elevated at the time of the experiment (BDI > 10) were excluded from all analyses. Thus, the final analyses were conducted on data from 62 participants. There were 28 participants in the never-dysphoric (ND) group (mean BDI = 5.4), and 34 participants in the previously dysphoric (PD) group (mean BDI = 5.7). The BDI scores of the two groups did not differ significantly [$t(60) < 1$]. However, to ensure that this variable did not influence subsequent results, we conducted analyses of covariance (ANCOVAs) using BDI scores as a covariate. In no case did the BDI scores alter any of the results reported later. For simplicity of presentation, therefore, we report the results of analyses conducted without the BDI as a covariate.

Efficacy of Mood-induction Procedures

Table 1 presents the descriptive statistics for overall mood ratings. To examine the effectiveness of the negative MIP, we conducted a 2 × 2 ANOVA with dysphoria history (ND vs. PD) as the between-subjects variable and time (baseline vs. immediately after the negative MIP) as the within-subject variable. The results of this analysis yielded a main effect of time, such that participants' mood ratings immediately after a negative MIP were significantly lower than at baseline [$F(1,60) = 82.1$, $P < .01$]. All other main effects and interactions failed to reach statistical significance. Similarly, to examine the effectiveness of the positive MIP, we conducted a 2 × 2 ANOVA with dysphoria history (ND vs. PD) as the between-subjects variable, and time (baseline vs. immediately after the positive MIP) as the within-subject variable. This analysis yielded a significant main effect of time, such that participants' mood ratings immediately after a positive MIP were significantly higher than at baseline [$F(1,60) = 51.9$, $P < .01$]. All other main effects and interactions failed to reach significance. These results indicate that both negative and positive MIPs were successful in modifying participants' mood.[1,2] They also

---

[1] Analyses of the unipolar mood scales yielded similar results.

[2] All of the analyses were conducted with order of mood inductions (PN vs. NP) as a between-subjects factor. However, because the effects of order and its interaction with other variables were not significant in any of the analyses, we did not include order as a factor in the following analyses.

TABLE 1

Group Means and (Standard Deviations) of Self-reported Overall Mood Ratings after the Positive and the Negative Mood-induction Procedures (MIPs)

Scale Name	Group	Time of Rating					
		Experiment 1			Experiment 2		
		Baseline[1]	Peak[2]	Delayed[3]	Baseline[4]	Peak[2]	Delayed[3]
Negative MIP	Never-dysphoric	10.6 (17.6)	−12.4 (13.9)	−2.4 (11.3)	16.1 (18.6)	−11.3 (18.6)	4.8 (16.1)
	Previously Dysphoric	5.2 (15.5)	−16.2 (13.9)	−9.6 (13.2)	15.7 (12.4)	−16.8 (16.2)	−5.0 (16.1)
Positive MIP	Never-dysphoric	10.6 (17.6)	26.6 (15.0)	8.4 (16.5)	16.1 (18.6)	28.3 (14.1)	15.4 (15.8)
	Previously Dysphoric	5.2 (15.5)	20.4 (15.9)	6.1 (15.7)	15.7 (12.4)	25.8 (14.0)	14.6 (15.5)

[1] Mood ratings after the neutral MIP. The ratings in the positive and negative MIPs refer to the same baseline ratings.

[2] Mood ratings immediately after a MIP.

[3] Mood ratings 5 minutes after a MIP.

[4] "Walk-in" mood ratings. The ratings in the positive and negative MIPs refer to the same baseline ratings.

suggest that ND and PD individuals did not differ from one another in their immediate reactions to either positive or negative MIPs.

Individual Differences in Affect Persistence

We predicted that PD participants would experience more protracted dysphoric mood in response to a negative MIP than would ND participants. In fact, the delayed mood ratings of the PD participants were more negative than were those of ND participants (see Table 2). It is possible, however, that several factors might have contributed to this effect. First, PD participants might have lower overall baseline mood ratings than do ND participants. Second, PD participants may have lower overall peak mood ratings after a negative MIP than do ND participants. Third, PD individuals may have drawn on more intensely negative experiences during the MIP than did ND individuals. Finally, differences in current depressive symptomatology (as measured by BDI) might also contribute to the observed differences in delayed mood ratings. To control statistically for these factors, we conducted multiple analyses of covariance (ANCOVAs) with dysphoria group as the between-subjects factor, with the following variables as covariates: (a) baseline mood ratings; (b) peak mood ratings; (c) intensity of the recalled negative experiences; (d) BDI; and (e) all of the above. Table 2 presents the adjusted mean ratings of delayed overall mood. As can be seen from Table 2, after controlling for all of the variables simultaneously, the difference between delayed mood ratings of PD and ND participants fell just short of statistical significance.

We also postulated that the protracted persistence of mood following a MIP in PD participants is specific to negative, not to positive, mood. Consistent with our prediction, there were no differences between PD and ND participants' delayed overall mood ratings following the positive MIP [$t(60) < 1$].

Individual Differences in Stroop Interference

Extreme RT scores (i.e. RTs longer than 2500msec or shorter than 333msec) were eliminated from analyses. Excluded responses occurred on 4% of the trials and did not differ as a function of word type or dysphoria group. In addition, data from two participants were excluded from the analyses because they had excessively high (above 10%) error rates (e.g. excessively short or long colour-naming times). Thus, reaction time data from 60 participants were analysed. These data are presented in Table 3.

TABLE 2
Adjusted Group Means of Delayed Self-reported Overall
Mood Ratings after the Negative Mood-induction
Procedure

Covaried Variables	Exp. 1		Exp. 2	
	ND	PD	ND	PD
None	-2.4_a	-9.6_b	4.8_a	-5.0_b
Baseline	-3.0_a	-9.1_a**	4.7_a	-4.9_b
Peak	-3.4_a	-8.7_b	3.4_a	-3.1_b
Intensity*	-3.2_a	-8.9_a**	5.1_a	-5.4_b
BDI	-2.6_a	-9.3_b	3.9_a	-3.8_b
Baseline + Peak + BDI + Intensity	-4.3_a	-7.9_a	3.9_a	-3.9_b

Note: ND, never-dysphoric; PD, previously dysphoric. Within each pair, means with different subscripts are significantly different from each other ($P < .05$), after covariance of the appropriate variable.

   * Intensity of the recalled negative experience.

   ** Within these pairs, the differences are significant at $P < .07$.

TABLE 3
Group Means and (Standard Deviations) of Reaction Times (msec) in the Stroop
Task

MIP Type	Mood-induction Procedure					
	Experiment 1 (N = 60)			Experiment 2 (N = 82)		
	Negative	Positive	Neutral	Negative	Positive	Neutral
Negative MIP	732$_a$	720$_b$	730$_a$	711$_a$	693$_b$	695$_b$
	(128)	(129)	(130)	(157)	(145)	(141)
Positive MIP	704$_a$	715$_b$	725$_b$	688$_a$	689$_a$	689$_a$
	(127)	(129)	(124)	(135)	(130)	(141)

Note: Within each triple, means with different subscripts are significantly different from each other at $P < .05$.

We predicted that PD participants would exhibit greater Stroop inter-ference with negative materials than would ND participants following a negative, but not following a positive, MIP. To test this hypothesis, we conducted a 2 × 2 × 3 ANOVA with dysphoria history (ND vs. PD) as the between-subjects factor and MIP (positive vs. negative) and stimulus valence (neutral, negative, positive) as within-subject factors. This analy-sis yielded a significant main effect for valence [$F(2,116) = 4.41$, $P < .05$]. Importantly, this main effect for valence was qualified by a significant interaction of MIP and valence [$F(2,116) = 4.84$, $P < .05$]. Planned follow-up comparisons indicated that, in the negative MIP, RTs to negative words were greater than to positive or neutral words, whereas this pattern was reversed in the positive MIP [$F(1,58) = 9.06$, $P < .05$ and $F(1,58) = 5.85$, $P < .05$, respectively]. This finding indicates that the effects of the mood inductions extended beyond self-report measures to affect perfor-mance on the Stroop task. Specifically, following a mood induction, participants exhibited greater attention to mood-congruent than to mood-irrelevant stimuli. There were no other significant main effects or interac-tions (all $Ps < .05$). Thus, contrary to our expectations, the PD participants did not differ from the ND participants with respect to their performance on the Stroop task.

In sum, the results of Experiment 1 suggest that the subjective effects of a negative MIP are more persistent for individuals with a history of dysphoria than for individuals without such a history. However, it is possible that these differences are mediated by other affect variables. Furthermore, in contrast to Ingram et al.'s (1994) findings of vulnerabil-ity-related differences on a dichotic listening task, we found no differences between PD and ND participants with respect to their performance on the emotion Stroop task following a negative mood induction.

OVERVIEW OF EXPERIMENT 2

Experiment 2 was designed to replicate and extend the results of Experiment 1. Because Experiment 1 assessed Stroop interference continuously, it forced all participants to engage in the same activity following the MIPs, thus interfering with their natural affect regulation strategies. It is possible, therefore, that more pronounced individual differences in affect persistence would emerge in the absence of continuous administration of the Stroop task. In addition, Experiment 1 used participants' mood ratings following a neutral MIP as their baseline ratings. Because a neutral MIP might have served as a self-focus manipulation, it is possible that participants' ratings after that induction did not provide an accurate measure of their baseline (i.e. typical neutral) mood. Thus, Experiment 2 was designed to avoid these possible confounds by: (1) including a brief period following the MIPs in which participants were left to use their own affect regulation strategies; and (2) assessing participants' "walk-in" mood as a measure of their neutral affective state. Specifically, in this experiment, participants began the Stroop task two minutes after completing the MIP. Consistent with our previous findings, we postulated that, compared with ND participants, PD participants would experience more persistent effects of the negative, but not the positive, MIP. In addition, we postulated that PD participants would exhibit greater Stroop interference with negative materials after the negative MIP than would ND participants. Finally, to examine the association between depression and memory for negative stimuli (e.g. Gotlib & MacLeod, 1997), we included an incidental memory measure for the Stroop stimuli. Consistent with Williams et al.'s (1988) model of elaborative cognitive biases in depression, we postulated that PD participants, compared with ND participants, would exhibit a negative bias in their delayed incidental memory for negative materials.

EXPERIMENT 2

Method

Participants

A total of 102 individuals participated in the experiment as part of a course requirement. Data from three participants were lost due to equipment failure. The participant selection procedure was identical to that used in Experiment 1.

Materials and Apparatus

The materials consisted of 75 experimenter-provided words. There were 25 words in each of the following three categories: neutral (e.g. "verbal", "temporal"); negative (e.g. "hopeless", "gloomy"); and positive (e.g. "friendly", "cheerful"). As in Experiment 1, the positive and negative words were equated for frequency, length, and emotionality based on John's (1988) ratings.

The apparatus was identical to that used in Experiment 1.

Procedure

As was the case in Experiment 1, this experiment consisted of four phases: an introductory phase, two experimental phases, and a final, mood-neutralising phase.

Introductory Phase.   After a brief introduction to the study, participants completed 20 practice trials of the Stroop task, which were the same as the experimental trials described later, except that the stimulus words were all neutral words (e.g. "one"). Participants then rated their mood, which was taken to represent their baseline affective state. Thus, in contrast to Experiment 1, the baseline mood in this experiment is participants' natural "walk-in" mood, rather than their mood following a recall of neutral autobiographical experience.

Experimental Phases.   Except for the two-minute delay following the administration of the MIP, the structure of these two phases was identical to that of Experiment 1. Specifically, after undergoing a MIP (negative in the NP condition and positive in the PN condition) participants rated their mood. They were then told that the computer was "loading data" for their next task. After a two-minute period, participants were instructed to begin the Stroop colour-naming task. During this task participants were presented with 75 stimuli. Participants' colour-naming response terminated a stimulus display. A two-second interval separated consecutive trials. This task took about two minutes to complete. After completing the Stroop task, the participants rated their mood. After completing the first experimental phase and a filler task (same as that used in Experiment 1), participants proceeded to the second experimental phase. Again, except for the valence of the mood-induction procedure (positive in the NP condition and negative in the PN condition), the structure of the second experimental phase was identical to the first (i.e. a MIP, mood-rating, two-minute delay, a Stroop task, and a final mood rating).

Neutralising Phase.   After completing both experimental phases, participants were given an incidental recall task in which they were requested to recall as many of the words that appeared in the Stroop task as possible. They were given three minutes to complete this task. Next, participants relived a neutral experience in order to neutralise their mood, and then completed the BDI. Finally, participants were debriefed and thanked for their participation.

Results and Discussion

Current Depressive Symptomatology

Eight participants whose BDI scores were significantly elevated at the time of the experiment (BDI > 10) were excluded from all analyses. There were 53 participants in the never-dysphoric (ND) group and 38 participants in the previously dysphoric (PD) group. Mean BDI scores of these groups were 3.7 and 5.3, respectively. A *t*-test indicated that the BDI scores of the PD participants were significantly higher than those of the ND participants $[t(90) = 2.5, P < .05]$. To ensure that this difference did not influence subsequent results, we conducted analyses of covariance (ANCOVAs) using the participants' BDI scores as a covariate. As in Experiment 1, in no analysis did the BDI scores alter any of the results reported later. Thus, we generally do not report the results of analyses involving BDI.

Efficacy of Mood-induction Procedures

As in Experiment 1, we examined the effectivenss of the negative MIP by conducting a 2 × 2 ANOVA with dysphoric history (ND vs. PD) as the between-subjects variable and time (baseline vs. immediately after the negative MIP) as the within-subject factor. This analysis yielded a main effect of time, such that participants' mood ratings immediately after the negative MIP were significantly lower than they were at baseline $[F(1,89) = 248.8, P < .01]$. No other main effects or interactions reached statistical significance. Similarly, to examine the effectiveness of the positive MIP, we conducted a 2 × 2 ANOVA on participants' mood ratings. This analysis too yielded a main effect of time, such that participants' mood ratings immediately after the positive MIP were significantly higher than at baseline $[F(1,89) = 61.4, P < .01]$. No other main effects or interactions were significant. Consistent with the findings of Experiment 1, these results suggest that both negative and positive MIPs were successful in modifying participants' mood, and that ND and PD individuals did not differ from one another with respect to their immediate reactions to either positive or negative MIP.

Individual Differences in Affect Persistence

As in Experiment 1, we examined differences between PD and ND participants' experience of negative affect by conducting a series of ANCOVAs with dysphoria group as the between-subjects factor, and baseline mood, peak mood, intensity of recalled negative experience, and concurrent depressive symptomatology (as measured by the BDI), and all of these variables combined, as covariates. As presented in Table 2, under all of these conditions the difference in the delayed mood ratings remained significant (all $Ps < .05$). Importantly, even after statistically controlling for all four potential factors that could influence delayed mood ratings, the difference between the PD and ND participants' ratings remained significant.

We postulated that the protracted persistence of mood after an MIP in the PD participants would be specific to negative mood. Consistent with this prediction, there were no differences between PD and ND participants' delayed overall mood ratings following the positive MIP [$t(89) < 1$].

Individual Differences in Stroop Interference

Our data reduction procedure eliminated all RTs above 2500msec and below 333msec. In addition, data from nine participants were excluded from the analyses because they had excessively high (above 10%) error rates (e.g. excessively short or long colour-naming times). Thus, Stroop interference data from 82 participants were analysed.

We predicted that PD participants would demonstrate greater Stroop interference with negative materials than would ND participants following the negative, but not the positive, MIP. To test this hypothesis, we conducted a $2 \times 2 \times 3$ ANOVA with dysphoria history (ND vs. PD) as the between-subjects factor, and MIP (positive vs. negative) and word stimulus valence (neutral, negative, positive) as within-subject factors. As in Experiment 1, this analysis yielded a significant interaction of MIP and stimulus valence [$F(2,156) = 4.27$, $P < .05$], (see Table 3). Planned follow-up comparisons indicated that, in the negative MIP, RTs to negative words were greater than to positive or neutral words [$F(1,78) = 8.9$, and $F(1,78) = 5.5$, respectively, both $Ps < .05$]. In the positive MIP condition, there were no significant differences among the three types of stimuli. Again, therefore, following a negative mood induction, participants exhibited greater attention to mood-congruent than to mood-irrelevant stimuli. There were no other significant main effects or interactions (all $Ps > .05$). In particular, as in Experiment 1, PD participants did not differ from ND participants with respect to their performance on the Stroop task.

Individual Differences in Incidental Recall

Table 4 presents descriptive statistics for the recall data. We expected that PD participants would recall more negative than neutral or positive words, whereas such a bias would not be observed with ND participants. Further, we postulated that this memory bias would be independent of participants' most recent mood. To investigate individual differences in participants' incidental memory for the Stroop stimuli, controlling for the effects of their most recent mood, the recall data were submitted to a 2 × 3 ANCOVA with dysphoria history as the between-subjects factor, stimulus valence (negative, positive, and neutral) as the within-subject factor, and overall mood ratings preceding the incidental memory task as a covariate. This analysis yielded a significant main effect of dysphoria history, such that PD participants remembered more words overall than did ND participants $[F(1,89) = 5.6, P < .05]$. The analysis also yielded a significant main effect of stimulus valence $[F(2,178) = 20.5, P < .01]$. Planned follow-up comparisons indicated that participants' memory for positive and negative stimuli was stronger than was their memory for neutral stimuli $[F(1,88) = 34.9,$ and $F(1,88) = 45.1,$ respectively, both $Ps < .01]$; memory for negative and positive stimuli did not differ $[F(1,88) < 1.4, P > .05]$. Most important, as predicted, the analysis also yielded a significant interaction of stimulus valence and dysphoria history $[F(2,176) = 6.04, P < .05]$. Planned follow-up comparisons indicated that PD participants demonstrated significantly better memory for negative words than did ND participants $[F(1,88) = 11.4, P < .01]$; the two groups did not differ with respect to their memory for either positive or neutral materials (both $Fs < 1$). There was no significant main effect of, or interaction involving, most recent mood. Thus, PD participants' superior recall of negative words cannot be explained by more negative mood prior to participating in the recall procedure.

TABLE 4
Group Means and (Standard Deviations) for the
Number of Words Recalled in an Incidental Memory
Task

Participant Group	Stimulus Type		
	Negative	Positive	Neutral
Never-depressed	1.25	1.48	.66
	(.22)	(.18)	(.76)
Previously Depressed	2.37	1.58	.76
	(.26)	(.21)	(.13)

GENERAL DISCUSSION

The results of the present studies confirmed two of our three hypotheses. We postulated that previously dysphoric participants would demonstrate better memory for negative information than would never-dysphoric participants, and that the two groups would not differ in their memory for positive or neutral stimuli. This hypothesis was confirmed. The results of several studies suggest that memory retrieval operations may not be completely normalised on recovery from a significant dysphoric episode (e.g. Bradley & Mathews, 1988; Hedlund & Rude, 1995; Teasdale & Dent, 1987). Moreover, the results of several prospective studies suggest that memory biases both precede and follow depressive episodes (e.g. Bellew & Hill, 1991; Brittlebank, Scott, Williams, & Ferrier, 1993; Dent & Teasdale, 1988). Such evidence is generally lacking with respect to attentional and judgement biases (see, however, Ingram et al., 1994). It is possible that, although biases in both attentional and memory processes are characteristic of a dysphoric state, only biases in memory functioning are associated with a persistent vulnerability to dysphoria. Should further research confirm this association, memory biases would be effective markers of vulnerability to depression.

We also postulated that PD participants would report more protracted negative affect than would ND participants. This hypothesis was confirmed in both experiments. Importantly, in Experiment 2, the differences between PDs and NDs were maintained after controlling statistically for several theoretically relevant variables, namely, the intensity of the recalled experience, concurrent depressive symptomatology, and levels of peak and baseline moods. Thus, it is unlikely that differences in delayed mood ratings can be attributed to the possibility that PD participants drew on more distressing memories than did ND participants, or that PD participants had more negative mood to begin with than did ND participants.

Protracted experience of negative affect might contribute to depressive vulnerability in several ways. First, prolonged dysphoric mood is likely to enhance the effects of cognitive biases and contribute to both the consolidation of negative self-schemata and the attenuation of positive self-schemata. Second, the duration of emotional reactions might affect the way such emotional experiences are interpreted and remembered (Gilboa & Revelle, 1994). For example, longer emotional experiences are more likely to be perceived as important and meaningful, and thus are more likely to affect an individual's self-perception. Transient negative states, in contrast, are unlikely to alter self-perception. Similarly, with respect to memory, longer affective experiences are more likely to be recalled than are shorter ones. Because individuals with a history of dysphoria tend to have more protracted negative than positive experiences, they might also be more likely to retrieve negative than positive experiences. This retrieval pattern might, in turn, negatively affect their subsequent mood.

Third, because the protracted duration of the emotional response provides more opportunities for noticing, and subsequently focusing on, one's emotional state, individuals with a tendency to experience such episodes might develop ruminative response characteristics such as those described by Nolen-Hoeksema (1991). As we mentioned earlier, Roberts et al. (in press) found that individuals with a history of depression report more ruminative tendencies than do individuals without such history. Considered together with laboratory studies in which rumination is manipulated experimentally (e.g. Morrow & Nolen-Hoeksema, 1990), the findings of the present studies suggest that protracted emotional reactions act as a trait vulnerability factor to depression. Future research should examine more explicitly the association between protracted emotional reactions and specific affect regulation strategies used by remitted dysphorics.

Finally, we postulated that, following a negative MIP, individuals with a history of dysphoria would exhibit greater attention to negative stimuli on the Stroop task than would never-dysphoric individuals. This hypothesis was not confirmed. Both PD and ND participants selectively processed negative information following a negative, but not a positive, mood-induction procedure. Because reaction times were affected by variation in mood, it is unlikely that the lack of group differences on the emotion Stroop task is due to the insensitivity of this measure.

The present results, like those Hedlund and Rude (1995), failed to reveal attentional differences between vulnerable and nonvulnerable individuals, and thus stand in contrast to the findings reported by Ingram et al. (1994). This inconclusive pattern of results extends beyond vulnerability studies to investigations utilising clinically depressed samples: Whereas some researchers have found differences between depressed and nondepressed participants with respect to attentional functioning (e.g. Gotlib & Cane, 1987; Gotlib, McLachlan, & Katz, 1988; McCabe & Gotlib, 1995; Williams & Nulty, 1986), others have not (e.g. Hill & Knowles, 1991; Mogg et al., 1993). It is likely that the nature and strength of association between depression and attentional biases depends critically on several variables. First, attentional biases might be due to a high level of comorbid anxiety in depressed individuals (e.g. Gotlib & MacLeod, 1997; Williams et al., 1988; but see also Bradley, Mogg, Millar, & White, 1995). Second, such biases may be more likely to emerge with stimuli strongly related to depressive concerns (Gotlib et al., in press; Williams & Nulty, 1986). Third, stimulus presentation that facilitates more elaborate semantic-processing (e.g. grouped presentation of semantically related stimuli on a single card) appears to lead to larger differences between emotional-disorder and normal groups than does random stimulus presentation (e.g. Dalgleish, 1995). Finally, it is becoming apparent that single-stimulus tasks, such as the Stroop task, yield a different pattern of results than do tasks involving multiple stimuli, such as the deployment-of-attention task, the dot-probe task, or the dichotic listening task. In particular, the association between depression and attentional bias appears to be stronger when stimulus presentation explicitly offers two distinct processing options than when attention is concentrated on a single stimulus (see MacLeod & Mathews, 1991). These formulations are tentative, however, and it remains for future research to examine them more explicitly.

In closing, we should note several limitations of the present study. First, our samples consisted of undergraduates whose previous dysphoria was assessed through retrospective self-reports. Clearly, replication of our findings with participants whose major depressive episodes were ascertained using clinical interviews would contribute to their reliability and validity. Second, the specific stimuli used on the Stroop task might be responsible for the absence of group differences. It is possible that the use of stimuli that are more specifically relevant to depressive schemata would have revealed differences between PDs and NDs. As we noted earlier, however, depression-associated differences on the Stroop task are not always found even when such stimuli are used (e.g. Mogg et al., 1993). Moreover, we did find group differences in incidental memory using these stimuli. Finally, an autobiographical mood induction, although effective in activating participants' idiosyncratic negative self-schemata, may introduce several theoretical complications. For example, such a manipulation introduces demand characteristics, calling into question the validity of results that rely on self-report measures. It is important to note, however, that the autobiographical MIP has been shown to influence nonself-report measures, such as mood-congruent Stroop performance (in the present studies; also in Gilboa, Revelle, & Gotlib, submitted) and memory recall (Meerum-Terwogt, Kremer, & Stegge, 1991; Salovey, 1992). Undoubtedly, a replication of the present findings with more standardised MIPs (e.g. using films or music) would contribute to a clearer delineation of differences in affect persistence between PD and ND participants.

In sum, our data indicate that remitted dysphorics demonstrate several emotional and cognitive characteristics that differ from those exhibited by never-dysphoric individuals. Consistent with Beck's (1976) formulation, memory biases are not simply concomitants of a depressive state; rather, they continue to be present after the depressive episode remits and, when activated, may mediate relapse. Consistent with Teasdale's differential activation hypothesis, affect regulation strategies may also play a causal role in vulnerability to depression. Future research should examine how temporal components of affective reactions interact with cognitive processes to produce memory and affect regulation patterns that outlast depressive episodes.

REFERENCES

APA (American Psychiatric Association) (1980). *Diagnostic and statistical manual of mental disorders: DSMIII* (3rd ed.). Washington, DC: Author.

APA (American Psychiatric Association) (1987). *Diagnostic and statistical manual of mental disorders: DSMIII-R* (3rd rev. ed.). Washington, DC: Author.

Andersen, S.M., Spielman, L.A., & Bargh, J.A. (1992). Future-event schemas and certainty about the future: Automaticity in depressive's future-event predictions. *Journal of Personality and Social Psychology, 63,* 711–723.

Beck, A.T. (1976). *Cognitive therapy and the emotional disorders.* New York: International Universities Press.

Beck, A.T., Rush, A.J., Shaw, B.T., & Emery, G. (1979). *Cognitive therapy of depression.* New York: Guilford.

Bellew, M., & Hill, B. (1991). Negative recall bias as predictor of susceptibility of depression following childbirth. *Personality and Individual Differences, 12,* 943–949.

Bradley, B., & Mathews, A. (1988). Memory bias in recovered clinical depressives. *Cognition and Emotion, 2,* 235–246.

Bradley, B.P., Mogg, K., Millar, N., & White, J. (1995). Selective processing of negative information: Effects of clinical anxiety, concurrent depression, and awareness. *Journal of Abnormal Psychology, 104,* 532–536.

Brittlebank, A.D., Scott, J., Williams, J.M. & Ferrier, I.N. (1993). Autobiographical memory in depression: State or trait marker? *British Journal of Psychiatry, 162,* 118–121.

Constans, J.I., & Mathews, A.M. (1993). Mood and the participative risk of future events. *Cognition and Emotion, 7,* 545–560.

Dalgleish, T. (1995). Performance of the emotional Stroop task in groups of anxious, expert, and control participants: A comparison of computer and card presentation formats. *Cognition and Emotion, 9,* 326–340.

Dent, J., & Teasdale, J.D. (1988). Negative cognitions and the persistence of depression. *Journal of Abnormal Psychology, 97,* 29–34.

Gilboa, E., & Revelle, W. (1994). Personality and the structure of emotional responses. In S. Van Goozen, N.E. Van de Poll, & A. Sargent (Eds.), *Emotions: Essays on emotion theory* (pp. 135–161). Hillsdale, NJ: Lawrence Erlbaum Associates Inc.

Gilboa, E., Revelle, W., & Gotlib, I.H. (submitted). *Stroop interference following mood induction: Emotionality, mood congruence, concern relevance, and persistence.*

Gotlib, I.H., & Cane, D.B. (1987). Construct accessibility and clinical depression: A longitudinal approach. *Journal of Abnormal Psychology, 96,* 199–204.

Gotlib, I.H., Gilboa, E., & Sommerfield, B.K. (in press). Cognitive functioning in depression: Nature and origins. In R.J. Davidson (Ed.), *Wisconsin symposium on emotion* (Vol. 1). New York: Oxford University Press.

Gotlib, I.H., & MacLeod, C. (1997). Information processing in anxiety and depression: A cognitive developmental perspective. In J. Burack & J. Enns (Eds.), *Attention, development, and psychopathology* (pp. 350–378). New York: Guilford Press.

Gotlib, I.H., & McCann, C.D. (1984). Construct accessibility and depression: An examination of cognitive and affective factors. *Journal of Personality and Social Psychology, 47,* 427–439.

Gotlib, I.H., McLachlan, A.L., & Katz, A.N. (1988). Biases in visual attention in depressed and nondepressed individuals. *Cognition and Emotion, 2,* 185–100.

Hammen, C.L. (1991). *Depression runs in families: The social context of risk and resilience in children of depressed mothers.* New York: Springer.

Hedlund, S., & Rude, S. (1995). Evidence of latent depressive schemas in formerly depressed individuals. *Journal of Abnormal Psychology, 104,* 517–525.

Hill, A.B., & Knowles, T.H. (1991). Depression and the 'emotional' Stroop effect. *Personality and Individual differences, 12,* 481–485.

Ingram, R.I., Bernet, C.Z., & McLaughlin, S.C. (1994). Attentional allocation processes in individuals at risk for depression. *Cognitive Therapy and Research, 18,* 317–332.

John, C.H. (1988). Emotionality ratings and free association norms of 240 emotional and nonemotional words. *Cognition and Emotion, 2,* 49–70.

Keller, M.B. (1985). Chronic and recurrent affective disorders: Incidence, course, and influencing factors. In D. Kemali & G. Recagni (Eds.), *Chronic treatments in neuropsychiatry* (pp. 111–120). New York: Raven.

MacLeod, C., & Mathews, A. (1991). Biased cognitive operations in anxiety: Accessibility of information or assignment of processing priorities? *Behaviour Research and Therapy, 29,* 599–610.

Martin, M. (1985). Neuroticism as a cognitive predisposition toward depression: A cognitive mechanism. *Personality and Individual Differences, 6,* 353–365.

Mathews, A., & MacLeod, C. (1994). Cognitive approaches to emotions and emotional disorders. *Annual Review of Psychology, 45,* 25–50.

Matt, G.E., Vazquez, C., & Campbell, W.K. (1992). Mood congruent recall of affectively tones stimuli: A meta-analytic review. *Clinical Psychology Review, 12,* 227–255.

McCabe, S.B., & Gotlib, I.H. (1993). Attentional processing in clinically depressed participants: A longitudinal investigation. *Cognitive Therapy and Research, 17,* 1–19.

McCabe, S.B., & Gotlib, I.H. (1995). Selective attention in clinical depression: Performance on a selective attention task. *Journal of Abnormal Psychology, 104,* 241–245.

Meerum Terwogt, M., Kremer, H.H., & Stegge, H. (1991). Effects of children's emotional state on their reactions to emotional expressions: A search for congruency effects. *Cognition and Emotion, 5,* 109–121.

Miranda, J., Persons, J.B., & Byers, C.N. (1990). Endorsement of dysfunctional beliefs depends on current mood-state. *Journal of Abnormal Psychology, 99,* 237–241.

Mogg, K., Bradley, S.D., Williams, R., & Mathews, A. (1993). Subliminal processing of emotional information in anxiety and depression. *Journal of Abnormal Psychology, 102,* 304–312.

Morrow, J., & Nolen-Hoeksema, S. (1990). Effects of responses to depression on the remediation of depressive affect. *Journal of Personality and Social Psychology, 58,* 519–527.

Nolen-Hoeksema, S. (1987). Sex differences in unipolar depression: Evidence and theory. *Psychological Bulletin, 101,* 256–282.

Nolen-Hoeksema, S. (1991). Responses to depression and their effect on the duration of depressive episodes. *Journal of Abnormal Psychology, 100,* 569–582.

Persons, J.B., & Miranda, J. (1992). Cognitive theories of vulnerability to depression: Reconciling negative evidence. *Cognitive Therapy and Research, 16,* 485–502.

Roberts, J.E., Gilboa, E., & Gotlib, I.H. (in press). Ruminative response style and vulnerability to depressive episodes: Factor components, mediating processes, and episode duration. *Cognitive Therapy and Research.*

Salovey, P. (1992). Mood-induced self-focused attention. *Journal of Personality and Social Psychology, 62,* 699–707.

Segal, Z.V., & Ingram, R.E. (1994). Mood priming and construct activation in tests of cognitive vulnerability to unipolar depression. *Clinical Psychology Review, 14,* 663–695.

Teasdale, J.D. (1988). Cognitive vulnerability to persistent depression. *Cognition and Emotion, 2,* 247–274.

Teasdale, J.D., & Barnard, P.G. (1993). *Affect, cognition, and change: Remodelling depressive thought*. Hove, UK: Lawrence Erlbaum Associates Ltd.

Teasdale, J.D., & Dent, J. (1987). Cognitive vulnerability to depression: An investigation of two hypotheses. *British Journal of Clinical Psychology, 26*, 113–126.

Williams, J.M.G. (1992). Autobiographical memory and emotional disorders. In S.A. Christianson (Ed.), *The handbook of emotion and memory* (pp. 451–476). Hillsdale, NJ: Lawrence Erlbaum Associates Inc.

Williams, J.M.G., & Nulty, D.D. (1986). Construct accessibility, depression, and the emotional Stroop task: Transient mood or stable structure? *Personality and Individual Differences, 7*, 485–491.

Williams, J.M.G., Watts, F.N., MacLeod, C., & Mathews, A. (1988). *Cognitive psychology and the emotional disorders*. Chichester: Wiley.

Zimmerman, M., & Coryell, W. (1987). The inventory to diagnose depression, lifetime version. *Acta Psychiatrica Scandinavica, 75*, 495–499.

Zimmerman, M., & Coryell, W. (1988). The validity of a self-report questionnaire for diagnosing major depressive disorder. *Archives of General Psychiatry, 45*, 738–740.

Zimmerman, M., Coryell, W., Corenthal, C., & Wilson, S. (1986). A self-report scale to diagnose major depressive disorder. *Archives of General Psychiatry, 43*, 1076–1081.

COGNITION AND EMOTION, 1997, *11* (5/6), 539–568

Self-referent Information-processing in Individuals at High and Low Cognitive Risk for Depression

Lauren B. Alloy

Temple University, Philadelphia, USA

Lyn Y. Abramson

University of Wisconsin–Madison, USA

Laura A. Murray and Wayne G. Whitehouse

Temple University, Philadelphia, USA

Michael E. Hogan

University of Wisconsin–Madison, USA

Whereas prior work has demonstrated that depressed persons exhibit preferential processing of negative self-referent information, the present study investigated whether persons who are cognitively vulnerable to depression show similar negative self-referent processing. Nondepressed participants in the Temple–Wisconsin Cognitive Vulnerability to Depression Project who were at hypothesised high or low cognitive risk for depression based on their dysfunctional attitudes and inferential styles were administered a Self-referent Information Processing Task Battery that yielded five information-processing measures: judgements of self-descriptiveness ("Me/Not Me") of trait words; response times for these judgements; past behavioural examples for self-descriptive words; future behavioural predictions; and correct recall of the trait words. Each dependent measure yielded scores for four types of stimuli in a Valence × Content design: positive and negative stimuli that

Requests for reprints should be sent to either Dr Lauren B. Alloy, Department of Psychology, Temple University, Weiss Hall, 13th Street and Cecil B. Moore Avenue, Philadelphia, PA 19122, USA; or Dr Lyn Y. Abramson, Department of Psychology, University of Wisconsin, 1202 W. Johnson Street, Madison, WI 53706, USA.

This article was supported by National Institute of Mental Health Grants MH 48216 to Lauren B. Alloy and MH 43866 to Lyn Y. Abramson. We would like to thank the following CVD Project interviewers for their contributions to this article: Michelle Armstrong, Monica Calkins, Mark Cenite, Judith Cronholm, Patricia Donovan, Kimberly Eberbach, Teresa Gannon, Nancy Just, Ray Kim, Christine Klitz, Alan Lipman, Catherine Panzarella, Matthew Robinson, Donna Rose, Pamela Shapiro, Janet Shriberg, and Aaron Torrance. The first two authors contributed equally to this article.

were either relevant or irrelevant to a depressive self-concept. Consistent with prediction, relative to low cognitive risk participants, high cognitive risk participants exhibited greater processing of negative self-referent information and less processing of positive self-referent information on all measures. Moreover, there was some evidence that risk group differences in self-referent processing biases were greater for depression-relevant than for depression-irrelevant content domains. The findings are discussed with respect to theoretical and methodological implications for the cognitive theories of depression.

INTRODUCTION

Cognitive vulnerability-stress theories of depression, such as Beck's (1967, 1987) cognitive theory and the hopelessness theory of depression (Abramson, Metalsky, & Alloy, 1989; Alloy, Abramson, Metalsky, & Hartlage, 1988), hypothesise that particular negative cognitive patterns increase individuals' likelihood of developing episodes of depression, in particular, episodes of a cognitively mediated subtype of depression (Abramson & Alloy, 1990; Abramson et al., 1989), when they experience stressful life events. According to these cognitive theories, people who possess such maladaptive cognitive patterns are vulnerable to depression because they tend to engage in negatively toned information-processing about themselves and their experiences when they encounter stressful events.

In Beck's theory (1967, 1987; Beck, Rush, Shaw, & Emery, 1979), for example, depression-prone people are hypothesised to possess negative self-schemata revolving around themes of inadequacy, failure, loss, and worthlessness. Such negative content is represented as a set of dysfunctional attitudes or self-worth contingencies in which the depression-prone person subscribes to maladaptive beliefs such as his/her happiness and success depend on being perfect or on others' approval. Consistent with cognitive science and social cognition perspectives on the operation of schemata (e.g. Alba & Hasher, 1983; Brewer & Nakamura, 1984; Taylor & Crocker, 1981), Beck (1967) hypothesised that depressive self-schemata guide the perception, interpretation, and memory of personally relevant experiences, with the result being a negatively biased construal of one's personal world. When activated by the occurrence of stressful life events, depressive self-schemata lead to the development of depressive symptoms through their effect on preferential encoding and retrieval of negative self-referent information.

In the hopelessness theory (Abramson et al., 1989; Alloy et al., 1988), people who exhibit a depressogenic inferential style, in which they characteristically attribute negative life events to stable and global causes, infer that negative consequences will follow from a current negative event, and infer that the occurrence of a negative event in their lives means that they are fundamentally flawed or worthless, are hypothesised to be vulnerable to developing episodes of depression, in particular "hopelessness depression", when they confront negative life events. This is because individuals who exhibit a depressogenic inferential style should be more likely to generate negative inferences regarding the causes, consequences, and self-implications of stressful events than individuals who do not possess this style, thereby increasing the likelihood that they will develop hopelessness and, in turn, symptoms of hopelessness depression. Similar to Beck's model, then, the hypothesised cognitive vulnerability in the hopelessness theory operates to increase risk for depression through its effects on processing or appraisals of personally relevant life experiences.

Cognitive Vulnerability and Self-referent Information-processing

In studies examining the cross-sectional or longitudinal relation between cognitive vulnerability and depression, investigators have typically used one of two strategies for measuring the cognitive vulnerabilities featured in Beck's theory and hopelessness theory: (1) self-report questionnaires designed to assess the content of self-schemata or cognitive styles; or (2) laboratory tasks adapted from cognitive psychology designed to assess the information-processing biases associated with the operation of self-schemata or cognitive styles.[1] For example, numerous studies have investigated whether dysfunctional beliefs as measured by the Dysfunctional Attitudes Scale (DAS; Weissman & Beck, 1978) or depressogenic attributional styles as measured by the Attributional Style Questionnaire (ASQ; Seligman, Abramson, Semmel, & von Baeyer, 1979) are associated concurrently with depression, remain elevated following remission from depression, or predict future depression alone or in interaction with stressful events (see, for example, Barnett & Gotlib, 1988 for a review). More recently, some researchers have turned to cognitive psychology paradigms modified for use with emotion-relevant stimuli, such as the Self-referent Encoding task (SRET; Craik & Tulving, 1975; Derry & Kuiper, 1981; Markus, 1977) or the Stroop task (Stroop, 1935; Gotlib & McCann, 1984; Segal & Vella, 1990), as an alternative approach for examining cognitive vulnerability in currently depressed, previously depressed, or future depressed individuals.

---

[1] Although self-report inventories are typically used to measure the content of cognitive vulnerabilities and laboratory tasks are generally used to measure the processing effects of these vulnerabilities, this is not a necessary distinction between the two types of methodologies. For example, some studies have assessed information-processing biases with self-report questionnaires (e.g. Alloy & Ahrens, 1987; Haack, Metalsky, Dykman, & Abramson, 1996).

What is the association between cognitive patterns as assessed by self-reports and information-processing as assessed by laboratory tasks? Specifically, in the present study, we examined whether individuals at hypothesised high and low vulnerability for depression based on the presence versus absence of dysfunctional attitudes and negative inferential styles also differ in their processing of self-referent information. We believe this issue is important for three major reasons.

First, the issue of whether information-processing biases associated with depression are actually reflective of an underlying vulnerability is of central concern to cognitive models of depression. Several theorists (e.g. Beck, 1967, 1987; Ingram & Wisnicki, 1991; Williams, Watts, MacLeod, & Mathews, 1988) have proposed that self-schema guided dysfunctional information-processing plays a causal role in depression. Prior work has demonstrated that depressed persons often show preferential processing of negative self-referent information (e.g. Segal, 1988), including greater endorsement and recall of depressive-content self-referent trait adjectives (e.g. Derry & Kuiper, 1981; Greenberg & Alloy, 1989; Greenberg & Beck, 1989; Ingram, Fidaleo, Freidberg, Shenk, & Bernet, 1995; Ingram, Smith, & Brehm, 1983; Kuiper & MacDonald, 1982), faster decision times for negative self-referent stimuli (e.g. Greenberg & Alloy, 1989; MacDonald & Kuiper, 1984), increased accessibility of negative constructs (e.g. Bargh & Tota, 1988; Dobson & Shaw, 1987; Gotlib & Cane, 1987; Gotlib & McCann, 1984), and preferential attention to negative or emotional stimuli (e.g. Dobson & Shaw, 1987; Gotlib, McLachlan, & Katz, 1988; Ingram, Bernet, & McLaughlin, 1994a; McCabe & Gotlib, 1993). However, these information-processing biases may be the result of the depressed episode rather than an indicator of vulnerability to depression. The finding of negative, self-referent processing biases in nondepressed individuals who are vulnerable to depression by virtue of possessing negative cognitive styles would be consistent with, although not fully indicative of, a vulnerability function for these biases.

Several investigators have attempted to determine whether self-schema processing is indicative of underlying vulnerability to depression by assessing information-processing in persons who have remitted from depression (e.g. Bradley & Mathews, 1988; Dobson & Shaw, 1987; Gotlib & Cane, 1987; Hammen, Marks, de Mayo, & Mayol, 1985; Hammen, Miklowitz, & Dyck, 1986; Hedlund & Rude, 1995; Ingram et al., 1994a; McCabe & Gotlib, 1993; Teasdale & Dent, 1987; Williams & Nulty, 1986). However, approaches to identifying self-referent processing biases associated with vulnerability to depression based on remitted depression paradigms are problematic in at least one respect (see Just, Abramson, & Alloy, submitted, for other problems with remitted depression designs). Not all formerly depressed persons would be expected to have exhibited the cognitively mediated subtype of depression featured in Beck's and hopelessness theory (Abramson & Alloy, 1990; Abramson et al., 1989) and thus, only a subset of remitted depressives would possess the putative information-processing biases reflective of cognitive vulnerability (Just et al., submitted). An alternative strategy for identifying information-processing effects associated with cognitive vulnerability is to use a behavioural high-risk design (Alloy, Lipman, & Abramson, 1992; Just et al., submitted) in which one directly selects nondepressed persons with and without the negative cognitive styles featured as diatheses in the cognitive theories of depression and then compares these high and low cognitive risk groups for differences in their processing of self-referent stimuli. This is the approach we adopted in the present study. Of course, further support for the vulnerability status of information-processing biases associated with maladaptive cognitive styles depends on demonstrating that those cognitive styles are themselves associated with past or future depression.

Second, from the perspective of Beck's theory and hopelessness theory, an association between self-report assessments of cognitive styles and laboratory task assessments of information-processing is important because negatively biased processing of self-referent material is presumed to be a mediating mechanism by which depressive self-schemata or inferential styles increase vulnerability to depression. If depressive cognitive styles do, in fact, increase the likelihood of depressive symptoms through their effects on encoding, interpretation, and/or retrieval of personally relevant material, then cognitively vulnerable and invulnerable individuals should differ in their self-referent information-processing. In particular, relative to persons at low cognitive risk for depression, high cognitive risk persons should be more likely to exhibit greater processing of negatively valenced and less processing of positively valenced, depression-relevant information about the self.

Finally, the issue of whether self-referent processing differences are associated with the presence versus absence of dysfunctional attitudes and inferential styles is significant from a methodological perspective. In his cogent appraisal of self-schema studies in depression, Segal (1988) argued that self-report questionnaires such as the DAS are not optimal for assessing cognitive vulnerability as represented by self-schemata, in part, because they may reflect fluctuations in negative verbalisations rather than underlying cognitive structure. Similarly, other investigators (e.g. Ingram & Reed, 1986; McCabe & Gotlib, 1993) have criticised self-report measures of cognitive vulnerability as subject to individuals' motivations and expectations or as only likely to tap conscious or controlled cognitive processes, whereas cognitive vulnerability may be reflected more strongly in automatic cognitive-processing (Hartlage, Alloy, Vazquez, & Dykman, 1993; Ingram et al., 1995; Ingram, Partridge, Scott, & Bernet, 1994b;

Teasdale, 1983, 1988). To the extent that negative versus positive attitudes and inferential styles as measured by the DAS and a revised ASQ are associated with actual differences in self-referent information-processing as measured by laboratory tasks adapted from cognitive psychology, the construct validity of both the self-report questionnaires and the laboratory information-processing tasks is increased. Several studies have reported significant correlations between DAS scores and other self-report measures of presumed cognitive biases (e.g. Blackburn, Jones, & Lewin, 1987; Giles & Rush, 1983; Hollon, Kendall, & Lumry, 1986); however, whether such associations would also occur when the cognitive biases are assessed with information-processing tasks remains to be investigated.

We assessed self-referent information-processing both in depression-relevant and depression-irrelevant content domains because Beck's (1967, 1987) theory suggests that depression-prone individuals have specific negative self-schemata related, for example, to autonomous themes of incompetence, worthlessness, and low motivation, but do not have negative schemata in all content domains (Dykman, Abramson, Alloy, & Hartlage, 1989; Greenberg & Alloy, 1989; McClain & Abramson, 1995). Thus, Beck's content-specificity hypothesis would suggest that information-processing biases should be limited to stimulus material congruent with the content embodied in the self-schemata.

Overview of the Present Study and Hypotheses

To examine whether individuals with maladaptive attitudes and inferential styles do, in fact, process information about themselves more negatively than do those with positive styles, we gave a Self-referent Information Processing (SRIP) Task Battery to high and low cognitive risk participants in the Temple–Wisconsin Cognitive Vulnerability to Depression (CVD) Project (Alloy & Abramson, submitted). In the CVD Project, university freshmen who were nondepressed and had no other current Axis I psychopathology at the outset of the study, but who were selected to be at high or low risk for depression based on their cognitive styles, were followed prospectively every 6 weeks for 2 years and then every 16 weeks for 3 more years with assessments of stressful life events, cognitions, and symptoms and diagnosable episodes of psychopathology. The SRIP Battery was administered at the start of the prospective phase of the project. The battery consisted of four tasks based on the work of Derry and Kuiper (1981) and Markus (1977) that yielded five dependent measures: judgements ("Me/Not Me") of self-descriptiveness of trait words; response latencies for these decisions; behavioural descriptions; behavioural predictions; and incidental recall of the trait words. Each task utilised four types of stimuli representing a 2 (Valence) × 2 (Content) design: Positively and negatively valenced stimuli that were either relevant or irrelevant to a depressive self-concept. Consistent with cognitive theories of depression, we hypothesised that relative to low cognitive risk participants, high cognitive risk participants would show better processing of negative words (i.e. greater and faster endorsement, more behavioural descriptions, higher behavioural predictions, and higher correct recall) and less processing of positive words. Moreover, based on Beck's content specificity hypothesis, we predicted that these risk group differences would be more pronounced for depression-relevant than irrelevant content domains. Thus, we predicted a Risk × Content × Valence triple interaction on each of the self-referent processing measures.

METHODS

Participants

Participants for the CVD Project were selected based on a two-phase screening procedure. In Phase I, we administered the Cognitive Style Questionnaire (CSQ), a revision of the ASQ (Seligman et al., 1979) that assesses styles for inferring causes, consequences, and self-characteristics for hypothetical positive and negative events, the DAS (Weissman & Beck, 1978), and a demographics questionnaire to 5378 freshmen at Temple University (TU) and the University of Wisconsin (UW). The CSQ and DAS assess the cognitive diatheses featured in hopelessness theory and Beck's theory, respectively. Potential participants were screened through classes, dormitories, campus activities, and campus media advertisements from 9/90 to 6/92. Freshmen with scores in the highest quartile (most negative) of the Phase I screening sample on *both* the DAS and CSQ composite of the stability, globality, consequences, and self-dimensions for negative events were designated the potential high-risk (HR) group; whereas those with scores in the lowest quartile (most positive) on *both* the DAS and CSQ negative event composite were the potential low-risk (LR) group.

A random subset of the 619 HR and 585 LR freshmen who met the Phase I criteria and were less than 30 years old were invited for the Phase II screening, in which they were administered the current episode and lifetime portions of a modified Schedule for Affective Disorders and Schizophrenia–Lifetime (mod-SADS-L) interview (Endicott & Spitzer, 1978). A total of 313 Phase I-eligible HR and 236 LR freshmen participated in the Phase II screening. Participants were excluded from the final sample if they met *Diagnostic and Statistical Manual of Mental Disorders, 3rd Edition-Revised* (DSMIII-R; APA, 1987) *or* Research Diagnostic Criteria (RDC; Spitzer, Endicott, & Robins, 1978) for any of the following based on the mod-SADS-L: (1) Current diagnosis of any episodic mood disorder [e.g. major (MD) or minor (MiD) depressive disorder, bipolar disorder (Bi) with a current episode of either MD or mania (Ma) or hypomania (Hyp)] or any chronic mood disorder [e.g. dysthymia (Dys), intermittent depressive disorder (IDD), or cyclothymia (Cyc)]; (2) Current diagnosis of any other psychiatric disorder (e.g. anxiety disorder, alcohol or drug use disorder); (3) Current psychotic symptoms; (4) Past history of Ma, Hyp, Bi, or Cyc; and (5) Serious medical illness that would preclude participation in a longitudinal study. Freshmen who met DSMIII-R or RDC criteria for a past unipolar mood disorder (e.g. past MD, MiD, Dys, IDD), but who had remitted for a minimum of two months, were retained in the final sample in order not to be left with an unrepresentative sample of HR participants.[2] The 209 eligible HR and 207 eligible LR participants who met all of the Phase II criteria were invited to participate in the prospective phase of the CVD Project. Of these eligible participants, 17 HR and 13 LR refused participation in the prospective phase and another 19 HR and 18 LR were dropped by us prior to entry into the prospective follow-up period.[3] The final CVD Project sample included 173 HR (83 at TU; 90 at UW) and 176 LR (87 at TU; 89 at UW) freshmen. The final sample was administered the SRIP Task Battery, along with the Beck Depression Inventory (BDI; Beck, Ward, Mendelson, Mock, & Erbaugh, 1961) at the outset of the prospective phase (Time 1), within one month of the Phase II screening.

Table 1 displays demographic and cognitive style characteristics of the final sample at each site. The two cohorts were similar on sex ratio and the cognitive style measures across the sites, but differed on ethnic composition and socioeconomic status (SES), as indicated by parental education and income. The TU cohort had a significantly higher proportion of minority participants (37.1%; 26.4% Afro-American, 3.6% Hispanic, 4.2% Asian, 3.0% Other) than did the UW cohort (6.2%; 1.7% Afro-

---

[2] Our logic in including participants who were nondepressed currently but had a past depression is that by excluding such people, we might be excluding the very people who are most likely to develop the hypothesised cognitively mediated subtype of depression (e.g. hopelessness depression). If Beck's theory and hopelessness theory are correct, then HR participants, by virtue of their negative cognitive styles, should more often be at risk and thus more likely to have experienced past depression than LR participants (a result we did obtain: Alloy et al., submitted). If we excluded such individuals, we might be left with an unrepresentative HR group consisting of participants, who, despite possessing very negative cognitive styles, do not readily become depressed, perhaps because they have other protective factors. Thus, in order not to bias the CVD Project against the cognitive theories by possibly excluding participants who are at risk for hopelessness depression, we included nondepressed participants with past depression.

[3] Participants were dropped from the study for any of three reasons: inability to locate the participant; five or more missed appointments; or poor English-speaking ability.

TABLE 1
Final CVD Project Sample: Demographic and Cognitive Style Characteristics

Temple site	High-risk (N = 83)		Low-risk (N = 87)	
DAS mean item score	4.39	(.55)	2.17	(.29)
CSQ-NEG. COMP. mean item score	5.05	(.47)	2.71	(.43)
Age (yrs)	18.45	(1.40)	19.57	(2.98)
Average parental educ. (yrs)	13.76	(2.47)	13.45	(2.26)
Combined parental income	$48,061	($36,013)	$39,882	($25,906)
Sex	67.5% F		66.7% F	
Ethnic group	68.3% Cauc.		57.7% Cauc.	

Wisconsin site	High-risk (N = 90)		Low Risk (N = 89)	
DAS mean item score	4.50	(.44)	2.23	(.33)
CSQ-NEG. COMP. mean item score	5.15	(.40)	2.78	(.37)
Age (yrs)	18.67	(.37)	18.77	(1.14)
Average parental educ. (yrs)	15.20	(2.17)	15.03	(2.27)
Combined parental income	$82,911	($100,473)	$71,782	($53,219)
Sex	68.9% F		67.4% F	
Ethnic group	95.6% Cauc.		92.1% Cauc.	

Note: DAS, Dysfunctional Attitudes Scale; CSQ-NEG. COMP., Cognitive Style Questionnaire Composite for Negative Events; standard deviations are in parentheses.

American, 0.6% Hispanic, 3.4% Asian, 0.6% Other), $[\chi^2(1) = 47.97, P < .0001]$. The TU cohort also had lower mean parental education and combined parental income than did the UW cohort $[F(1,333) = 36.50, P < .0001]$ for parental education, and $[F(1,263) = 18.26, P < .0001]$ for parental income.[4] The HR and LR groups did not differ on sex, ethnic composition, or SES, but the LR group was significantly older than the HR group $[F(1,342) = 10.33, P < .002]$, and the men were older than the women $[F(1,341) = 5.90, P < .02]$. In addition, there was a significant Risk $\times$ Site interaction $[F(1,341) = 7.38, P < .01]$, in which the TU LR group was older than the TU HR group and the UW LR and HR groups.

The final sample did not differ significantly from the Phase I screening sample on age or ethnic composition, but did have a higher proportion of women (67.1% at TU; 68.2% at UW) than did the Phase I screening sample (56.8% at TU; 60.7% at UW), $[\chi^2(1) = 9.86, P < .01]$. In turn, the Phase I screening samples did not differ from the entire freshmen classes at each university on age or ethnic composition, but also had a higher proportion of women than the freshmen classes as a whole (51% women at each university). The female bias in both the Phase I screening sample and our final

---

[4] The degrees of freedom for the comparison on parental income are small because many participants did not provide this information.

sample is probably due to women being more likely than men to volunteer for research studies in general. Our final sample also did not differ significantly on demographics or CSQ and DAS scores from eligible participants who either refused participation or were dropped by us prior to the prospective phase of the project. Thus, the final sample of HR and LR participants was generally representative of the populations from which it was drawn on demographics (but obviously not on cognitive styles) and was unbiased relative to other eligible freshmen who did not participate in the prospective phase. Further details regarding the rationale for: screening, characteristics, and representativeness of the CVD Project sample may be found in Alloy and Abramson (submitted).

Screening Instruments

Cognitive Style Questionnaire (CSQ; Abramson, Metalsky, & Alloy, in prep). The CSQ is an expanded and modified version of the ASQ (Seligman et al., 1979) that assesses the degree to which individuals make internal, stable, and global attributions for 6 positive and 6 negative achievement and interpersonal events. There were two major modifications of the ASQ to create the CSQ. First, the number of hypothetical events was increased to 12 positive and 12 negative (6 achievement and 6 interpersonal of each) events of relevance to college students. Second, ratings of two additional inferences featured as vulnerabilities to depression in the hopelessness theory (Abramson et al., 1989) were added about each of the 24 events: inferences about the consequences and self-worth implications of the events. Mean item scores on the CSQ can range from 1 to 7. Internal consistency for the CSQ composites (stability + globality + consequences + self-implication) for positive and negative events is good, with alphas = .86 and .88, respectively. Predictive validity data for the CSQ are presented later (see Validation of Cognitive Risk Status). The CSQ composite score for negative events was used in conjunction with the DAS to select HR and LR participants for the CVD Project.

Dysfunctional Attitudes Scale (DAS; Weissman & Beck, 1978). The DAS is a 40-item self-report questionnaire that is designed to assess maladaptive attitudes involving concern with evaluation, perfectionistic standards of performance, causal attributions, and so on. It is used frequently as a measure of the content of self-schemata relevant to depression. The DAS has demonstrated reliability and validity in both student and patient samples (e.g. Dobson & Breiter, 1983; Hammen & Krantz, 1985). The DAS was used along with the CSQ to select HR and LR participants at Phase I.

Modified SADS-L Interview (Endicott & Spitzer, 1978). A modified SADS-L interview was used to make current and lifetime RDC and DSMIII-R diagnoses of depression and other disorders at the Phase II screening; participants who met criteria for any current Axis I disorder were excluded from the final sample. The SADS-L interview was modified for the CVD Project as follows. (1) We added additional probes to allow for DSMIII-R as well as RDC diagnoses. (2) We added additional items that assessed the precise number of days a person felt depressed and for what percent of waking hours each day he/she felt depressed. (3) We expanded and improved on the probes in the anxiety disorders section by incorporating aspects of the Anxiety Disorders Interview Schedule (DiNardo et al., 1985). (4) We grouped together all items relevant to a given diagnosis and presented items about past episodes of a given disorder immediately after the items for a current episode of that disorder; participants found this modified format less confusing. All project interviewers were *blind* to participants' risk group status. They participated in an intensive interviewer training program for the administration of the mod-SADS-L (and the other project interviews) and the assignment of DSMIII-R and RDC diagnoses modelled after ideal programs (Amenson & Lewinsohn, 1981; Gibbon, McDonald-Scott, & Endicott, 1981). Inter-rater reliability was calculated by means of the kappa statistic (Cohen, 1960). Based on joint ratings of 80 mod-SADS-L interviews, we obtained kappas $\geq$ .90 for all diagnoses. Further details regarding the mod-SADS-L, interviewer training, diagnostic calibration, and diagnostic reliability may be found in Alloy and Abramson (submitted) and Alloy et al. (submitted).

Beck Depression Inventory (BDI; Beck et al., 1961). The BDI was administered at the start of the prospective phase of the project, along with the SRIP Task Battery, to assess initial levels of depressive symptoms. The BDI has high internal consistency, test-retest reliability, and validity with both psychiatric and normal samples (Beck, Steer, & Garbin, 1988).

Selection and Matching of Self-referent Task Stimuli

Depression-relevant (competence, self-worth, motivation) and irrelevant (politeness, predictability) content domains were those used successfully by Greenberg and Alloy (1989) and McClain and Abramson (1995). Potential depression-relevant domains were initially generated based on clinical descriptions of the depressive self-concept (e.g. Beck, 1967; Bibring, 1953; Lewinsohn, 1974; Seligman, 1975), whereas potential irrelevant or control domains were never mentioned in clinical descriptions of the depressive self-concept. We then administered a Self Perception Questionnaire (SPQ; Greenberg & Alloy, 1989), consisting of bipolar adjective dimensions from each of the potential relevant and irrelevant domains, to a separate sample of 156 undergraduates along with the BDI. Those dimensions that most strongly correlated with BDI scores were chosen as the final depression-relevant domains for the present study, whereas those dimensions that were uncorrelated with BDI scores were chosen as the final irrelevant domains.[5]

Next, we generated a list of 250 words (mostly adjectives), 15 corresponding to the positive (e.g. competence) and 15 corresponding to the negative end-point (e.g. incompetence) of each of the 3 relevant and 2 irrelevant domains. We specifically avoided words that were affect descriptors (e.g. blue, dejected). Another separate sample of 170 undergraduates, unselected for depressed mood, rated each word on its degree of relationship to each of the positive and negative domains. The final pool of 80 words (8 for each of the positive and negative endpoints of the 5 relevant or irrelevant domains), contained those that were rated as most highly related to one domain and least highly related to the other domains. The positive words in the depression-relevant and irrelevant domains were equated for likeableness (Anderson, 1968), as were the negative words in the relevant and irrelevant domains. Finally, the words in each of the 4 Content × Valence sets [i.e. negative depression-relevant (NDR), positive depression-relevant (PDR), negative depression-irrelevant (NDI), positive depression-irrelevant (PDI)] were equated on word length and word frequency. Two equivalent forms (Form A and B) of 40 words each (12 NDR, 12 PDR, 8 NDI, 8 PDI), equated on word length, frequency, and likeableness, were created for use in the CVD Project to minimise practice effects when the SRIP Task Battery was repeated at yearly intervals during the prospective follow-up phase. The present findings are based on the first administration of the SRIP Battery (Form A) at the outset of the prospective phase. Table 2 presents the final set of words.

Procedure for the Self-referent Information Processing (SRIP) Task Battery

Participants were tested individually. The following four tasks, yielding five dependent measures, were completed as follows.

---

[5] Although we had generated several potential depression-irrelevant domains, only two of these domains (politeness and predictability) did not correlate empirically with BDI scores in our pre-test sample. Thus, we only used these two irrelevant domains in the SRIP Task Battery.

TABLE 2
Word Stimuli used in the Self-referent Information Processing Task Battery (SRIP)

Category	Content Domain	Form A	Form B
Positive Depression-relevant	Competence	competent	successful
		resourceful	confident
		intelligent	effective
		capable	qualified
	Motivation	motivated	enthusiastic
		active	ambitious
		dynamic	vigorous
		energetic	industrious
	Self-worth	worthy	good
		important	useful
		valuable	lovable
		winner	deserving
Negative Depression-relevant	Incompetence	failure	incompetent
		stupid	incapable
		ineffective	weak
		unskilled	unable
	Lack of motivation	lazy	unmotivated
		indifferent	lethargic
		passive	inactive
		apathetic	uninspired
	Worthlessness	bad	worthless
		nobody	unvaluable
		useless	unimportant
		unlovable	loser
Positive Depression-irrelevant	Politeness	polite	amiable
		courteous	thoughtful
		civil	congenial
		tactful	friendly
	Predictability	predictable	dependable
		reliable	prompt
		consistent	methodical
		steady	cautious
Negative Depression-irrelevant	Rudeness	offensive	rude
		nosy	impolite
		thoughtless	crude
		boastful	hostile
	Unpredictability	erratic	unpredictable
		irrational	wild
		frivolous	inconsistent
		fickle	changeable

Self-descriptiveness Judgements and Latency.   The trait words in Form A were presented to participants on Macintosh computers that were programmed to record two dependent variables: response choices and response times (RTs). Words were presented with an inter-stimulus interval of 4 seconds and each remained in the centre of the computer monitor until the participant responded. Participants were instructed to press the "Me" button on the computer keyboard if they believed the word was self-descriptive or the "Not Me" button if they judged that the word was not self-descriptive. The "Z" and "/" keys on the keyboard were labelled "Me" and "Not Me", counterbalanced so that half of the participants had the "Me" button on the right side (/ key) and half had it on the left side (Z key). Participants rested their index fingers on the response buttons when they were not responding. Participants were instructed to make their judgements according to how they usually viewed themselves and their RTs were recorded without their awareness. Each of the 40 words was presented twice in a different random order for each participant, with the condition that the entire set was presented once before any word was repeated.[6] The 40 target words presented twice were preceded and followed by 5 practice words, designed to familiarise participants with the task and to minimise primacy and recency effects in the later incidental recall task.

Behavioural Descriptions.   In Task 2, each participant received a booklet (Form A) containing the same three words, chosen at random, from each of the 4 Content × Valence types from Task 1. For each word they judged to be self-descriptive, they were asked to provide specific evidence of their own past behaviours that indicated why the word described them. For example, if a participant believed he/she was incompetent, he/she had to provide specific examples of past incompetent behaviours in his/her life. Markus (1977) found that behavioural examples are more accessible when an individual has a self-schema in that content domain. Participants were given unlimited time for this task and were asked to provide as many examples of past behaviour as possible. The dependent measure was the number of behavioural examples provided per word judged to be self-descriptive for each of the 4 Content × Valence types of words.

---

[6] The target words were each presented twice in order to examine the consistency of participants' "Me/Not Me" judgements. Prior studies have found more consistent "Me" judgements for content congruent with the self-schema (e.g. MacDonald & Kuiper, 1984). Participants' responses ("Me/Not Me") to the two presentations of the target words were consistent 96% of the time. Therefore, we simply combined the data from both presentations for purposes of analysis. Exclusion of the 4% of the cases with discrepant responses does not change any of the results reported here.

Behavioural Predictions. In Task 3, participants read 24 statements (Form A) describing hypothetical behaviours in each of the 4 Content × Valence types of domains (6 PDR, 6 NDR, 6 PDI, 6 NDI statements), for example, "You give an in class presentation and communicate your ideas clearly" (competence, PDR), or "You give up your seat on the bus for an old woman" (politeness, PDI). They were asked to judge on a 0% to 100% scale the probability that they would behave or react in the way described if they were in that situation in the future. The mean probability judgement for each of the four types of domains was the dependent measure. Markus (1977) reported that individuals give higher predictions for statements describing behaviours that are congruent with the content embodied in their self-schemata.

Free Recall. Task 4 was an incidental free recall test for the words participants had judged "Me" or "Not Me" in Task 1. The recall test followed Task 1 with a delay of two hours. Participants were handed a blank piece of lined paper and were instructed to recall in any order as many of the words they had seen on the computer monitor in Task 1 as they could. They were given five minutes for their free recall. The dependent measure was the proportion of words in each of the 4 Content × Valence categories that were correctly recalled.

RESULTS

Validation of Cognitive Risk Status

In order to validate that the cognitive HR and LR groups do, in fact, differ in their vulnerability to depression, we present *briefly* CVD Project data on the lifetime prevalence and prospective incidence of episodic unipolar depressive disorders here. The reader is referred to Alloy et al. (submitted) and Alloy and Abramson (1995) for the more detailed presentation and analysis of these data as well as data on other forms of psychopathology. Based on the mod-SADS-L interviews conducted at the Phase II screening, HR participants had significantly higher lifetime prevalences than LR participants of DSMIII-R major depression [42% vs. 17%; $F(1,340) = 27.7$, $P < .0001$], RDC major depression [40% vs. 16%; $F(1,340) = 29.4$, $P < .0001$], RDC minor depression [27% vs. 13%; $F(1,340) = 11.2$, $P < .001$], and of the subtype of hopelessness depression [46% vs. 13%; $F(1,340) = 50.9$, $P < .0001$]. In addition, *preliminary* prospective data based on the first two years of follow-up at the TU site only indicated that the HR group also had higher prospective incidence than the LR group of DSMIII-R major depression [17% vs. 5%; $F(1,161) =$

5.9, $P < .02$], RDC major depression [13% vs. 6%; $F(1,161) = 2.1$ $P < .15$], RDC minor depression [37% vs. 16%; $F(1,161) = 8.4$, $P < .004$], and hopelessness depression [39% vs. 16%; $F(1,161) = 10.3$, $P < .002$]. Moreover, the prospective incidence differences were even greater among the TU subsample with no prior history of depression: 22% HR vs. 0% LR for DSMIII-R major depression [$F(1,73) = 12.5$, $P < .001$]; 12% HR vs. 1% LR for RDC major depression [$F(1,73) = 3.4$, $P < .07$]; 28% HR vs. 7% LR for RDC minor depression [$F(1,73) = 4.8$, $P < .03$]; and 34% HR vs. 7% LR for hopelessness depression [$F(1,73) = 7.1$, $P < .01$]. Thus, HR participants were more vulnerable than LR participants to episodic unipolar depressive disorders and to the hypothesised cognitively mediated subtype of depression, in particular.

Overview of Hypothesis Testing Approach

Our hypothesis testing strategy involved three parts. First, we examined whether the critical predicted Risk × Content × Valence interaction was significant using an approach that was conservative in two respects. First, to protect against inflated experiment-wise error rate due to multiple statistical tests, we tested the predicted interaction by conducting a Risk (HR, LR) × Sex (male, female) × Site (TU, UW) × Content [depression-relevant (DR), depression-irrelevant (DI)] × Valence [positive (P), negative (N)] repeated-measures multivariate analysis of variance (MANOVA) on the five dependent measures (judgements, RTs, behavioural descriptions, behavioural predictions, and correct recall). As will be seen later, the Risk × Content × Valence interaction was significant in the MANOVA; thus, we then felt justified in examining further this interaction in individual ANOVAs on each of the dependent variables.[7] The second way in which our approach was conservative was that we used two-tailed tests of significance, despite the fact that we had clear-cut directional predic-

---

[7] For dependent measures in which it was possible to examine participants' information-processing as a function of their responses ("Me/Not Me") on the self-descriptiveness judgement task (i.e. RTs and correct recall), we included Response as a factor in the ANOVA design. This allowed us to determine whether the pattern of decision times and recall was opposite for words judged self-descriptive vs. non-descriptive. Given that participants should exhibit faster RTs and better recall for words consistent with the content embodied in their self-schemata (e.g. NDR words judged "Me" and PDR words judged "Not Me" by HR participants vs. PDR words judged "Me" and NDR words judged "Not Me" by LR participants), we expected an opposite pattern of RTs and recall performance for "Me" vs. "Not Me" positively and negatively valenced words. Thus, for RTs and correct recall, we conducted Risk × Sex × Site × Content × Valence × Response repeated-measures ANOVAs.

tions. Significant interactions (or marginal interactions if predicted) in the ANOVAs on individual dependent measures were decomposed with simple effects tests. As the second component of our hypothesis testing strategy, in both the initial MANOVA and the subsequent ANOVAs on individual dependent measures, we examined whether the predicted Risk × Content × Valence interaction (or the predicted Risk × Content × Valence × Response interaction, see footnote 7) was further modified by any higher order interactions involving Sex or Site. We did not decompose interactions that did not further modify or otherwise compromise the interpretation of the predicted interactions involving Risk Group.[8]

The third component of our hypothesis testing strategy was designed to investigate whether any residual differences in depressive symptom levels between HR and LR participants at the time of the SRIP Task Battery could account for our risk group effects. Thus, we reconducted both the initial MANOVA and the ANOVAs on the individual dependent measures with the BDI as a covariate. We report whether the predicted Risk × Content × Valence interaction (or 4-way interaction with Response) remains significant with the BDI as a covariate and whether the BDI interacts with Content and Valence (and Response) in the same way that Risk does. Inasmuch as the HR and LR groups differed on age, we computed Pearson correlations to test whether age predicted any of the dependent measures. Given that age did not predict any of the dependent measures significantly (rs ranged from $-.106$ to $.102$, n.s.), it was not necessary to include age as a covariate in the analyses. Degrees of freedom differ slightly across the ANOVAs on individual dependent variables due to missing data on some measures.

SRIP Task Battery Analyses

MANOVA Results.   The Risk × Sex × Site × Content × Valence repeated-measures MANOVA on judgements of self-descriptiveness, RTs for these judgements, behavioural descriptions, behavioural predictions, and correct recall yielded the following significant multivariate effects: Risk [$F(4,298) = 8.30, P < .0001$]; Site [$F(4,298) = 15.71, P < .0001$]; Content [$F(4,298) = 43.12, P < .0001$]; Valence [$F(4,298) = 515.10, P < .0001$]; Risk × Content [$F(4,298) = 2.74, P < .03$]; Risk × Valence

---

[8] Given the complexity of our experimental design potentially allowing for multiple higher order interactions, we only present the decomposition of the theoretically predicted interactions involving Risk or interactions that further modify the predicted interactions involving Risk in order not to detract from a clear description of the theoretically meaningful findings.

$[F(4,298) = 13.77, P < .0001]$; Sex $\times$ Content $[F(4,298) = 2.91, P < .03]$; Site $\times$ Content $[F(4,298) = 35.10, P < .0001]$; Content $\times$ Valence $[F(4,298) = 13.83, P < .0001]$; Risk $\times$ Content $\times$ Valence $F(4,298) = 4.26, P < .002]$; Sex $\times$ Content $\times$ Valence $[F(4,298) = 2.77; P < .03]$; and Site $\times$ Content $\times$ Valence $[F(4,298) = 3.45, P < .01]$. All of these effects remained significant, including the critical predicted Risk $\times$ Content $\times$ Valence interaction $[F(4,295) = 3.59, P < .007]$, when the BDI was included as a covariate in the analysis and, in turn, the BDI $\times$ Content $\times$ Valence interaction was not reliable $[F(4,295) = 0.24, \text{n.s.}]$. Given that the predicted Risk $\times$ Content $\times$ Valence interaction was significant and was not modified by higher order interactions with Sex or Site, we examined this interaction further in ANOVAs on the individual dependent measures.

Judgements of Self-descriptiveness. A Risk $\times$ Sex $\times$ Site $\times$ Content $\times$ Valence ANOVA on the proportion of words of each type judged as self-descriptive (i.e. "Me") yielded the predicted Risk $\times$ Content $\times$ Valence interaction $[F(1,325) = 10.38, P < .001]$, unmodified by any higher order interactions. Further, this interaction remained significant $[F(1,300) = 3.98, P < .05]$, when the BDI was included as a covariate and the BDI $\times$ Content $\times$ Valence interaction was not significant $[F(1,300) = 0.48, \text{n.s.}]$. Table 3 displays the means and standard deviations (SDs) for the proportion of "Me" judgements. To examine whether the interaction conformed to prediction, we decomposed it. The Risk $\times$ Valence 2-way interaction was significant both for DR content $[F(1,325) = 42.98, P < .0001]$, and DI content $[F(1,325) = 9.92, P < .002]$, although it was stronger for DR content. As predicted, HR participants endorsed fewer positive DR (PDR) words $[F(1,325) = 41.25, P < .0001]$, and more negative DR (NDR) words, $[F(1,325) = 26.08, P < .0001]$, than did LR participants. They also endorsed fewer positive DI (PDI) words $[F(1,325) = 8.59, P < .004]$, and more negative DI (NDI) words $[F(1,325) = 4.44, P < .04]$, than LR participants, but the group differences were smaller for the DI words.

Response Times (RTs) for Self-descriptiveness Judgements. The ANOVA on RTs included Response (Me/Not Me) as a factor because we expected the pattern of decision times to be opposite for words judged "Not Me" versus "Me" (see footnote 7). The predicted Risk $\times$ Content $\times$ Valence $\times$ Response interaction was significant for RTs $[F(1,326) = 12.29, P < .001]$, and was not modified further by Sex or Site. This 4-way interaction was still significant when the BDI was included in the ANOVA $[F(1,323) = 10.48, P < .001]$, and the BDI $\times$ Content $\times$ Valence $\times$ Response interaction was not reliable $[F(1,323) = 0.10, \text{n.s.}]$. The RT means and SDs are shown in Table 3. To examine whether the interaction

TABLE 3
Words Judged "Me" and "Not Me" and Response Times for these Judgements

	Low Risk		High Risk	
	Mean	(SD)	Mean	(SD)
Self-descriptiveness judgements				
Me response				
Positive DR	.92	(.02)****	.78	(.02)
Negative DR	.09	(.01)****	.17	(.01)
Positive DI	.86	(.01)***	.80	(.01)
Negative DI	.19	(.02)**	.23	(.02)
Not Me response				
Positive DR	.08	(.01)****	.22	(.01)
Negative DR	.91	(.02)****	.83	(.02)
Positive DI	.14	(.01)***	.20	(.01)
Negative DI	.81	(.02)**	.77	(.02)
Response times for judgements				
Me response				
Positive DR	1902.45	(121.55)****	2581.40	(123.47)
Negative DR	4261.83	(249.34)*	3633.00	(253.29)
Positive DI	2250.89	(178.67)	2536.16	(181.50)
Negative DI	3563.76	(267.69)	3841.50	(271.93)
Not Me response				
Positive DR	4574.49	(253.94)*	3957.64	(257.96)
Negative DR	2205.97	(108.69)***	2656.48	(110.41)
Positive DI	3323.84	(141.52)	3881.27	(143.76)
Negative DI	2492.17	(98.29)	2898.43	(99.85)

Note: DR, depression-relevant; DI, depression-irrelevant. Response times are given in msecs. Proportion of "Not Me" judgements are the inverse of proportion of "Me" judgements.
*P < .10; ** P < .05; *** P < .01; **** P < .001.

conformed to prediction, we conducted separate analyses for words judged "Me" and "Not Me" and found that the Risk × Content × Valence interaction was reliable for both "Me" [$F(1,326) = 5.29$, $P < .02$], and "Not Me" words [$F(1,326) = 8.18$, $P < .005$]. Simple effects tests showed that the Risk × Valence interaction was significant for DR content for both "Me" [$F(1,326) = 12.31$, $P < .001$], and "Not Me" rated words [$F(1,326) = 8.49$, $P < .004$], but not for DI content for either type of response. As predicted, compared to the LR group, the HR group was significantly slower in responding "Me" to PDR words [$F(1,326) = 15.36$, $P < .001$] and "Not Me" to NDR words [$F(1,326) = 8.46$, $P < .004$]. They also showed a trend to be faster than the LR group in responding "Me" to NDR words [$F(1,326) = 3.13$, $P < .08$] and "Not Me" to PDR words [$F(1,326) = 2.90$, $P < .09$].

Behavioural Descriptions.   The Risk × Content × Valence interaction was also significant in the ANOVA on behavioural descriptions [$F(1,321)$ = 6.67, $P < .01$], and was not modified further by Sex or Site (see Table 4 for means and SDs). This interaction remained significant when the BDI was added as a covariate [$F(1,319) = 5.12$, $P < .03$], and the BDI did not interact with Content and Valence [$F(1,319) = 0.12$, n.s.]. We decomposed the interaction to determine whether it conformed to prediction. The 2-way Risk × Valence interaction was significant for DR content [$F(1,321)$ = 6.93, $P < .009$], but not for DI content. As predicted, HR participants tended to provide fewer behavioural examples from their past lives for why PDR words were self-descriptive [$F(1,321) = 3.54$, $P < .06$], and more past behavioural examples for why NDR words were self-descriptive [$F(1,321) = 3.64$, $P < .06$], than did LR participants.

TABLE 4
Behaviour Descriptions and Behaviour Predictions

	Low Risk		High Risk	
	Mean	*(SD)*	*Mean*	*(SD)*
Behaviour descriptions				
Behaviour examples				
Positive DR	2.39	(.09)*	2.14	(.10)
Negative DR	0.56	(.04)*	0.67	(.04)
Positive DI	1.63	(.07)	1.78	(.08)
Negative DI	0.15	(.04)	0.26	(.04)
Words judged self-descriptive				
Positive DR	2.80	(.46)****	2.44	(.86)
Negative DR	0.73	(.55)**	0.87	(.69)
Positive DI	2.47	(.72)**	2.30	(.79)
Negative DI	0.22	(.58)***	0.45	(.77)
Behaviour predictions				
Positive DR	78.21	(0.97)****	71.66	(1.00)
Negative DR	20.44	(1.09)****	38.12	(1.13)
Positive DI	79.60	(1.14)***	75.10	(1.18)
Negative DI	23.45	(1.55)****	33.56	(1.61)

Note: DR, Depression-relevant; DI, Depression-irrelevant. For the behaviour descriptions task-behaviour examples, the numbers in the table represent the number of behavioural examples provided per self-descriptive word for each type of content. For the behaviour descriptions task-words judged self-descriptive, the numbers in the table represent the number of words out of 3 possible for each type of content that were judged as self-descriptive. For behaviour predictions, the numbers in the table represent the predicted probability (0–100%) of future behaviour for each type of content.
*$P < .06$; ** $P < .05$; *** $P < .01$; **** $P < .001$.

Behavioural Predictions.   There was also a significant Risk × Content × Valence interaction on behavioural predictions [$F(1,322) = 11.58$, $P < .001$], unmodified by Sex or Site, that remained significant when the BDI was in the analysis [$F(1,320) = 7.38$, $P < .007$]. Moreover, the BDI × Content × Valence interaction was not reliable [$F(1,320) = 0.45$, n.s.], (see Table 4 for means and SDs). Again, to test whether the interaction conformed to prediction, we decomposed it. The Risk × Valence interaction was highly significant for both DR [$F(1,322) = 84.56$, $P < .0001$] and DI content [$F(1,322) = 22.33$, $P < .0001$], although the effect was stronger for DR content. As hypothesised, HR participants predicted that they would be more likely to behave in negative DR ways [$F(1,322) = 127.54$, $P < .0001$] and negative DI ways [$F(1,322) = 20.55$, $P < .0001$], and less likely to behave in positive DR ways [$F(1,322) = 22.03$, $P < .0001$] and positive DI ways [$F(1,322) = 6.99$, $P < .01$] in the future than did LR participants.

Correct Recall.   Given that we expected the pattern of recall of "Me" and "Not Me" rated words to be mirror images of each other (see footnote 7), we included Response as a factor in the ANOVA on the proportion of words correctly recalled. The 4-way Risk × Content × Valence × Response interaction was significant for correct recall [$F(1,319) = 4.66$, $P < .03$], was not modified further by Sex or Site, and remained significant with the BDI in the analysis [$F(1,316) = 3.95$, $P < .05$]. The BDI × Content × Valence × Response interaction was not significant [$F(1,316) = 0.02$, n.s.], (recall means and SDs are displayed in Table 5). We decomposed this interaction to test whether it conformed to prediction. The Risk × Content × Valence interaction was almost significant for "Me" rated words [$F(1,319) = 3.51$, $P < .06$], but was not reliable for "Not Me" rated words [$F(1,319) = 2.60$, $P < .11$].[9] For "Me" rated words, the Risk × Valence interaction was reliable for DR content [$F(1,319) = 8.29$, $P < .004$], but not for DI content. Whereas HR and LR participants did not differ in their recall of negative DR words judged "Me" [$F(1,319) = 2.20$, n.s.], the HR group recalled significantly fewer positive DR words judged "Me" than the LR group [$F(1,319) = 6.46$, $P < .01$].

---

[9] Given that the Risk × Content × Valence interaction for "Not Me" rated words was quite marginal, we examined this interaction in an exploratory fashion. The Risk × Valence interaction for "Not Me" words was reliable for DR content [$F(1,319) = 5.17$, $P < .02$], but not for DI content. The HR group recalled more positive DR words judged "Not Me" than the LR group [$F(1,319) = 13.91$, $P < .0001$], but the risk groups did not differ in their recall of negative DR words judged "Not Me".

TABLE 5
Correct Recall

	Low Risk		High Risk	
	Mean	(SD)	Mean	(SD)
Proportion of words recalled				
Me response				
Positive DR	.30	(.01)***	.26	(.01)
Negative DR	.05	(.01)	.06	(.01)
Positive DI	.28	(.01)	.29	(.01)
Negative DI	.05	(.01)	.07	(.01)
Not Me response				
Positive DR	.02	(.01)****	.06	(.01)
Negative DR	.17	(.01)	.17	(.01)
Positive DI	.04	(.01)	.04	(.01)
Negative DI	.14	(.01)	.14	(.01)
Actual number of words recalled				
Me response				
Positive DR	3.58	(1.52)	3.16	(1.75)
Negative DR	0.60	(0.74)	0.78	(0.92)
Positive DI	2.17	(1.10)	2.31	(1.24)
Negative DI	0.36	(0.64)	0.54	(0.84)
Not Me response				
Positive DR	0.30	(0.63)	0.78	(1.23)
Negative DR	2.10	(1.24)	2.15	(1.32)
Positive DI	0.30	(0.63)	0.28	(0.65)
Negative DI	1.12	(1.07)	1.13	(1.09)

Note: DR, Depression-relevant; DI, Depression-irrelevant. Analyses were performed only on the proportion of words recalled because the number of words recalled for each type of content is confounded by different numbers of words seen in the relevant vs. irrelevant categories.
*** $P < .01$; **** $P < .001$.

DISCUSSION

To summarise our major findings, relative to participants at low cognitive risk for depression, those at high cognitive risk for depression exhibited greater processing of negative self-referent information and less processing of positive self-referent information. This was evidenced by a significant Risk × Content × Valence (or Risk × Content × Valence × Response) interaction on the overall MANOVA and on all five of the individual information-processing measures. Moreover, there was some evidence that risk group differences in self-referent processing were greater for depression-relevant than for depression-irrelevant content. Specifically, HR participants were more likely to endorse as self-descriptive, tended to be faster in endorsing, retrieved more past behavioural examples of, and tended to correctly recall more self-descriptive negative depression-relevant words than LR participants. In addition, HR participants predicted that they would be more likely to engage in future negative depression-relevant behaviours than LR participants. Perhaps even more consistent across the different dependent measures, HR participants also were less likely to endorse as self-descriptive, were slower in endorsing, retrieved fewer past behavioural examples of, predicted less future behaviour in the domain of, and correctly recalled fewer positive depression-relevant words than LR participants. Indeed, a perusal of the means displayed in Tables 3–5 shows that both HR and LR participants exhibited preferential endorsement, processing, and retrieval of positive over negative self-referent information; HR participants simply showed significantly less of this processing bias in favour of positive self-referent material than did LR participants. The consistency of the pattern of self-referent processing biases exhibited by HR versus LR participants across the dependent measures is impressive and gives added confidence to the reliability of the findings. It is also noteworthy that the risk group differences in self-referent processing remained even when current levels of depressive symptoms were controlled and that participants' depressive symptom levels did not interact with the content and valence of the stimuli in the same manner as did their cognitive styles. These findings suggest that the self-referent processing differences associated with cognitive risk status are not attributable to any residual differences in HR and LR participants' depressive symptoms.

Our finding of self-referent information-processing differences between individuals who were at high versus low cognitive risk for depression based on their dysfunctional attitudes and inferential styles has important theoretical and methodological implications for cognitive theories of depression (e.g. Abramson et al., 1989; Beck, 1967, 1987). First, the findings indicate that negatively toned self-referent processing previously demonstrated to be characteristic of depressed individuals (e.g. Derry & Kuiper, 1981; Gotlib & Cane, 1987; Greenberg & Beck, 1989; Ingram et al., 1994b; Segal, 1988) also occurs among persons who are hypothesised to be vulnerable to depression by virtue of possessing negative cognitive styles. Given that these negative cognitive styles were found to be predictive of past and future depressive episodes in the CVD Project, our findings suggest that negatively biased processing of information about the self may also be an indicator of cognitive vulnerability to depression. Of course, further evidence that relatively negative encoding and retrieval of self-referent information provides vulnerability to depression would come from studies that showed that such negatively biased processing itself predicted future depressive episodes. Second, the fact that differences in participants' cognitive styles predicted concomitant differences in the way they processed information about themselves is consistent with, although not fully demonstrative of, the hypothesis that negative cognitive styles may function to increase vulnerability to depression in part through mechanisms such as encoding, accessibility, and memory for self-referent information. That is, the relatively negative information-processing biases observed in HR participants serve to elaborate more fully the concept of negative cognitive style. With future prospective data from the CVD Project, it will be possible to test directly whether the ability of participants' cognitive risk status to predict prospective onsets of depressive episodes either alone or in interaction with stressful life events is mediated, at least in part, by their differential self-referent information-processing. Finally, from a methodological perspective, the present findings are significant because they provide converging evidence for information-processing effects of cognitive styles on laboratory tasks adapted from cognitive science paradigms (e.g. Ingram & Reed, 1986; McCabe & Gotlib, 1993; Segal, 1988). As such, the findings further support the construct validity of the cognitive style questionnaire measures employed here and in many other studies of cognition and depression.

That HR participants showed less preferential processing of positive versus negative self-referent information than LR participants is reminiscent of a related finding in the depression literature. Whereas nondepressed persons have been found to be highly susceptible to "self-serving" or "beneffectance" biases (e.g. Bradley, 1978; Greenwald, 1980; Miller & Ross, 1975), in which they take credit for successes and deny responsibility for failures and attribute more positive than negative characteristics to themselves, depressed persons often fail to succumb to such asymmetric biases or show them to a smaller degree (Alloy & Abramson, 1988). The present findings suggest that the reduced asymmetry of positive over negative self-referent processing associated with depression may also be characteristic of persons who are cognitively vulnerable to depression but are not currently in a depressive episode. Future research will be needed to determine whether individuals who are cognitively vulnerable to depression also exhibit reduced susceptibility to other forms of self-serving biases.

In addition, based on Beck's (1967) content specificity hypothesis and earlier work demonstrating that depressed individuals do not possess negative self-schemata in all content domains (e.g. Dykman et al., 1989; Greenberg & Alloy, 1989; McClain & Abramson, 1995), we hypothesised that risk group differences would be more pronounced for depression-relevant content involving themes of competence, self-worth, and motivation than for depression-irrelevant domains of politeness and predictability. Although there were larger HR–LR differences in processing positive and negative depression-relevant stimuli than positive and negative depression-irrelevant stimuli, respectively, on the judgement, RT, behaviour descriptions, predictions, and recall measures (see Tables 3–5), HR and LR participants did, in fact, also differ significantly on the irrelevant stimuli on the judgement and behaviour prediction measures. It is of interest that the two measures on which we obtained risk group differences in the processing of depression-irrelevant content may both be viewed as intentional tasks, in which the individual makes a conscious decision about self-descriptiveness or a conscious prediction about likely future behaviour. In contrast, two of the measures (RTs and recall) on which there were no risk group differences in the processing of irrelevant content involved tasks that were incidental to the participants' adjective rating task and thus participants were unaware that their RTs or memory for the words would be assessed. Cognitive conceptualisations of depression emphasise the automatic nature of self-schema based processing (Ingram et al., 1994b, 1995). It is possible that whereas individuals who are cognitively vulnerable to depression may consciously endorse or predict any negative characteristic about themselves, they may only unintentionally elaborate and process negative self-referent information that is congruent with core themes embodied in their self-schemata.

Limitations of the Present Study and Directions for Future Research

In interpreting the present findings, it is important to recall that participants' status, with respect to cognitive vulnerability, was determined on the basis of both dysfunctional attitudes (representing cognitive vulnerability in Beck's theory) and inferential styles (representing cognitive vulnerability in hopelessness theory). Therefore, it is not possible to determine whether the relatively negative self-referent processing biases associated with high cognitive risk status obtained here are attributable to the presence of dysfunctional attitudes alone, negative inferential styles alone, or some combination of both.

Although we obtained predicted differences in the processing of self-referent depression-relevant content as a function of cognitive vulnerability status on all five of our dependent measures, a stronger and theoretically more consistent test of the cognitive theories' information-processing predictions would involve an examination of self-referent processing in the context of life events. According to the hopelessness theory of depression (Abramson et al., 1989), individuals hypothesised to be cognitively vulnerable to depression by virtue of possessing a depressogenic inferential style are hypothesised to engage in negatively biased self-referent processing in response to negative life events. Similarly, the dysfunctional attitudes featured as a vulnerability factor in Beck's (1967; Beck et al., 1979) theory involve self-worth contingencies in which maladaptive self-referent conclusions are dependent on the occurrence of certain negative situations (e.g. making a mistake or others' disapproval). Consequently, a more clear-cut prediction of these cognitive theories is that negatively toned self-referent processing in cognitively vulnerable individuals would occur in the context of negative events, but not positive events. Moreover, both Beck's theory and the hopelessness theory contain a "specific vulnerability" or "matching" hypothesis in which negative events that are congruent with the content of the depression-prone individual's inferential style or self-schema (e.g. a social rejection for a sociotropic or interpersonally vulnerable person) are especially likely to elicit negatively biased information-processing and, ultimately, depression. Although the present demonstration of self-referent processing differences between cognitively vulnerable and invulnerable individuals provides important support for the cognitive theories of depression, we hope that future investigations of information-processing biases associated with depression-proneness will go beyond the present study by providing more fine-grained tests of the theories' hypotheses regarding the eliciting role of vulnerability-congruent negative life events in negative self-referent processing biases.

REFERENCES

Abramson, L.Y., & Alloy, L.B. (1990). Search for the "negative cognition" subtype of depression. In D.C. McCann & N. Endler (Eds.), *Depression: New directions in theory, research, and practice* (pp. 77–109). Toronto: Wall & Thompson.

Abramson, L.Y., Metalsky, G.I., & Alloy, L.B. (1989). Hopelessness depression: A theory-based subtype of depression. *Psychological Review, 96*, 358–372.

Abramson, L.Y., Metalsky, G.I., & Alloy, L.B. (in prep.). *The Cognitive Style Questionnaire: A measure of the diatheses featured in the hopelessness theory of depression.* University of Wisconsin–Madison.

Alba, J.W., & Hasher, L. (1983). Is memory schematic? *Psychological Bulletin, 93*, 207–231.

Alloy, L.B., & Abramson, L.Y. (1988). Depressive realism: Four theoretical perspectives. In L.B. Alloy (Ed.), *Cognitive processes in depression* (pp. 223–265). New York: Guilford Press.

Alloy, L.B., & Abramson, L.Y. (1995, September). *The Temple–Wisconsin Cognitive Vulnerability to Depression (CVD) Project: Psychopathology and self-referent information processing in individuals at high and low cognitive risk for depression.* Paper presented at the NIMH Workshop on "The Cognitive Psychology of Depression", Bethesda, MD.

Alloy, L.B., & Abramson, L.Y. (submitted). *The Temple–Wisconsin Cognitive Vulnerability to Depression (CVD) Project: Conceptual background, design, and methods.*

Alloy, L.B., Abramson, L.Y., Hogan, M.E., Whitehouse, W.G., Rose, D.T., Kim, R.S., & Lapkin, J.B. (submitted). *The Temple–Wisconsin Cognitive Vulnerability to Depression*

(CVD) Project: Lifetime history of psychopathology in individuals at high and low cognitive risk for depression.

Alloy, L.B., Abramson, L.Y., Metalsky, G.I., & Hartlage, S. (1988). The hopelessness theory of depression: Attributional aspects. *British Journal of Clinical Psychology, 27*, 5–21.

Alloy, L.B., & Ahrens, A.H. (1987). Depression and pessimism for the future: Biased use of statistically relevant information in predictions for self versus others. *Journal of Personality and Social Psychology, 52*, 366–378.

Alloy, L.B., Lipman, A.J., & Abramson, L.Y. (1992). Attributional style as a vulnerability factor for depression: Validation by past history of mood disorders. *Cognitive Therapy and Research, 16*, 391–407.

Amenson, C.S., & Lewinsohn, P.M. (1981). An investigation into the observed sex difference in prevalence of unipolar depression. *Journal of Abnormal Psychology, 90*, 1–13.

APA (American Psychiatric Association) (1987). *Diagnostic and statistical manual of mental disorders: DSMIII-R* (3rd. rev. ed.). Washington, DC: Author.

Anderson, N.H. (1968). Likeableness ratings of 555 personality-trait words. *Journal of Personality and Social Psychology, 9*, 272–279.

Bargh, J.A., & Tota, M.E. (1988). Context-dependent automatic processing in depression: Accessibility of negative constructs with regard to self but not others. *Journal of Personality and Social Psychology, 54*, 925–939.

Barnett, P.A., & Gotlib, I.H. (1988). Psychosocial functioning and depression: Distinguishing among antecedents, concomitants, and consequences. *Psychological Bulletin, 104*, 97–126.

Beck, A.T. (1967). *Depression: Clinical, experimental, and theoretical aspects.* New York: Harper & Row.

Beck, A.T. (1987). Cognitive models of depression. *Journal of Cognitive Psychotherapy: An International Quarterly, 1*, 5–37.

Beck, A.T., Rush, A.J., Shaw, B.F., & Emery, G. (1979). *Cognitive therapy of depression.* New York: Guilford Press.

Beck, A.T., Steer, R.A., & Garbin, M.G. (1988). Psychometric properties of the Beck Depression Inventory: Twenty-five years of evaluation. *Clinical Psychology Review, 8*, 77–100.

Beck, A.T., Ward, C.H., Mendelson, M., Mock, J., & Erbaugh, J. (1961). An inventory for measuring depression. *Archives of General Psychiatry, 4*, 53–63.

Bibring, E. (1953). The mechanism of depression. In P. Greenacre (Ed.), *Affective disorders* (pp. 13–48). New York: International Universities Press.

Blackburn, I.M., Jones, S., & Lewin, R.J.P. (1987). Cognitive style in depression. *British Journal of Clinical Psychology, 25*, 241–251.

Bradley, B.P., & Mathews, A. (1988). Memory bias in recovered clinical depressives. *Cognition and Emotion, 2*, 235–245.

Bradley, G.W. (1978). Self-serving biases in the attribution process: A reexamination of the fact or fiction question. *Journal of Personality and Social Psychology, 36*, 56–71.

Brewer, W.F., & Nakamura, G.V. (1984). The nature and functions of schemas. In R.S. Wyer & T.K. Srull (Eds.), *Handbook of social cognition* (Vol. 1, pp. 119–160). Hillsdale, NJ: Lawrence Erlbaum Associates Inc.

Cohen, J. (1960). A coefficient of agreement for nominal scales. *Educational and Psychological Measurement, 20*, 37–46.

Craik, F.I.M., & Tulving, E. (1975). Depth of processing and the retention of words in episodic memory. *Journal of Experimental Psychology: General, 104*, 268–294.

Derry, P.A., & Kuiper, N.A. (1981). Schematic processing and self-reference in clinical depression. *Journal of Abnormal Psychology, 90*, 286–297.

DiNardo, P.A., Barlow, D.H., Cerny, J., Vermilyea, B.B., Vermilyea, J.A., Himadi, W., & Waddell, M. (1985). *Anxiety disorders interview schedule-revised (ADIS-R)*. Albany, NY: Phobia and Anxiety Disorders Clinic, State University of New York at Albany.

Dobson, K.S., & Breiter, H.J. (1983). Cognitive assessment of depression: Reliability and validity of three measures. *Journal of Abnormal Psychology, 92*, 107–109.

Dobson, K.S., & Shaw, B.F. (1987). The specificity and stability of self-referential encoding in clinical depression. *Journal of Abnormal Psychology, 96*, 34–40.

Dykman, B.M., Abramson, L.Y., Alloy, L.B., & Hartlage, S. (1989). Processing of ambiguous feedback among depressed and nondepressed college students: Schematic biases and their implications for depressive realism. *Journal of Personality and Social Psychology, 56*, 431–445.

Endicott, J., & Spitzer, R.A. (1978). A diagnostic interview: The schedule for affective disorders and schizophrenia. *Archives of General Psychiatry, 35*, 837–844.

Gibbon, M., McDonald-Scott, P., & Endicott, J. (1981). *Mastering the art of research interviewing: A model training procedure for diagnostic evaluation*. New York: Biometrics Research, New York State Psychiatric Institute.

Giles, D.E., & Rush, A.J. (1983). Cognitions, schemas, and depressive symptomatology. In M. Rosenbaum, C.M. Franks, & Y. Jaffe (Eds.), *Perspectives on behaviour therapy* (pp. 184–199). New York: Springer.

Gotlib, I.H., & Cane, J.B. (1987). Construct accessibility and clinical depression: A longitudinal investigation. *Journal of Abnormal Psychology, 96*, 199–204.

Gotlib, I.H., & McCann, C.D. (1984). Construct accessibility and depression: An examination of cognitive and affective factors. *Journal of Personality and Social Psychology, 47*, 427–439.

Gotlib, I.H., McLachlan, A.L., & Katz, A.N. (1988). Biases in visual attention in depressed and nondepressed individuals. *Cognition and Emotion, 2*, 185–200.

Greenberg, M.S., & Alloy, L.B. (1989). Depression versus anxiety: Processing of self- and other-referent information. *Cognition and Emotion, 3*, 207–223.

Greenberg, M.S., & Beck, A.T. (1989). Depression versus anxiety: A test of the content specificity hypothesis. *Journal of Abnormal Psychology, 98*, 9–13.

Greenwald, A.G. (1980). The totalitarian ego: Fabrication and revision of personal history. *American Psychologist, 35*, 603–618.

Haack, L.J., Metalsky, G.I., Dykman, B.M., & Abramson, L.Y. (1996). Use of current situational information and causal inference: Do dysphoric individuals make "unwarranted" causal inferences? *Cognitive Therapy and Research, 20*, 309–331.

Hammen, C., & Krantz, S.E. (1985). Measures of psychological processes in depression. In E.E. Beckham & W.R. Leber (Eds.), *Handbook of depression: Treatment, assessment, and research* (pp. 408–444). Homewood, IL: Dorsey.

Hammen, C., Marks, T., DeMayo, P., & Mayol, A. (1985). Self-schemas and risk for depression: A prospective study. *Journal of Personality and Social Psychology, 49*, 1147–1159.

Hammen, C., Miklowitz, D.J., & Dyck, D.G. (1986). Stability and severity parameters of depressive self-schema responding. *Journal of Social and Clinical Psychology, 4*, 23–45.

Hartlage, S., Alloy, L.B., Vazquez, C., & Dykman, B.M. (1993). Automatic and effortful processing in depression. *Psychological Bulletin, 113*, 247–278.

Hedlund, S., & Rude, S.R. (1995). Evidence of latent depressive schemas in formerly depressed individuals. *Journal of Abnormal Psychology, 104*, 517–525.

Hollon, S.D., Kendall, P.C., & Lumry, A. (1986). Specificity of depressotypic cognitions in clinical depression. *Journal of Abnormal Psychology, 95*, 52–59.

Ingram, R.E., Bernet, C.Z., & McLaughlin, S.C. (1994a). Attentional allocation processes in individuals at risk for depression. *Cognitive Therapy and Research, 18*, 317–332.

Ingram, R.E., Fidaleo, R.A., Friedberg, R., Shenk, J.L., & Bernet, C.Z. (1995). Content and mode of information processing in major depressive disorder. *Cognitive Therapy and Research, 19*, 281–294.

Ingram, R.E., Partridge, S., Scott, W., & Bernet, C.Z. (1994b). Schema specificity in subclinical syndrome depression: Distinctions between automatically versus effortfully encoded state and trait depressive information. *Cognitive Therapy and Research, 18*, 195–209.

Ingram, R.E., & Reed, M.J. (1986). Information encoding in depression: Findings, issues, and future directions. In R.E. Ingram (Ed.), *Information processing approaches to clinical psychology*. Orlando, FL: Academic Press.

Ingram, R.E., Smith, T.W., & Brehm, S.S. (1983). Depression and information processing: Self-schemata and the encoding of self-referent information. *Journal of Personality and Social Psychology, 45*, 412–420.

Ingram, R.E., & Wisnicki, K.S. (1991). Cognition in depression. In P.A. Magaro (Ed.), *Annual review of psychopathology*. Newbury Park, CA: Sage.

Just, N., Abramson, L.Y., & Alloy, L.B. (submitted). *Remitted depression paradigms as tests of the cognitive vulnerability hypotheses of depression onset: A critique and conceptual analysis.*

Kuiper, N.A., & MacDonald, M.R. (1982). Self and other perception in mild depressives. *Social Cognition, 1*, 223–239.

Lewinsohn, P.M. (1974). A behavioral approach to depression. In R.J. Friedman & M. Katz (Eds.), *The psychology of depression: Contemporary theory and research* (pp. 112–139). Washington, DC: Winston-Wiley.

MacDonald, M.R., & Kuiper, N.A. (1984). Self-schema decision consistency in clinical depressives. *Journal of Social and Clinical Psychology, 2*, 264–272.

Markus, H. (1977). Self-schemata and processing information about the self. *Journal of Personality and Social Psychology, 35*, 63–78.

McCabe, S.B., & Gotlib, I.H. (1993). Attentional processing in clinically depressed subjects: A longitudinal investigation. *Cognitive Therapy and Research, 17*, 359–378.

McClain, L., & Abramson, L.Y. (1995). Self-schemas, stress, and depressed mood in college students. *Cognitive Therapy and Research, 19*, 419–432.

Miller, D.T., & Ross, M. (1975). Self-serving biases in the attribution of causality: Fact or fiction? *Psychological Bulletin, 82*, 213–225.

Peterson, C., & Villanova, P. (1988). An expanded attributional style questionnaire. *Journal of Abnormal Psychology, 97*, 87–89.

Segal, Z.V. (1988). Appraisal of the self-schema construct in cognitive models of depression. *Psychological Bulletin, 103*, 147–162.

Segal, Z.V., & Vella, D.D. (1990). Self-schema in major depression: Replication and extension of a priming methodology. *Cognitive Therapy and Research, 14*, 161–176.

Seligman, M.E.P. (1975). *Helplessness: On depression, development, and death*. San Francisco, CA: Freeman.

Seligman, M.E.P., Abramson, L.Y., Semmel, A., & von Baeyer, C. (1979). Depressive attributional style. *Journal of Abnormal Psychology, 88*, 242–247.

Spitzer, R.L., Endicott, J., & Robins, E. (1978). Research diagnostic criteria: Rationale and reliability. *Archives of General Psychiatry, 35*, 773–782.

Stroop, J.R. (1935). Studies of interference in serial verbal reactions. *Journal of Experimental Psychology, 18*, 643–662.

Taylor, S.E., & Crocker, J. (1981). Schematic bases of social information processing. In E.T. Higgins, P. Herman, & M.P. Zanna (Eds.), *The Ontario symposium in personality and social psychology* (Vol. 1, pp. 81–134). Hillsdale, NJ: Lawrence Erlbaum Associates Inc.

Teasdale, J.D. (1983). Negative thinking in depression: Cause, effect, or reciprocal relationship? *Advances in Behaviour Research and Therapy, 5,* 3–25.

Teasdale, J.D. (1988). Cognitive vulnerability to persistent depression. *Cognition and Emotion, 2,* 247–274.

Teasdale, J.D., & Dent, J. (1987). Cognitive vulnerability to depression: An investigation of two hypotheses. *British Journal of Clinical Psychology, 26,* 113–126.

Weissman, A., & Beck, A.T. (1978). *Development and validation of the Dysfunctional Attitude Scale: A preliminary investigation.* Paper presented at the meeting of the American Educational Research Association, Toronto, Canada.

Williams, J.M.G., & Nulty, D.D. (1986). Construct accessibility, depression and the emotional Stroop task: Transient mood or stable structure? *Personality and Individual Differences, 7,* 485–491.

Williams, J.M.G., Watts, F.N., MacLeod, C., & Mathews, A. (1988). *Cognitive psychology and emotional disorders.* Chichester, UK: Wiley.

COGNITION AND EMOTION, 1997, *11* (5/6), 569–583

On the Contributions of Deficient Cognitive Control to Memory Impairments in Depression

Paula T. Hertel

Trinity University, San Antonio, USA

Research on cognitive biases in depression suggests that deficient control of attention underlies impairments in memory for emotionally neutral events. Such impairments might result from general difficulties in focusing and sustaining attention, specific and habitual priorities to attend to matters of personal concern, or both. This paper considers these alternative means of impairment in the context of a review of selected theories and findings; a test of the framework is illustrated; and related considerations are discussed.

INTRODUCTION

The research domain of depression and memory has been defined by two almost independent lines of inquiry. The more active line has focused on findings of particularly good memory for emotionally negative events, whereas the other has pursued issues of impaired memory for emotionally neutral events. When the question about the relationship between these lines arises, it is generally assumed that the propensity for negative or self-focused thinking in depression provides a rich context for elaborating mood-related material but intrudes during the processing of neutral material to produce interference (e.g. Ellis & Ashbrook, 1988; Gotlib, Roberts, & Gilboa, 1996; Ingram, 1990). Compared to the bias assumption, however, the intrusion assumption is less well developed theoretically and more neglected empirically, in spite of the importance of understanding

Requests for reprints should be sent to Paula Hertel, Department of Psychology, Trinity University, 715 Stadium Drive, San Antonio, TX 78212, USA; e-mail: phertel@trinity.edu.

The author is grateful to Mary Blehar and Howard Kurtzman of the National Institute of Mental Health for organising the (September 1995) workshop on the cognitive psychology of depression, to the workshop participants who stimulated portions of this paper, and to three anonymous reviewers for their helpful comments. This work was partly supported by Discretionary Faculty Development Funds allocated by Mary Stefl and Edward Roy of Trinity University.

memory impairment in depression. The point of this paper is to examine the means by which intrusive thoughts might impair memory for emotionally neutral events.

The effects of thought intrusions on memory for neutral events can occur, roughly, at two general stages and for two different reasons. First, such thoughts might redirect attention during the initial processing episode and thereby detract from processes that enhance deliberate retrieval later on. Second, even when the events are well attended initially, intrusions during the retention interval and at the time of the test might impair deliberate retrieval. These and other effects of thought intrusions, moreover, might occur primarily because a depressed person's self-concerns are more compelling or attention-demanding than are those of a nondepressed person. In other words, the effect might be related specifically to the attentional priorities and current concerns associated with depression (see Klinger, 1982). Alternatively or in addition, the effects might reflect a more pervasive problem. Reduced synaptic activity in the prefrontal cortex is associated both with difficulties in sustaining attention and self-initiation (e.g. Posner, 1992; Duncan, Emslie, & Williams, 1996) and with depressed states (e.g. Henriques & Davidson, 1991; Resnick, 1992). Therefore, a reasonable hypothesis is that frontal hypoactivation in depression makes it difficult to sustain attention, regardless of one's motivation to focus on the task. Perhaps *any* off-task thoughts would engender more memorial difficulties for depressed people than for others. Self-focused ruminations typify off-task thoughts in depression (Ingram, 1990) and perhaps produce a higher frequency of intrusive thoughts, but the consequence might be more profound for depressed people than for others, due to fundamental difficulties in redirecting attention to the task at hand.

BACKGROUND

Depression-related Deficits in Memory for Neutral Events

Burt, Zembar, and Niederehe's (1995) meta-analysis across 147 studies of recall and recognition in clinically depressed and nondepressed samples revealed clear evidence of depression-related deficits in remembering neutral material. Other, less formal reviews have concluded that the deficits can be predicted by reference to the continuum of controlled to automatic processing (e.g. Hartlage, Alloy, Vazquez, & Dykman, 1993; Williams, Watts, MacLeod, & Mathews, 1988). Cognitive processes are categorised broadly according to the degree of attention they require (e.g. Hasher & Zacks, 1979). Those processes that require little or no attention or awareness are said to be automatic, and those that require more attention are called controlled processes. Controlled processes compete with each other in a limited capacity system. That is, we cannot think about very many things at the same time. Controlled procedures, however, become more automatic through practice and thereby require less attention for their enactment.

The continuum of controlled to automatic processes is relevant to memory at two primary stages: initial exposure to the material and later testing. At initial exposure, materials are processed with varying degrees of attentional control; merely reading words is relatively automatic, for example, whereas making deliberate judgements about their meaning is more controlled. In general, initial procedures that promote later recall, such as elaboration or distinction, tend to be more attention-demanding (e.g. Tyler, Hertel, McCallum, & Ellis, 1979). A number of published experiments have shown depression-related impairments in deliberate memory for neutral materials that had been presented in attention-demanding tasks (for recent reviews see Gotlib et al., 1996; Hartlage et al., 1993). Such deficits occur typically in tests of free recall and are less frequently found in recognition. In this regard, the continuum of controlled to automatic processes is also relevant to retrieval conditions.

Performance on memory tests is influenced both by controlled, deliberate reflection on the past episode and by automatic effects of prior exposure (e.g. target words pop into mind or feel familiar; see Jacoby, Toth, & Yonelinas, 1993). Controlled retrieval processes are thought to dominate tests of free recall, where deficits are most typically found. Recognition tests less frequently show deficits because they are good examples of the joint operation of automatic and controlled retrieval processes (i.e. a word feels familiar because it is fluently processed, the source of familiarity is remembered, or both; see Jacoby, 1991). By using Jacoby's (1991) procedures for separating the controlled and automatic components of retrieval on recognition tests, Hertel and Milan (1994) showed that only the controlled component was disrupted in a sample of dysphoric students. Similarly, tests of implicit memory, which are designed to side-step controlled reflection and to reflect primarily automatic influences of past experience, rarely reveal impairments associated with depression or dysphoria (e.g. Danion et al., 1991; Hertel & Hardin, 1990; Watkins, Mathews, Williamson, & Fuller, 1992). In summary, attention-demanding cognitive procedures, performed during initial exposure or testing, lie at the heart of depression-related impairments in memory. Theoretical issues now pertain to the nature of their role.

The review by Hartlage et al. (1993) emphasised two theoretical perspectives and referred to them as the capacity-reduction hypothesis and the attention-narrowing hypothesis. In brief, the capacity-reduction hypothesis, as exemplified by Weingartner and colleagues (e.g. Weingartner, Cohen, Murphy, Martello, & Gerdt, 1981), claims that depression reduces the amount of processing capacity available for allocation to cognitive tasks, whereas the attention-narrowing hypothesis claims that memory deficits occur because attention is focused on personal concerns, rather than on the task at hand. (The resource-allocation hypothesis—Ellis & Ashbrook, 1988—was described as a combination of these two hypotheses.) At this point, the available evidence suggests that the capacity-reduction hypothesis is inadequate. First, depressed people have sufficient capacity to perform well when experimental materials are self-relevant and congruent with their current mood (see Bower, 1992). Similarly, the social judgement literature contains evidence that, compared to others, dysphoric students engage *more* effortful procedures in situations that threaten their sense of social control (see Weary, Marsh, Gleicher, & Edwards, 1993, for review). Third, several studies have shown depression-related impairments under easier processing conditions with relatively lax external control (e.g. Hertel, 1994b, on implicit memory; Smith, Tracy, & Murray, 1993, on categorisation), but not under more difficult but better controlled conditions (e.g. Hertel & Rude, 1991a; Smith et al., 1993). More generally, capacity accounts of memory difficulties have been criticised on theoretical grounds (see Hasher & Zacks, 1988, who emphasise impaired inhibitory processes instead).

Although the capacity account is an insufficient account of memory impairments in depression, the notion that there are limits on how much can be attended to at any one time, regardless of mood or psychopathology, is important. This notion, moreover, is essential to the attention-narrowing account of depressive memory and to yet another account, briefly mentioned by Hartlage et al. (1993) as the motivation account. Motivation accounts of *depression* (such as the hopelessness theory of Abramson, Metalsky, & Alloy, 1989; also see Kuhl & Helle, 1986) do not address cognitive control in the present sense, but by emphasising perceived lack of control in general, they suggest that depressed people often do not voluntarily initiate controlled procedures. It is this impairment in cognitive control that serves as the central feature of the cognitive initiative account of depressive deficits in memory (Hertel & Hardin, 1990).

Cited by Hartlage et al. (1993) as exemplifying motivation accounts, the cognitive initiative framework is perhaps better viewed as a blend of attention and motivation accounts. It claims that depression-related impairments in remembering occur when attention during the initial task or during the test is not well controlled by external means. Under these lax or unconstrained conditions, depressed people are less likely than others to employ controlled, attention-demanding procedures on their own initiative. Depression-related deficits in recall of word lists, for example, occur under conditions of medium structure, where the initiative to organise can pay off, rather than on completely unstructured lists, where it does not (Channon, Baker, & Robertson, 1993; Watts, Dalgleish, Bourke, & Healy, 1990). Other support for the initiative framework has come from experiments showing that depression-related impairments can be eliminated when depressed participants are instructed to do what others seem to do on their own initiative—in other words, when attention is under better environmental control (see Hertel, 1994a).

Consider an experiment in which participants were either required or not required to sustain attention to words in sentence contexts during an incidental learning task (Hertel & Rude, 1991a). Compared to the non-depressed participants, the depressed participants who were not required to sustain attention showed impaired subsequent recall of words from more difficult or distinctive trials, whereas those who were required to sustain attention showed *no* impairment in remembering words from those trials. Based on such evidence, we have argued that the deficiencies are understood better in terms of impaired attentional control than in terms of resource limitations; depressed participants clearly were capable of allocating *sufficient* resources on the more effortful processing trials. We had also speculated that unconstrained conditions produce deficits because they offer windows of opportunity for attending to matters other than the task at hand. The main difficulty with the initiative account is that, although studies have shown that depressed people are capable of attending in beneficial ways when appropriately guided, we do not yet understand why they fail to do so voluntarily. Does the failure reflect a general impairment in cognitive control (regardless of motivation), or a more specific set of priorities for attention that are motivated by personal concerns?

Priorities for Attention, Automatic Thoughts, and Rumination

Evidence for mood-congruent recall suggests that depressed people are indeed motivated to attend to matters related to their concerns and to initiate processes that help them to remember (e.g. Bradley & Mathews, 1983). In this case, off-task thoughts that are mood-related presumably provide routes useful in controlled retrieval. To explain such evidence of mood-congruent recall, investigators often refer to Bower's (1981) network model, in which emotion nodes are linked to concept nodes when concurrently activated. The model has been adopted by cognitively oriented depression theorists (e.g. Ingram, 1984) to describe how negative self views influence performance on cognitive tasks and *adapted* to incorporate features of Beck's schema theory of depression (Beck, Rush, Shaw, & Emery, 1979), with its emphasis on negatively toned, automatic thoughts. Although the model has organised and inspired a great deal of research on mood and memory, the default assumption—that moods *automatically* activate associated information—has been challenged (see Mathews & MacLeod, 1994; Williams et al., 1988). The challenges include several failures to show depression-congruent effects on implicit tests of memory (e.g. Watkins et al., 1992) and mixed evidence for emotional Stroop effects in depression (see Gotlib et al., 1996; Mathews & MacLeod, 1994). In general, a simple version of the network model cannot easily accommodate evidence that controlled elaborative processes are biased in depression (but not in anxiety disorders) and that automatic pre-attentive processes are biased in anxiety disorders (but not so clearly in depression, except when highly correlated symptoms of anxiety may mediate). Still, the depression researcher is left with the problem of explaining the clinical phenomenon of automatic thoughts that earlier seemed to be well described by network theory. Perhaps the issues related to automaticity have been oversimplified and we should therefore reconsider the nature of automatic thoughts and rumination in depression (see Haaga, Dyck, & Ernst, 1991).

The occurrence of automatic thoughts has been simulated in a series of experiments on thought suppression in which dysphoric participants are less successful than others in suppressing thoughts of neutral or depressive content (e.g. Conway, Howell, & Giannopoulus, 1991; Wenzlaff, Wegner, & Roper, 1988). Note that the thought-suppression paradigm captures an important aspect of automaticity: The process occurs even when one is trying to do the opposite (see Jacoby, 1991; Wegner, 1994). Furthermore, although such thoughts might spring to mind automatically, they provide cues for more sustained ruminations that characterise depressive episodes (Ingram, 1990). Therefore, there is good reason to retain Beck's notions of both automatic thoughts and ruminations in current cognitive formulations of depression. However, to say that negative thoughts come to mind automatically is not to demand evidence of negative biases in well-constrained tests like the emotional Stroop task or stem-completion tests of implicit memory. Such thoughts more likely arise in unconstrained situations that allow mind-wandering. Intrusive thoughts arise automatically because they have been practised well under similarly unconstrained conditions. Their initiation is automatically cued by unfilled intervals, but further ruminations spurred by these thoughts clearly occupy attention. In this way, automatic thoughts during unconstrained conditions can invite rumination and provide sources of interference in ongoing tasks that require attention.

Rumination and Memory

Are depressive ruminations associated with memory difficulties? Seibert and Ellis (1991) experimentally induced dysphoric states in college students and found that recall was negatively correlated with the number of irrelevant thoughts voiced aloud during exposure to task materials or reported later. A similar relationship had earlier been found in clinically depressed people who were instructed to report losses of concentration (Watts & Sharrock, 1985). However, in the first case the induction procedure itself included instructions to free associate to any thoughts that came to mind as the participants attempted to place themselves in negative mood states, and in the second case participants were alerted to concentration difficulties by the procedures. Therefore, these findings are difficult to generalise to uninstructed situations, but they do strongly suggest that if ruminations occur in the absence of instruction to focus on them, they would likely impair controlled retrieval of task materials.

Summary

The phenomena of automatic thoughts and subsequent rumination play potentially important roles in blending the two lines of research on depression and memory. Negative thoughts act as uninvited visitors during conditions of lax attention (see Bower, 1992). Due to practice, they know the way in. Now, we should concentrate on the consequences of the visit for ongoing and upcoming procedures. Are such thoughts detrimental because they are particularly interesting visitors or because depressed people have trouble showing anyone the door? This metaphor illustrates a central question yet to be addressed empirically by those of us who wish to understand the relationship between thought intrusions and impaired memory for neutral events: Is personal relevance necessary or merely sufficient to disrupt memory for neutral events? A set of experiments in progress is aimed to address this question. Next, I offer some aspects of their design as an illustration of ways in which the present framework can guide investigations.

EXAMPLE OF AN EXPERIMENTAL TEST

Depression-related difficulties in controlling attention and avoiding intrusive thoughts are likely to occur during attempts to remember. Do these difficulties derive primarily from the particularly compelling nature of depressive concerns, or might they also reflect more pervasive deficits? To address this question, an experiment nearing completion consists of three phases, the first and last being initial exposure and the memory test. Phase 2 contains the variation that is critical to the issues at hand and so it is described first.

The unconstrained or "free" condition of Phase 2 is designed to mimic ideal conditions for rumination; subjects sit quietly and do nothing. Any current concerns could easily come to mind and occupy attention, but in the absence of such concerns or worries, the participants might take a break (or a nap!), or think about the previous task and rehearse for the upcoming test, about which they are forewarned. Depressed participants are more likely to ruminate (see Fennell & Teasdale, 1984). They should also remember fewer words on the subsequent test, because the act of ruminating should introduce general interference during the test phase. The point of the design, however, is to link these two phenomena— rumination and poor memory—and for this purpose two additional conditions are included.

These conditions, derived from procedures used by Nolen-Hoeksema and colleagues, instruct separate groups of both depressed and nondepressed participants to think either about their current feelings and personal characteristics (in the self-focused task) or about geographical locations and objects (in the neutral task). In a number of experiments, the self-focused task has increased ratings of negative moods made by depressed or dysphoric participants only, whereas the neutral task has decreased them (e.g. Lyubomirsky & Nolen-Hoeksema, 1995; Nolen-Hoeksema & Morrow, 1993). The point of the manipulation for the purpose at hand, however, is to determine if the self-focused task also impairs controlled components of retrieval, to a greater degree in a depressed sample than in a nondepressed sample, by establishing a ruminative cycle. The point is also to determine if the neutral task affects controlled retrieval in both samples, due to its distracting nature, or whether the depressed sample might still suffer a relative impairment, due to general difficulties in switching attention to the task at hand. The outcomes from each of these tasks should inform us about the processes that occur freely in the unconstrained condition.

Phases 1 and 3 are modelled closely on an experiment by Jacoby (1996). For the present purposes, one important feature of the method is the quick presentation of Phase-1 materials under instructions merely to read aloud. Little "room" is allowed for mind-wandering or rumination during this phase. Another important feature is the use of process-dissociation procedures for separating controlled and automatic components of memory. Estimates of these components—from performance on inclusion and exclusion tests of fragment completion[1]—serve as the dependent variables in separate analyses of the effects of the Phase-2 manipulation. The procedure itself is called "process dissociation" because a number of independent or grouping variables have been shown to affect estimates of one component while leaving the other component invariant. For example, only the controlled component of retrieval is reduced by experimentally dividing attention during the study phase or the test phase (Jacoby et al., 1993) and by using an older sample of participants (Jennings & Jacoby, 1993). More to the present point, dysphoric college students have shown deficits in the controlled (but not the automatic) component of recognition memory (Hertel & Milan, 1994).

The process dissociation procedure is an important feature of the design, due to its greater sensitivity when compared to explicit tests of memory, such as cued recall or recognition. For example, Hertel and Milan's (1994) experiment did not show evidence of an overall recognition deficit. Moreover, only the controlled, attention-demanding aspect of remembering should be affected by distractions, regardless of whether the deficiency is caused by attentional priorities or is more pervasive. Automatic uses of the past come into play regardless of one's cognitive control (as is evident in automatic thoughts more generally).

The separation of controlled and automatic retrieval processes first permits a test of whether automatic uses of the past (A) remain unaffected by depression or distraction. Showing no depression-related differences in estimates of A would corroborate our findings in the recognition paradigm (Hertel & Milan, 1994). Showing no effect of distraction on the automatic component would parallel evidence from research on directed forgetting (e.g. Russo & Andrade, 1995). The advantage is to show such null findings

---

[1]On each inclusion test trial, participants are instructed to complete the fragment in a word/fragment pair (e.g. *building s_o_e*) with a word from Phase 1 that is associatively related to the first word of the pair (e.g. *stone*). If they cannot recollect such a word, they should complete with the first word that comes to mind that fits the fragment and is related. The probability of completing with a Phase-1 word on inclusion trials is assumed to be equal to the probability that the word is consciously recollected (C) or, in the absence of recollection, the probability that it comes to mind automatically (A): Inclusion = $C + (1 - C)A$. On exclusion trials, participants are instructed to avoid using a word from Phase 1 to complete the fragment. They are encouraged to remember such a word but to use a different word that is also associatively related to the first word in the pair (e.g. *store* instead of *stone*). The probability of *erroneously* completing the fragment with a Phase-1 word on exclusion trials is assumed to be equal to the probability that the word comes to mind automatically in the absence of conscious recollection: Exclusion = $(1 - C)A$. An estimate of C is obtained for each participant by subtracting the proportion of Phase-1 words used on exclusion trials from the proportion used on inclusion trials; then an estimate of A is calculated by substitution in one of the equations. See Jacoby (1996) for a fuller explanation.

on the same task that reveals differences in controlled retrieval associated with depression and the experimental manipulations.

The predictions of greater interest pertain to estimates of controlled retrieval (C). To the extent that nondepressed participants entertain few task-irrelevant thoughts in the unconstrained condition, their performance should be best in that condition[2]; otherwise we would not expect differences across the three Phase-2 conditions for nondepressed participants.

How should depressed participants perform? The unconstrained condition is the point of reference; that condition should produce lower estimates of C, relative to the nondepressed participants. Even though all participants are forewarned about the memory test, the unconstrained interval, nevertheless, should invite mind-wandering in the depressed sample. Second, estimates should be as low or lower in the self-focused condition, because any tendency toward off-task thoughts would be exacerbated by the self-focused task. The interesting condition is the neutral one. Similar to the distracting condition in Nolen-Hoeksema and colleagues' research, it contains materials that improve mood-ratings in depressed samples. Will estimates of controlled retrieval similarly benefit by distraction from potentially intrusive thoughts, or will more general difficulties in redirecting attention to the Phase-1 words keep performance depressed? Preliminary evidence gathered from dysphoric and non-dysphoric college students supports the priorities account; estimates of controlled retrieval produced by dysphoric participants in the neutral condition are reliably higher than in the other Phase-2 conditions, and comparable to those produced by nondysphoric participants in the neutral condition.[3] Evidence for general difficulties in cognitive control, however, may very well depend on issues yet to be considered.

OTHER CONSIDERATIONS

The extent to which either source of difficulty in control characterises performance by depressed people should vary with the severity of the depressive episode. Severity exaggerates deficits in standard recall tasks (Johnson & Magaro, 1987) in which performance clearly depends on controlled procedures for both initial processing and retrieval. Furthermore, there is some evidence that severity is associated with mind-wandering (e.g. Watts & Sharrock, 1985), but whether increased mind-wandering is caused by

---

[2] This prediction relies on the classic finding by Jenkins and Dallenbach (1924) of retroactive interference when participants were occupied with task irrelevant matters.

[3] If the pattern of means would show improvement in the neutral depressed group relative to the unconstrained depressed group but not to the level of the neutral nondepressed group, it would suggest joint effects of general and specific (prioritised) difficulties.

attentional priorities, frontal dysfunction, or both is yet to be determined. A safe bet is that frontal hypoactivation would be evidenced more clearly in severely depressed people (see Henriques & Davidson, 1991) and would be atypical in a sample of dysphoric college students.

Even less is known about the relationship between the duration of depressive episodes and memory performance. The present framework suggests that practice in entertaining negative thoughts, perhaps as a function of duration of the episode, should increase the extent to which they occur automatically in unfilled intervals. Duration of the present episode, however, might not be as important a consideration as past history of depression. In this regard, Miranda, Persons, and Byers (1990) found that variations in reports of dysfunctional beliefs were direct functions of negative mood states in asymptomatic individuals who had previously been depressed. Although reports of dysfunctional beliefs do not directly index how automatically such thoughts spring to mind, the finding helps raise the question of whether prior *practice* in negative thinking contributes to impaired control in negative mood states.

These considerations of severity and duration might invite the reader to wonder whether mood induction techniques, shown to cause impaired memory following unconstrained tasks (e.g. Ellis, Thomas, & Rodriguez, 1984; Hertel & Rude, 1991b), do so by establishing task-irrelevant priorities for attention. Induction techniques are used for the purpose of making causal statements about depressed mood and memory, so researchers are motivated to assume that inductions provide adequate models of depression for the purpose of studying memory. Induction techniques sometimes, however, produce different patterns of results from those obtained with depressed or dysphoric samples. In an experiment similar to one reported by Ellis et al. (1984), for example, Hertel and Rude (1991b) found different patterns of recall deficits, depending on whether negative mood states were induced or measured. Moreover, similar patterns of impairment (from inductions vs. natural mood states) can, on logical grounds, have different causes. For example, although some induction procedures used to establish memory deficits instruct subjects to ruminate and encourage them to feel lethargic, they probably do not mimic general impairments in cognitive control.

On the other hand, induction procedures can open the door to previously well-practised thoughts, as seen in the recent use of mood inductions to inform issues related to cognitive vulnerability for relapse in remitted samples (see Gotlib et al., 1996; Segal & Ingram, in press). Along the same lines, if remitted groups were asked to participate in the experiment on self-focused versus neutral distraction just described, we could investigate differential effects of that manipulation on controlled retrieval (in comparison to never-depressed control groups). In other words, induction techniques can serve us better if we focus on the processes by which they should affect performance than if we merely assume that their effects mimic processes associated with depression more generally.

Finally, it is also important to consider whether this proposed account of depressive memory impairment extends to other affective disorders and to thought disorders. Impairments on memory tasks requiring controlled procedures are common in schizophrenia, for example, but not in anxiety disorders (see Burt et al., 1995; Williams et al., 1988). Moreover, anxiety-disordered samples show some skill in directing attention away from sources of threat (see Mathews & MacLeod, 1994) and increased attention to the task at hand (although reduced efficiency; Eysenck & Calvo, 1992), whereas such control seems fundamentally impaired in schizophrenia. Clearly, these possible differences deserve further investigation as we attempt to distinguish among diagnoses of psychopathology in cognitive terms (see Ingram, 1984).

IMPLICATIONS FOR INTERVENTION

Investigations of impaired cognitive control in depression also suggest guidelines for intervention. Several lines of research converge in this direction. Teasdale et al. (1995a) have shown evidence of disruptions in depressive ruminations caused by well-constrained cognitive tasks, and thinking about neutral events improves the mood of depressed participants (Fennell, Teasdale, Jones, & Damle, 1987; Nolen-Hoeksema & Morrow, 1993). What seems to be missing is an examination of possible therapeutic advantages in understanding associated effects on memory for neutral events and in seeking to overcome deficient performance in neutral tasks (see Williams, 1992). In everyday cognitive activities requiring controlled use of memory for neutral events, depressed people complain about poor performance. Success on these nonemotional tasks therefore should improve mood by short-circuiting cycles of hopelessness (Abramson et al., 1989). And in the context of cognitive-behavioural therapy, recollection of neutral events is crucial in order to establish new interpretations (Teasdale, Segal, & Williams, 1995b). In this regard, the type of control difficulty experienced by depressed people carries important implications. If the control of attention is generally impaired, improved performance during depressive episodes should depend on the degree of external control built into the intervention, but otherwise meaningful levels of improvement might await recovery. On the other hand, if the difficulties are at least partially responsive to priorities established by prior practice, interventions should motivate and train thought control (while avoiding the pitfalls of simple thought suppression; see Wegner, 1994). Practice in redirecting attention offers hope by establishing new habits for reacting to intrusive thoughts in the typically unconstrained tasks of everyday life (Teasdale et al., 1995b).

REFERENCES

Abramson, L.Y., Metalsky, G.I., & Alloy, L.B. (1989). Hopelessness depression: A theory-based subtype of depression. *Psychological Review, 96*, 358–372.

Beck, A.T., Rush, A.J., Shaw, B.F., & Emery, G. (1979). *Cognitive therapy of depression.* New York: Guilford Press.

Bower, G.H. (1981). Mood and memory. *American Psychologist, 36*, 129–148.

Bower, G.H. (1992). How might emotions affect learning? In S. Christianson (Ed.), *The handbook of emotion and memory: Research and theory* (pp. 3–31). Hillsdale, NJ: Lawrence Erlbaum Associates Inc.

Bradley, B.P., & Mathews, A.M. (1983). Negative self-schemata in clinical depression. *British Journal of Clinical Psychology, 22*, 173–181.

Burt, D.B., Zembar, M.J., & Niederehe, G. (1995). Depression and memory impairment: A meta-analysis of the association, its pattern, and specificity. *Psychological Bulletin, 117*, 285–305.

Channon, S., Baker, J.E., & Robertson, M.M. (1993). Effects of structure and clustering on recall and recognition memory in clinical depression. *Journal of Abnormal Psychology, 102*, 323–326.

Conway, M., Howell, A., & Giannopoulous, C. (1991). Dysphoria and thought suppression. *Cognitive Therapy and Research, 15*, 153–166.

Danion, J-M., Willard-Schroeder, D., Zimmermann, M-A., Grange, D., Schlienger, J-L., & Singer, L. (1991). Explicit memory and repetition priming in depression. *Archives of General Psychiatry, 48*, 707–711.

Duncan, J., Emslie, H., & Williams, P. (1996). Intelligence and the frontal lobe: The organization of goal-directed behavior. *Cognitive Psychology, 30*, 257–303.

Ellis, H.C., & Ashbrook, P.W. (1988). Resource allocation model of the effects of depressed mood states on memory. In K. Fiedler & J. Forgas (Eds.), *Affect, cognition and social behavior* (pp. 25–43). Toronto: Hogrefe.

Ellis, H.C., Thomas, R.L., & Rodriguez, I.A. (1984). Emotional mood states and memory: Elaborative encoding, semantic processing and cognitive effort. *Journal of Experimental Psychology: Learning, Memory, and Cognition, 10*, 470–482.

Eysenck, M.W., & Calvo, M.G. (1992). Anxiety and performance: The processing efficiency theory. *Cognition and Emotion, 6*, 409–434.

Fennell, M.J.V., & Teasdale, J.T. (1984). Effects of distraction on thinking and affect in depressed patients. *British Journal of Clinical Psychology, 23*, 65–66.

Fennell, M.J.V., Teasdale, J.D., Jones, S., & Damle, A. (1987). Distraction in neurotic and endogeneous depression: An investigation of negative thinking in major depressive disorder. *Psychological Medicine, 17*, 441–452.

Gotlib, I.H., Roberts, J.E., & Gilboa, E. (1996). Cognitive interference in depression. In I.G. Sarason, G.R. Pierce, & B.R. Sarason, (Eds.), *Cognitive interference: Theories, methods, and findings* (pp. 347–377). Mahwah, NJ: Lawrence Erlbaum Associates Inc.

Haaga, D., Dyck, M.J., & Ernst, D. (1991). Empirical status of cognitive theory of depression. *Psychological Bulletin, 110*, 215–236.

Hartlage, S., Alloy, L.B., Vazquez, C., & Dykman, B. (1993). Automatic and effortful processing in depression. *Psychological Bulletin, 113*, 247–278.

Hasher, L., & Zacks, R.T. (1979). Automatic and effortful processses in memory. *Journal of Experimental Psychology: General, 108*, 356–388.

Hasher, L., & Zacks, R.T. (1988). Working memory, comprehension, and aging: A review and a new view. In G.H. Bower (Ed.), *The psychology of learning and motivation* (Vol. 22, pp. 193–225). New York: Academic Press.

Henriques, J.B., & Davidson, R.J. (1991). Left frontal hypoactivation in depression. *Journal of Abnormal Psychology, 100*, 535–545.

Hertel, P.T. (1994a). Depression and memory: Are impairments remediable through attentional control? *Current Directions in Psychological Science, 3*, 190–193.

Hertel, P.T. (1994b). Depressive deficits in world identification and recall. *Cognition and Emotion, 8*, 313–327.

Hertel, P.T., & Hardin, T.S. (1990). Remembering with and without awareness in a depressed mood: Evidence of deficits in initiative. *Journal of Experimental Psychology: General, 119*, 45–59.

Hertel, P.T., & Milan, S. (1994). Depressive deficits in recognition: Dissociation of recollection and familiarity. *Journal of Abnormal Psychology, 103*, 736–742.

Hertel, P.T., & Rude, S.S. (1991a). Depressive deficits in memory: Focusing attention improves subsequent recall. *Journal of Experimental Psychology: General, 120*, 301–309.

Hertel, P.T., & Rude, S.S. (1991b). Recalling in a state of natural or induced depression. *Cognitive Therapy and Research, 15*, 103–127.

Ingram, R.E. (1984). Toward an information processing analysis of depression. *Cognitive Therapy and Research, 8*, 443–478.

Ingram, R.E. (1990). Self-focused attention in clinical disorders: Review and a conceptual model. *Psychological Bulletin, 107*, 156–176.

Jacoby, L.L. (1991). A process dissociation framework: Separating automatic from intentional uses of memory. *Journal of Memory and Language, 30*, 513–541.

Jacoby, L.L. (1996). Dissociating automatic and consciously controlled effects of study/test compatibility. *Journal of Memory and Language, 35*, 32–52.

Jacoby, L.L., Toth, J., & Yonelinas, A. (1993). Separating conscious and unconscious influences of memory: Measuring recollection. *Journal of Experimental Psychology: General, 122*, 139–154.

Jennings, J.M., & Jacoby, L.L. (1993). Automatic versus intentional uses of memory: Aging, attention and control. *Psychology and Aging, 8*, 283–293.

Johnson, M.H., & Magaro, P.A. (1987). Effects of mood and severity on memory processes in depression and mania. *Psychological Bulletin, 101*, 28–40.

Klinger, E. (1982). On the self-management of mood, affect, and attention. In P. Karoly & F.H. Kanfer (Eds.), *Self-management and behavior change* (pp. 129–164). Elmsford, NY: Pergamon.

Kuhl, J., & Helle, L. (1986). Motivational and volitional determinants of depression: The degenerated-intention hypothesis. *Journal of Abnormal Psychology, 95*, 247–251.

Lyubomirsky, S., & Nolen-Hoeksema, S. (1995). Effects of self-focused rumination on negative thinking and interpersonal problem solving. *Journal of Personality and Social Psychology, 69*, 176–190.

Mathews, A., & MacLeod, C. (1994). Cognitive approaches to emotion and emotional disorders. *Annual Review of Psychology, 45*, 25–50.

Miranda, J., Persons, J.B., & Byers, C.N. (1990). Endorsement of dysfunctional beliefs depends on current mood state. *Journal of Abnormal Psychology, 99*, 237–241.

Nolen-Hoeksema, S., & Morrow, S. (1993). The effects of rumination and distraction on naturally occurring depressed moods. *Cognition and Emotion, 7*, 561–570.

Posner, M.I. (1992). Attention as a cognitive and neural system. *Current Directions in Psychological Science, 1*, 11–14.

Resnick, S.M. (1992). Positron Emission Tomography in psychiatric illness. *Current Directions in Psychological Science, 1*, 92–98.

Russo, R., & Andrade, J. (1995). The directed forgetting effect in word-fragment completion: An application of the process-dissociation procedure. *Quarterly Journal of Experimental Psychology, 48A*, 405–423.

Segal, Z.V., & Ingram, R.E. (in press). Mood priming and construct activation in tests of cognitive vulnerability to unipolar depression. *Clinical Psychology Review*,

Seibert, P.S., & Ellis, H.C. (1991). Irrelevant thoughts, emotional mood states, and cognitive task performance. *Memory and Cognition, 19*, 507–513.

Smith, J.D., Tracy, J.I., & Murray, M.J. (1993). Depression and category learning. *Journal of Experimental Psychology: General, 122*, 331–346.

Teasdale, J.D., Dritschel, B.H., Taylor, M.J., Proctor, L., Lloyd, C.A., Nimmo-Smith, I., & Baddeley, A.D. (1995a). Stimulus-independent thought depends on central executive resources. *Memory and Cognition, 23*, 551–559.

Teasdale, J.D., Segal, Z., & Williams, J.M.G. (1995b). How does cognitive therapy prevent depressive relapse and why should attentional control (mindfulness) training help? *Behaviour Research and Therapy, 33*, 25–39.

Tyler, S.W., Hertel, P.T., McCallum, M.C., & Ellis, H.C. (1979). Cognitive effort and memory. *Journal of Experimental Psychology: Human Learning and Memory, 5*, 607–617.

Watkins, P.C., Mathews, A., Williamson, D.A., & Fuller, R.D. (1992). Mood-congruent memory in depression: Emotional priming or elaboration? *Journal of Abnormal Psychology, 101*, 581–586.

Watts, F.N., Dalgleish, T., Bourke, P., & Healy, D. (1990). Memory deficit in clinical depression: Processing resources and the structure of materials. *Psychological Medicine, 20*, 345–349.

Watts, F.N., & Sharrock, R. (1985). Description and measurement of concentration problems in depressed patients. *Psychological Medicine, 15*, 317–326.

Weary, G., Marsh, K.L., Gleicher, F., & Edwards, J.A. (1993). Depression, control motivation, and the processing of information about others. In G. Weary, F. Gleicher, & K.L. Marsh (Eds.), *Control motivation and social cognition* (pp. 255–287). New York: Springer.

Wegner, D.M. (1994). Ironic processes of mental control. *Psychological Review, 101*, 34–52.

Weingartner, H., Cohen, R.M., Murphy, D.L., Martello, J., & Gerdt, C. (1981). Cognitive processes in depression. *Archives of General Psychiatry, 38*, 42–47.

Wenzlaff, R., Wegner, D.M., & Roper, D. (1988). Depression and mental control: The resurgence of unwanted negative thoughts. *Journal of Personality and Social Psychology, 55*, 882-892.

Williams, J.M.G. (1992). Autobiographical memory and emotional disorders. In S. Christianson (Ed.), *The handbook of emotion and memory: Research and theory* (pp. 451–477). Hillsdale, NJ: Lawrence Erlbaum Associates Inc.

Williams, J.M.G., Watts, F.N., MacLeod, C., & Mathews, A. (1988). *Cognitive psychology and emotional disorders*. New York: Wiley.

COGNITION AND EMOTION, 1997, *11* (5/6), 585–605

Cognitive Vulnerability, Depression, and the Mood-state Dependent Hypothesis: Is Out of Sight Out of Mind?

Jeanne Miranda

Georgetown University, Washington, DC, USA

James J. Gross

Stanford University, USA

Cognitive theory holds that dysfunctional attitudes are an important risk factor for depression. Critics have challenged this view, pointing out that dysfunctional attitudes are not evident in vulnerable individuals who are currently asymptomatic. To address this criticism, Miranda and Persons (1988) advanced the mood-state dependent hypothesis, which holds that cognitive vulnerability factors for depression are present in vulnerable individuals who are not currently depressed, but are simply inaccessible until activated by negative mood. In this article, we review critically the empirical evidence relevant to the mood-state dependent hypothesis. On the basis of this review, we propose a somewhat more dynamic interpretation of the mood-state dependent hypothesis and suggest several directions for future research.

INTRODUCTION

One in five people become clinically depressed at some point in their lives (Kessler et al., 1994), and when depression strikes, the toll it takes is often exorbitant. Work performance deteriorates, subjective pain as intense as that associated with major medical illness must be endured, social relations are disrupted, and the risk for suicide increases dramatically (Depression Guideline Panel, 1993; Wells et al., 1989). Even in cold financial terms, the price of depression is staggering. The cost of major depressive disorder for

Requests for reprints should be sent to Jeanne Miranda, Department of Psychiatry, Georgetown University Medical Center, 3800 Reservoir Road NW, Washington, DC 20007, USA; e-mail: mirandj@medlib.georgetown.edu.

The authors wish to thank Jacqueline Persons whose continued collaboration and thoughtful discussions of these topics greatly benefited this paper.

the year 1990 alone was estimated at about \$44 billion (Greenberg, Stiglin, Finkelstein, & Berndt, 1993). Because of its immense impact on adaptive functioning, as well as its cost to society at large, depression has long been the focus of sustained scientific analysis. At the heart of this inquiry is a simple question: Why do some people become clinically depressed but others do not?

One answer is that people who become depressed tend to think about themselves and the world around them differently from people who are not vulnerable to depression (Beck, Rush Shaw, & Emery, 1979). This cognitive perspective has spawned a powerful therapeutic technique that treats depression by changing the way people think. Despite the immense practical success of this therapy, however, cognitive theory has not been uniformly supported by empirical research findings. Particularly troubling is the fact that people who are known to be at risk for future depression (but are currently asymptomatic) do not show increased signs of the dysfunctional thinking that is hypothesised to put them at risk for later clinical depression.

To reconcile cognitive theory with this evidence, Miranda and Persons (1988) proposed what they called the "mood-state dependent hypothesis". This hypothesis holds that although these depressogenic thoughts are out of sight, they are not out of mind. Indeed, these dysfunctional thoughts, attitudes, and beliefs are present in individuals who are vulnerable to depression, but are simply inaccessible until they have been activated by negative mood. In this article, we first review the origins of the mood-state dependent hypothesis and then review critically the empirical evidence bearing on this hypothesis. On the basis of this review, we suggest a somewhat more dynamic interpretation of the mood-state dependent hypothesis than we have employed previously, and suggest several directions for future research.

COGNITIVE THEORIES OF DEPRESSION

Cognitive theories of depression answer the question as to why some people get depressed whereas others do not by suggesting that those who become depressed evidence faulty thinking. That is, their beliefs, attitudes, and thought processes make them vulnerable to depression. These theories propose that it is not so much what happens to people that causes depression, as it is how they think about what happens. Thus, Beck's cognitive theory of depression (Beck, 1967, 1972) proposes that individuals who are vulnerable to depression have dysfunctional attitudes which, when activated by stressful life events, cause depression. Other cognitive theories have postulated that attributional style (Abramson, Metalsky, & Alloy, 1989; Abramson, Seligman, & Teasdale, 1978; Seligman, 1991), self-focused attention (Ingram & Smith, 1984), and rumination (Nolen-Hoeksema, 1987) are cognitive factors that put people at risk for depression.

In very general terms, these cognitive approaches draw support from two major lines of evidence. The first is that clinical depression is associated with increased dysfunctional thinking (APA, 1994). That is, in addition to sadness and/or anhedonia, clinical depression often is associated with negative thoughts about the self, the world, and the future (Beck et al., 1979). When people are depressed, they typically report more depressogenic cognitions than do people who are not depressed (for a review, see Haaga, Dyck, & Ernst, 1991).

The second line of evidence is that this theory has generated an extremely effective psychotherapeutic treatment for depression. Cognitive therapy (Beck et al., 1979) is an active, directive, educational approach in which patients learn to identify and then modify dysfunctional thoughts, attitudes, and beliefs. Outcome studies have repeatedly shown that cognitive therapy reduces the level of depression substantially faster than would occur without treatment (e.g. Dobson, 1989; Hollen, Shelton, & Davis, 1993; Persons, 1993; Robinson, Berman, & Neimeyer, 1990). In fact, cognitive therapy has been shown to be at least as effective as other short-term psychological or pharmacological treatments (for a review, see Persons, 1993), and several meta-analytic reviews have found cognitive therapy to be superior to other treatments for depression (Dobson, 1989; Robinson et al., 1990; Hollon, Shelton, & Loosen, 1991), particularly when it comes to protecting against relapse (Hollon et al., 1991; Shea et al., 1992).

Discrepant Evidence

Other evidence has accumulated, however, that is at odds with the cognitive perspective. Specifically, cognitive theory's tenet that dysfunctional thinking is a vulnerability factor for depression (i.e. vulnerable individuals hold certain beliefs or attitudes that tend to make them depressed when life circumstances interact with those beliefs) has not been well supported. For example, individuals who have never been depressed report similar levels of dysfunctional attitudes to those who have been previously depressed but are currently asymptomatic (Blackburn, Roxborough, Muir, Glabus, & Blackwood, 1990; Eaves & Rush, 1984; Hamilton & Abramson, 1983; Hollon, Kendall, & Lumry, 1986; Persons & Rao, 1985; Reda, Carpiniello, Secchiaroli, & Blanco, 1985; Simons, Garfield, & Murphy, 1984). Although most individuals endorse high levels of dysfunctional thinking when depressed, the dysfunctional attitudes seem to "remit" along with the depression. Even more troubling, in a longitudinal study of dysfunctional cognitions and depression in adults, Lewinsohn, Steinmetz, Larson, and

Franklin (1981) found that people who later developed depression did not report more dysfunctional cognitions while asymptomatic than persons who did not later become depressed. Similarly, in studies of pregnant women, dysfunctional attitudes have not generally predicted subsequent post-partum depression (Gotlib, Whiffen, Wallace, & Mount, 1991; O'Hara, Neunaber, & Zekoski, 1984; but see O'Hara, Schlechte, Lewis, & Varner, 1991).

Responses to the Discrepant Evidence

One response to this discrepant evidence has been to reject cognitive theory's central claim that dysfunctional attitudes play a causal role in depression. Thus, some critics have suggested that dysfunctional thinking may be *associated* with depression, but have no direct causal role in the onset of depression (e.g. Barnett & Gotlib, 1988; Coyne & Gotlib, 1983). Unfortunately, this response has the liability of leaving unanswered the question as to why cognitive therapies are so successful if the theories on which they are based are so fundamentally flawed.

A second, and quite different response to the tension between the manifest success of cognitive theories of depression and the evidence that individuals at risk for depression do not show elevated levels of dysfunctional thinking was suggested by Miranda and Persons (1988; Persons & Miranda, 1992). Drawing on the literature on mood and memory, they proposed what they called the mood-state dependent hypothesis.

MOOD AND MEMORY

It has long been known that external contextual factors (such as physical setting) influence learning and recall. Beginning in the 1970s, Bower and colleagues proposed that *internal* factors such as a person's mood at the time of encoding might exert similar effects (Bower, 1981, 1983; Bower, Monteiro, & Gilligan, 1978). In a series of studies, Bower and colleagues found evidence for what they termed mood-dependent retrieval, which refers to the fact that it is easier to recall memories if one is in the same mood state at the time of recall as one was when these memories were encoded. A study by Snyder and White (1982) illustrates this notion. In this study, positive or negative moods were induced in subjects, who were then subsequently asked (in what they thought was an unrelated experiment) for autobiographical events from the past two weeks. Sad subjects reported greater numbers of sad memories than happy memories, whereas happy subjects reported greater numbers of happy memories than sad memories.

On the basis of these findings, Bower and associates postulated that just as external contextual cues are associated with ongoing events in memory, so too are internal contextual cues such as mood. More recently, it has become clear that mood-dependent retrieval is more complex than initially imagined (Blaney, 1986; Bower, 1987; Bower & Mayer, 1985), but the notion that internal mood states might facilitate (or inhibit) memory nonetheless has had a profound impact on contemporary thinking about mood, memory, and depression.

THE MOOD-STATE DEPENDENT HYPOTHESIS

Influenced by the early mood-dependent findings, a number of theorists postulated that negative mood may "prime" negative beliefs and self-representations in persons vulnerable to depression (e.g. Ingram, 1984; Riskind & Rholes, 1984; Segal & Ingram, 1994; Teasdale, 1983, 1988). Among these theorists were Miranda and Persons (1988; Persons & Miranda, 1992), who reasoned that if the dysfunctional beliefs that predisposed vulnerable individuals to depression were tightly linked to negative mood, they might be difficult to access unless a negative mood were invoked. If dysfunctional attitudes were present in these vulnerable individuals, but simply difficult to access under normothymic conditions, this would help reconcile cognitive theory with evidence suggesting that vulnerable (but not currently depressed) individuals fail to report dysfunctional attitudes when they are in a euthymic mood state.

This reasoning led Miranda and Persons (1988; Persons & Miranda, 1992) to propose what they called the *mood-state dependent hypothesis*, which holds that cognitive vulnerability factors for depression are indeed present in individuals who are at risk for depression, but are simply inaccessible until they have been activated by negative mood. According to this view, when individuals who are vulnerable to depression are in a negative mood, the negative mood activates latent dysfunctional thinking, and this increases the probability that they will become depressed. In contrast, nonvulnerables who experience a negative mood do not have increased dysfunctional thinking, and thus are not placed at heightened risk for developing depression.

Empirical Evidence Relevant to the Mood-state Dependent Hypothesis

Since the mood-state dependent hypothesis was first introduced, empirical findings relevant to this hypothesis have gradually accumulated. Because these studies are still too few in number and too heterogeneous in kind to permit a meaningful formal (meta-analytic) review, we instead provide a qualitative review of studies either indirectly or directly relevant to this hypothesis.

Indirect Evidence. Indirect evidence for the mood-state dependent hypothesis comes from Teasdale and Dent (1987), who considered what happens to self-perception when vulnerable individuals experience a negative mood. They found that vulnerable women did not differ from nonvulnerable women in the number of negative self-descriptive adjectives they attributed to themselves following a sad music mood induction. However, a few moments later, vulnerable subjects recalled more of the negative self-descriptive adjectives than did nonvulnerables. This study was recently replicated (Myers, 1995) in a sample of men and women. In this replication, depression-prone subjects reported more negative self-attributes following the mood induction and recalled more negative self-attributes on the delayed recall task than did never-depressed individuals. These studies provide support for the notion that negative mood triggers negative thoughts about the self for vulnerable subjects, but they do not address the role of negative mood in revealing dysfunctional attitudes more generally.

Miranda (1992) also provided indirect support for the mood-state dependent hypothesis in a study relating stressful life events to dysfunctional thinking. As predicted, negative life events were linearly related to dysfunctional thinking for those with a history of depression, but were unrelated for those without a history of depression. Unfortunately, because the association of stressful life events to negative mood was not measured, we cannot be certain why vulnerable individuals showed heightened dysfunctional cognitions following the negative life events.

More convincing evidence for the mood-state hypothesis derives from two studies that were designed to test the hypothesis that self-focused attention may be the trigger for negatively biased information-processing among those who are vulnerable to depression (Ingram, Bernet, & McLaughlin, 1994). In one study, Hedlund and Rude (1995) found that formerly depressed individuals were negatively biased on two of three information-processing measures administered following a self-focus manipulation. Similarly, Ingram, Bernet, and McLaughlin (1994) found that students with a history of depression made more errors on a dichotic listening task following a self-focus manipulation; those without a history were not effected by the self-focus manipulation. These information-processing studies suggest that self-focused attention leads to different cognitive processes for those with a history of depression as compared to those less vulnerable to depression. Inasmuch as self-focus has been found to increase negative mood for depressives (Gibbons et al., 1985; Nolen-Hoeksema, 1987; Smith, Ingram, & Roth, 1985), these studies lend support for the mood-state hypothesis by demonstrating that self-focused attention—a manipulation that increases negative mood—leads to information-processing biases consistent with dysfunctional thinking.

Direct Evidence. More direct evidence regarding the mood-state dependent hypothesis was provided by Miranda, Persons, and Byers (1990). Miranda and colleagues reasoned that dysfunctional thinking should wax and wane as clinically depressed individuals' mood states varied over the course of the day. Accordingly, depressed patients (34 in-patients, 13 out-patients) identified the typical time of day during which they felt best and worst, and completed measures of mood and dysfunctional thinking at these two times of day. As predicted, dysfunctional thinking increased when mood was worse and decreased when mood was better. This study demonstrates that mood shifts are related to shifts in dysfunctional thinking for those who are vulnerable to depression; differences between vulnerables and invulnerables were not examined.

Evidence that mood and dysfunctional thinking are related for those vulnerable to depression but not for those not vulnerable comes from three studies. First, Miranda and Persons (1988) examined 43 female patients and visitors at San Francisco General Hospital. Vulnerability was measured by self-report of depressive symptomatology in the past. As predicted (and as shown in Fig. 1), for subjects with a history of depression, negative mood was positively related to dysfunctional cognitions. No such relation between current mood and level of dysfunctional thinking was evident for those without a history of depression. Miranda et al. (1990) conducted a more rigorous version of this study using the standardised National Institute of Mental Health Diagnostic Interview Schedule (DIS; Robins, Helzer, Croughan, & Ratcliff, 1981) to identify those vulnerable to depression based on history of major depressive episode. Again, reports of dysfunctional beliefs varied as a function of mood state for the vulnerable individuals but not for those who had never been depressed. Roberts and Kassel (1996) recently addressed this same issue in a large sample ($N = 162$) of undergraduates. Current negative affect was related to a variety of measures of dysfunctional thinking among remitted dysphorics (those who met symptom criteria for past major depression, but not duration criteria), but was not related to dysfunctional thinking among the never-dysphoric group. Although these studies support the mood-state dependent hypothesis, because mood and dysfunctional thinking were only examined correlationally, they do not indicate whether mood actually evokes, or causes, those who are vulnerable to depression to become more dysfunctional in their thinking.

To address this issue, Engel (1995) directly tested the hypothesis that increasing negative mood will result in higher reports of dysfunctional thinking and depressogenic attributional style for those who are vulnerable to depression. Engel measured dysfunctional thinking before and after a musical mood induction in college students with and without a history of depression. Dysfunctional attributional style (but not a measure of dysfunc-

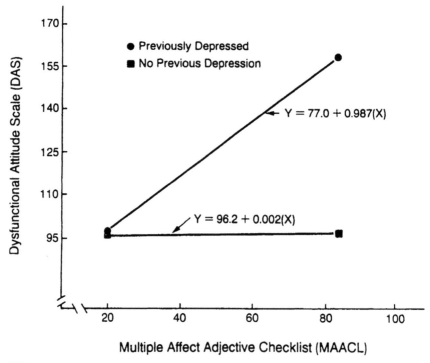

FIG. 1.   Estimated regression lines: relationship of dysfunctional attitudes (DAS) to current mood state (MAACL) for subjects with and without a history of previous depression (from Miranda & Persons, 1988).

tional thinking) was found to be significantly related to mood change following the induction for those with a history of depression, but not for those without a history of depression. Somewhat puzzlingly, baseline findings were not in accord with the mood-state dependent hypothesis: At baseline, mood was not significantly related to dysfunctional thinking for those with a history of depression, but was positively related to dysfunctional thinking for those without a history of depression.

To our knowledge, only one other study has actually manipulated mood in order to test the mood-state hypothesis. In this study, Miranda, Gross, Persons, and Hahn (in press) examined 100 adult women who were predominantly employees at San Francisco General Hospital (33 with and 67 without a history of depression). The women completed measures of mood and dysfunctional attitudes before and after viewing a film negative mood induction. As predicted (and as shown in Fig. 2), increased negative mood led to increased dysfunctional attitudes in vulnerable subjects. Unexpectedly, in nonvulnerable subjects, increased negative mood

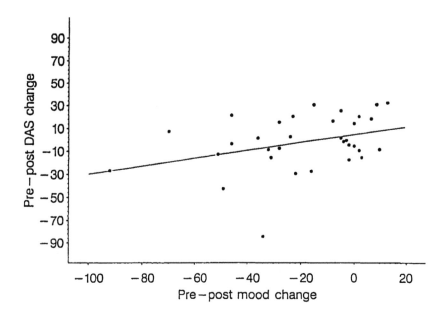

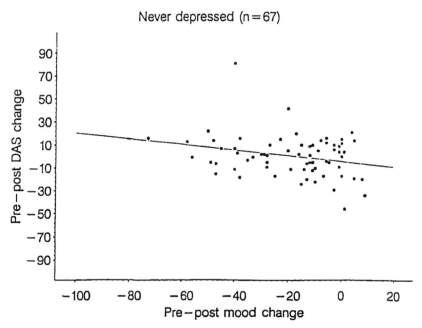

FIG. 2.   Scatter plots and estimated regression lines for the relationship of change in dysfunctional attitudes (measured on the Dysfunctional Attitude Scale; DAS) to change in mood state following a sad film mood induction in subjects who reported a history of depression compared with those who had never been depressed (from Miranda et al., in press).

led to decreased dysfunctional attitudes. Also unexpectedly, baseline dysfunctional thinking and mood were positively related both for vulnerable and nonvulnerable individuals.

Critical Evaluation of the Evidence

What do these studies tell us about the role of dysfunctional thinking in vulnerability to depression? Studies of the impact of acute changes in negative affect on depressogenic thinking have consistently supported the mood-state dependent hypothesis. Negative mood shifts are related to increased information-processing errors (Hedlund & Rude, 1995; Ingram et al., 1994), recall of negative self-attributes (Myers, 1995; Teasdale & Dent, 1987), dysfunctional thinking (Engel, 1995; Miranda et al., in press), and depressogenic attributional styles (Engel, 1995) in those vulnerable to depression but not in those who are less vulnerable to depression. A variety of affect inductions have produced this result, including self-focused attention (Hedlund & Rude, 1995; Ingram et al., 1994), sad music (Engel, 1995; Teasdale & Dent, 1987), and sad films (Miranda et al., in press). This result also is evident in clinical samples of currently depressed patients whose moods show acute spontaneous shifts across the day (Miranda et al., 1990).

Studies of dysfunctional thinking and tonic affect levels also are generally supportive of the mood-state dependent hypothesis, although this is more clearly the case for vulnerable individuals than for invulnerables. Four studies have shown that for vulnerables, baseline negative mood is positively related to dysfunctional thinking (Miranda & Persons, 1988; Miranda et al., 1990, in press; Roberts & Kassel, 1996). The one study that failed to show this relationship (Engel, 1995) used a college student sample and found that negative mood and dysfunctional thinking were unrelated for those vulnerable to depression at baseline. We are unsure why this study failed to find relations between negative mood and dysfunctional thinking, but, given the generally positive findings in this area and the modest effect sizes, it seems possible that this negative result is due to sampling error.

Interestingly, relations between dysfunctional thinking and tonic mood levels are less consistent for those classified as not vulnerable to depression. Three studies found the predicted lack of relationship between mood and dysfunctional thinking for those not vulnerable to depression (Miranda & Persons, 1988; Miranda et al., 1990; Roberts & Kassel, 1996). However, two studies found a positive relationship between negative mood and dysfunctional thinking in those not vulnerable to depression (Engel, 1995; Miranda et al., 1996). In both studies, participants were informed that a mood induction would later be conducted, and it may well be that when attention is called to mood, there is a suspension of typical emotion-regulatory processes. This possibility is suggested by the findings of Parrott and Sabini (1990), who showed that when college students (the majority of whom were probably nonvulnerable) were observed unobtrusively, they were more likely to remember positive past events when they were in a negative mood. When it was obvious that they were participating in a mood study, however, students showed mood-*congruent* recall of life events (and thus recalled more negative memories when in a negative mood), perhaps because they suspended efforts at mood regulation in order to comply with perceived experimental demands. We believe nonvulnerable individuals in mood-induction studies designed to test the mood-state dependent hypothesis also may temporarily suspend their usual mood regulation efforts, resulting in a positive association between tonic negative mood and depressogenic thinking.

REVISITING THE MOOD-STATE DEPENDENT HYPOTHESIS

After a careful literature review, we believe that the majority of studies in this area support the mood-state dependent hypothesis. However, our review also uncovered important puzzles and raised a number of questions that have yet to be resolved.

First, do the studies we have reviewed really demonstrate that dysfunctional thinking is related to negative *mood*? Most would say yes, in that one major finding in this area is that when affective state is manipulated (e.g. with a sad movie clip), vulnerables become more dysfunctional in their thinking whereas nonvulnerables do not. But emotion researchers now agree that the terms emotion and mood should not be used interchangeably (Ekman & Davidson, 1994). Some consensus exists that emotions are likely to have clear antecedents, be focal, and bias action rather than cognition. Moods, on the other hand, typically lack clear antecedents, are diffuse, and bias cognition rather than action. Using these consensual standards, the studies reviewed earlier might be seen as eliciting emotion rather than mood, thus providing good evidence for the notion that acute change in negative emotion leads to negative thinking in vulnerable individuals, but leaving largely unaddressed the relation between negative mood and dysfunctional thinking.

Does this mean that we should rename the mood-state dependent hypothesis the sadness-dependent hypothesis? We think not. At this point, we believe that it is valuable to note that vulnerables differ from nonvulnerables in terms of response to sad emotion. This may be one critical point at which vulnerable individuals begin the cascade into depression (Gross & Munoz, 1995). We suspect, however, that the differences would be even larger were actual mood assessed. That is, as vulnerable individuals come to be in an increasingly negative diffuse mood, we hypothesise that they become increasingly dysfunctional in thinking. We would predict that nonvulnerables could experience negative moods without reporting concomitant negative cognitions, although they may experience slight cognitive biases.

Is it *level* of negative effect or *change* in negative affect that results in dysfunctional thinking? We hypothesise that for negative emotion, acute change may be related to increases in dysfunctional thinking for those who are vulnerable to depression. However, for negative mood, we hypothesise that both level and change may be important to an understanding of dysfunctional thinking. Clearly, this is an issue that requires further examination.

Is all of the action in the vulnerable individuals? Previous interpretations of the mood-state dependent hypothesis have emphasised the activation of latent dysfunctional attitudes in vulnerables and have said little or nothing about nonvulnerables. We now believe that a more even-handed treatment of both groups may be required. When vulnerable individuals experience high levels of negative mood or have acute increases in negative mood or emotion, they think in more dysfunctional ways as a result. However, when less vulnerable individuals experience tonic negative moods or acute negative mood shifts, their thinking remains stable, and may even improve (Miranda et al., 1996; see also Smith & Petty, 1995). This highlights the importance of regulatory processes, ranging from low-level differential attention allocation to positive versus negative stimuli (e.g. Gotlib & McCabe, 1995; Matthews & Antes, 1992; Pyszczynski & Greenberg, 1987) through high-level cognitive strategies for coping with negative feelings (e.g. Morris & Reilly, 1987; Rippere, 1977). Similarly, if our hypothesis is correct that invulnerables are able to suspend their usual mood-regulatory responses under conditions when they know they are going to undergo a mood induction and wish to co-operate with the investigator, they may in fact have more flexibility in response to mood than do those who are vulnerable. That is, nonvulnerables may choose to respond in different ways to negative moods; whereas vulnerable individuals may simply become more dysfunctional in thinking in response to negative mood without being able to control this process.

Increasingly, we are inclined to believe that there may be multiple points in the depressive cascade at which vulnerables may become more dysfunctional in their thinking as compared with nonvulnerables. We envision a sequence in which an external situation or internal image is attended to and then evaluated, and whether a negative emotion arises will depend on what is attended to and how it is evaluated. During this evaluation stage, vulnerable individuals may engage in more biased thinking than nonvulnerables, thus leading them to incur more negative feelings than do non-vulnerables. Next, sadness precipitates brief episodes of dysfunctional thinking for those vulnerable to depression. These brief episodes of biased thinking may in fact inhibit those who are vulnerable from engaging in adaptive behaviours typical of those who are nonvulnerable to depression. Certain evaluations that trigger negative emotions, such as sadness, may, if the negative emotion is prolonged, potentiate a negative mood. This, in turn, may lead to changes in thought processes including an increase in dysfunctional thinking. Finally, this dysfunctional thinking may in turn influence the environment (e.g. others with whom the individual inter-acts) as well as subsequent evaluations of this new environment.

Within this scheme, we conceptualise the mood-state dependent hypoth-esis as focusing on just one of many points of difference between vulner-ables and invulnerables, who might in fact differ in typical evaluations, thresholds of activation of negative emotions, consequences of acute negative emotions for cognitive processes, the ease with which negative emotions are translated into negative moods, and cognitive consequences of such shifts in negative mood (see also Teasdale, 1988). By expanding the focus to consider multiple points of potential difference between vulnerable individuals and invulnerables, this conception preserves the mood-state dependent hypothesis's ability to reconcile cognitive theory with discrepant findings, but admits a much greater complexity of active emotion regulatory processes in vulnerables and nonvulnerables alike.

DIRECTIONS FOR FUTURE RESEARCH

The mood-state dependent hypothesis was developed in order to reconcile the cognitive theory of depression with evidence that appears to contradict its basic tenets. However, as is often the case, this hypothesis has in turn raised other questions and difficulties. In the following sections, we review the most important of these, relating to the conceptualisation and measure-ment of key constructs, design issues, and the nature of cognitive vulner-ability to depression. In so doing, we hope to point to what we believe to be some of the most promising directions for future research on cognitive vulnerability to depression.

Conceptualisation and Measurement Issues.   At this point, it is unclear whether it is most profitable to conceptualise emotion and mood in dimen-sional terms (e.g. negative and positive affect) or in discrete emotion terms (e.g. sadness and amusement). Typically, research on vulnerability to depression has taken a dimensional perspective, and one important ques-tion for future research on the mood-state dependent hypothesis is whether the affective shifts that reveal previously hidden dysfunctional attitudes in vulnerables are specific to specific emotions, such as sadness, or general, so that any negative emotion or mood may serve as a trigger.

In this work, it will be important to distinguish between emotion and mood. In general, an emotion is most likely to be present when subjective experience, expressive behaviour, and physiological responding show a co-ordinated pattern in response to a specifiable antecedent event. On the other hand, a mood is most likely to be present when there are diffuse subjective feelings, generalised behavioural changes (such as decreased activity levels), and slowed or biased cognitive-processing in the absence of a clearly identifiable antecedent event. It also will be important to distinguish between emotion or mood and depression, which includes the presence of certain emotions and moods (e.g. sadness, diffuse negative mood) and the absence of others (e.g. joy, diffuse positive mood), but also includes many other signs and symptoms such as changes in eating and suicidal ideation (for a contrary view, see Morris, 1992).

Difficulties also exist with the way cognitive vulnerability has been operationalised. Typically, studies in this area have relied on self-reported history of depression. This approach has several problems. First, self-reports may be unreliable (e.g. recall of episodes of depression may be related to current mood state; Goodwin & Sher, 1993). Second, even if reports of past episodes of depression were reliable, this factor would still be an imperfect proxy for vulnerability (which is really what is relevant to the mood-state dependent hypothesis). Someone who has had a previous episode of depression may or may not have another episode, and, clearly, many people who have never had a previous episode of depression become depressed. Third, the dichotomous approach that we and others have taken (which assumes that someone is either vulnerable to depression or not) is most likely an oversimplification. In reality, it seems much more likely that vulnerability is a continuous variable, with some individuals being easily depressed and others being very invulnerable to depression. For the time being, prior history of depression, treated dichotomously, may be the best vulnerability marker we have, but we expect that further conceptual advances in the assessment of vulnerability will be essential.

Another important area for future research concerns the measurement of dysfunctional attitudes. Currently, we and others use the Dysfunctional Attitudes Scale (Weissman, 1979). This measure is subject to the problems typical of self-report, including socially desirable response sets. There also may be more specific problems with the DAS. For example, there is now evidence that the two forms typically used may have different factor structures (Beck, Brown, Steer, & Weissman, 1991). In addition, the items may not address the particular core dysfunctional beliefs of some participants. Clearly, future work on measurement of depressogenic thinking is also needed.

Design Considerations. Investigators interested in testing the mood-state dependent hypothesis face a number of thorny design issues. Many of these stem directly from the fact that it is extremely unlikely that one would ever randomly assign subjects to a given cognitive vulnerability status or to a stressor that would be sufficient to overwhelm the emotion regulatory mechanisms of many of the research participants. One solution is to use analogue studies, in which the relation between mood change and cognition is studied in healthy (invulnerable) subjects. This has the advantage of protecting vulnerable subjects from unintended negative consequences of the experiment. Unfortunately, the mood-state dependent hypothesis posits a very special relationship between negative mood shifts and dysfunctional cognitions in those at risk for depression. For this reason, studying those known to be at risk for depression, as well as healthy controls, is essential to this work. Because tonic affect levels and acute affect reactivity may differentially relate to cognitive processes, carefully assessing both affect and dysfunctional attitudes at least two time points seems essential.

Acute mood shifts may be either naturally occurring or induced, but the latter has the advantage of allowing the investigator to tease apart the effects of mood from factors that give rise to those mood changes in everyday life. For the experimenter interested in experimentally inducing mood, a whole set of additional issues arise. The experimenter can shift the subject's mood in a negative direction, but only within limits. Many moderate affect induction procedures have been developed (e.g. Gerrards-Hesse, Spies, & Hesse, 1994; Gross & Levenson, 1995; Martin, 1990). In selecting a mood-induction procedure, one of the first issues to address is whether the subject should be aware that his/her mood is the focus of investigation. In vulnerable subjects, ethical considerations suggest the appropriateness of making this explicit, but doing so may obscure subtle relationships between mood change and cognitive vulnerability factors (see Parrott & Sabini, 1990). A second issue is how "cognitive" a mood induction to use. In the Velten mood-induction procedure, for example, subjects say affectively toned phrases out loud (Velten, 1968). One drawback of this procedure in the present context is that some of these phrases may be very similar to the dysfunctional attitudes that are meant to be the dependent measures. Thus, one is in the awkward position of trying to manipulate mood via cognitive means in order to assess whether the mood manipulation has any impact on cognitive factors. One alternative is to use music or films that have been carefully pre-tested. This allows one to make a clearer (although incomplete) separation between manipulated variables and dependent measures, inasmuch as the mood induction procedure is not directly targeting the very cognitive variables that are being assessed as dependent measures.

Whatever induction procedure one employs, some designs may require the induction of both negative and neutral moods. In addition, if hypotheses concerning alterations in the ability to manage positive emotions are also to be tested, this suggests the addition of a positive mood condition as well. Unfortunately, because we do not currently know very much about the temporal characteristics of the effects of negative mood shift on cognitive factors, presenting two or more inductions to the same subjects may be unwise. Between-subjects designs should be employed so as to avoid confusing the cognitive sequelae of one mood induction with that of another. Given that it is important to be able to compare vulnerable subjects' responses to those of subjects who are not vulnerable to depression, the induction of three mood states may mean that six experimental cells are required, and the essential question must always be whether the expected information gain associated with each additional cell justifies the additional expense and difficulty of finding large numbers of vulnerable, but asymptomatic, individuals.

To circumvent some of the difficulties associated with experimental designs, longitudinal designs may be used. These follow individuals over time, assessing mood and cognitive factors at multiple time points, then assessing who becomes depressed. Although such studies do not afford the sort of experimental control permitted by laboratory sessions, they do naturally circumvent the ethical limitations imposed on such studies, and may therefore take full advantage of naturally occurring negative life events. The subjects could be followed over time to see if those who have strong relationships between mood and dysfunctional thinking are more likely to become depressed than are those without such a relationship. In addition, prospective studies bypass the host of difficulties associated with contrasting formerly depressed patients with individuals who have never been depressed, in which case one is unable to evaluate whether the findings are the result of having an episode of depression or differences that were the cause of the episode of depression. However, given the expense of this sort of work, such studies may be most appropriate after some of the conceptual and methodological issues regarding measurement of key constructs have been further resolved.

What is the Core Risk Factor for Depression? Improvements in the conceptualisation and measurement of affect, cognitive vulnerability, and dysfunctional attitudes, as well as a richer appreciation of the complexities of designing adequate studies in this area should all contribute to an improved understanding of vulnerability to depression. These developments will be important, because at the moment the mood-state dependent hypothesis does not specify the precise content of the dysfunctional cognition. Is it specific beliefs, memories, attitudes, or ways of thinking?

If so, this raises the question as to what distinguishes the negative thoughts that are relevant to depression from other mental content and processes. In most cases, mood-dependent recall merely acts as an additional cue, facilitating the recall of events that were encoded through a match between current mood state and mood state at time of encoding. According to the mood-state dependent hypothesis, however, recall of dysfunctional attitudes are not just facilitated. Negative mood seems to be necessary. Why is this? And what is the difference between negative events that vulnerable subjects' presumably can recall despite current mood and dysfunctional attitudes unavailable for recall except under conditions of negative mood?

SUMMARY

In this article, we have described how the mood-state dependent hypothesis grew out of a need to reconcile cognitive theory with growing evidence that the vulnerability factors postulated by this theory were absent in vulnerable but currently asymptomatic individuals. This mood-state dependent hypothesis proposes that dysfunctional attitudes are present in vulnerable individuals, but remain inaccessible until they are activated by negative mood. According to this view, out of sight is not out of mind. Hidden dysfunctional attitudes are every bit as destructive once they have been activated by negative mood. Our review of the accumulating evidence relevant to the mood-state dependent hypothesis suggests a more dynamic interpretation of this hypothesis than provided previously. This interpretation highlights the importance of emotion regulation, and suggests that one reason why some people become clinically depressed, whereas others do not is that they fail to modulate appropriately the impact of negative mood on cognitive processes.

REFERENCES

Abramson, L.Y., Metalsky, G.I., & Alloy, L.B. (1989). Hopelessness depression: A theory-based subtype of depression. *Psychological Review, 96*, 358–372.

Abramson, L.Y., Seligman, M.E.P., & Teasdale, J. (1978). Learned helpless in humans: Critique and reformulation. *Journal of Abnormal Psychology, 87*, 102–109.

APA (Americal Psychiatric Association) (1994). *Diagnostic and statistical manual of mental disorders* (4th ed.). Washington, DC: Author.

Barnett, P.A., & Gotlib, I.H. (1988). Psychosocial functioning and depression: Distinguishing among antecedents, concomitants, and consequences. *Psychological Bulletin, 104*, 97–126.

Beck, A.T. (1967). *Depression: Clinical, experimental, and theoretical aspects.* New York: Harper & Row.

Beck, A.T. (1972). *Depression: Causes and treatment.* Philadelphia: University of Pennsylvania Press.

Beck, A.T., Brown, G., Steer, R.A., & Weissman, A.N. (1991). Factor analysis of the Dysfunctional Attitudes Scale in a clinical population. *Psychological Assessment, 3,* 478–483.

Beck, A.T., Rush, A.J., Shaw, B.F., & Emery, G. (1979). *Cognitive therapy of depression.* New York: Guilford Press.

Blackburn, I.M., Roxborough, H.M., Muir, W.J., Glabus, M., & Blackwood, D.H.R. (1990). Perceptual and physiological dysfunctional in depression. *Psychological Medicine, 20,* 95–103.

Blaney, P.H. (1986). Affect and memory: A review. *Psychological Bulletin, 99,* 229–246.

Bower, G.H. (1981). Mood and memory. *American Psychologist, 36,* 129–148.

Bower, G.H. (1983). Affect and cognition. *Philosophical Transactions of the Royal Society of London B, 302,* 387–402.

Bower, G.H. (1987). Commentary on mood and memory. *Behavioral Research and Therapy, 25,* 443–455.

Bower, G.H., & Mayer, J.D. (1985). Failure to replicate mood-dependent retrieval. *Bulletin of the Psychonomic Society, 23,* 39–42.

Bower, G.H., Monteiro, K.P., & Gilligan, S.G. (1978). Emotional mood as a context for learning and recall. *Journal of Verbal Learning and Verbal Behavior, 17,* 573–585.

Coyne, J.C., & Gotlib, I.H. (1983). The role of cognition in depression: A critical appraisal. *Psychological Bulletin, 94,* 472–505.

Depression Guideline Panel (1993). *Depression in primary care: Vol. 2. Treatment of major depression.* Rockville, MD: US Department of Health and Human Services.

Dobson, K.S. (1989). A meta-analysis of the efficacy of cognitive therapy for depression. *Journal of Consulting and Clinical Psychology, 57,* 414–419.

Eaves, G., & Rush, A.J. (1984). Cognitive patterns in symptomatic and remitted unipolar major depression. *Journal of Abnormal Psychology, 93,* 31–40.

Ekman, P., & Davidson, R.J. (Eds.) (1994). *The nature of emotion: Fundamental questions.* New York: Oxford University Press.

Engel, R. (1995, November). *Cognitive vulnerability to depression and the mood-state hypothesis: Is the endorsement of dysfunctional attitudes and attributional style mood-state dependent?* Poster presented at the annual meeting of the Association for the Advancement of Behavior Therapy, Washington, DC.

Gerrards-Hesse, A., Spies, K., & Hesse, F.W. (1994). Experimental inductions of emotional states and their effectiveness: a review. *British Journal of Psychology, 85,* 55–78.

Gibbons, F.X., Smith, T.W., Ingram, R.E., Pearce, K., Brehm, S.S., & Schroeder, D. (1985). Self-awareness and self-confrontation: Effects of self-focused attention on members of a clinical population. *Journal of Personality and Social Psychology, 48,* 662–675.

Goodwin, A.H., & Sher, K.J. (1993). Effects of induced mood on diagnostic interviewing: Evidence for a mood and memory effect. *Psychological Assessment, 5,* 197–202.

Gotlib, I.H., & McCabe, S.B. (1995). Selective attention and clinical depression: Performance on a deployment-of-attention task. *Journal of Abnormal Psychology, 104,* 241–245.

Gotlib, I.H., Whiffen, V.E., Wallace, P.M., & Mount, J.H. (1991). Prospective investigation of postpartum depression: Factors involved in onset and recovery. *Journal of Abnormal Psychology, 100,* 122–132.

Greenberg, P.E,. Stiglin, L.E., Finkelstein, S.N., & Berndt, E.R. (1993). The economic burden of depression in 1990. *Journal of Clinical Psychiatry, 54,* 405–418.

Gross, J.J., & Levenson, R.W. (1995). Emotion elicitation using films. *Cognition and Emotion, 9,* 87–108.

Gross, J.J., & Munoz, R.F. (1995). Emotion regulation and mental health. *Clinical Psychology: Science and Practice, 2,* 151–164.

Haaga, D.A.F., Dyck, M.J., & Ernst, D. (1991). Empirical status of cognitive theory of depression. *Psychological Bulletin, 110*, 215–236.

Hamilton, E.W,. & Abramson, L.Y. (1983). Cognitive patterns and major depressive disorder: A longitudinal study in a hospital setting. *Journal of Abnormal Psychology, 92*, 173–184.

Hedlund, S., & Rude, S.S. (1995). Evidence of latent depressive schemas in formerly depressed individuals. *Journal of Abnormal Psychology, 104*, 517–525.

Hollon, S.D., Kendall, P.C., & Lumry, A. (1986). Specificity of depressotypic cognitions in clinical depression. *Journal of Abnormal Psychology, 95*, 52–59.

Hollon, S.D., Shelton, R.C., & Davis, D.D. (1993). Cognitive therapy for depression: Conceptual issues and clinical efficacy. *Journal of Consulting and Clinical Psychology, 61*, 270–275.

Hollon, S.D., Shelton, R.C., & Loosen, P.T. (1991). Cognitive therapy and pharmacotherapy for depression. *Journal of Consulting and Clinical Psychology, 59*, 88–99.

Ingram, R.E. (1984). Toward an information-processing analysis of depression. *Cognitive Therapy and Research, 8*, 443–478.

Ingram, R.E., Bernet, C., & McLaughlin, S.C. (1994). Attention allocation processes in individuals at risk for depression. *Cognitive Therapy and Research, 18*, 317–332.

Ingram, R.E., & Smith, T.W. (1984). Depression and internal versus external focus of attention. *Cognitive Therapy and Research, 8*, 139–152.

Kessler, R.C., McGonagle, K.A., Zhao, S., Nelson, C.B., Hughes, M., Eshleman, S., Wittchen, H.U., & Kendler, K.S. (1994). Lifetime and 12-month prevalence of DSM-III-R psychiatric disorders in the United States: Results from the National Comorbidity Survey. *Archives of General Psychiatry, 51*, 8–19.

Lewinsohn, P.M., Steinmetz, J.I., Larson, D.W., & Franklin, J. (1981). Depression-related cognitions: Antecedents or consequence? *Journal of Abnormal Psychology, 90*, 213–219.

Martin, M. (1990). On the induction of mood. *Clinical Psychology Review, 10*, 669–697.

Matthews, G.R., & Antes, J.R. (1992). Visual attention and depression: Cognitive biases in the eye fixations of the dysphoric and the nondepressed. *Cognitive Therapy and Research, 16*, 359–371.

Miranda, J. (1992). Dysfunctional thinking is activated by stressful life events. *Cognitive Therapy and Research, 16*, 473–483.

Miranda, J., Gross, J., Persons, J., & Hahn, J. (in press). Mood matters: Negative mood induction activates dysfunctional attitudes in women vulnerable to depression. *Cognitive Therapy and Research.*

Miranda, J., & Persons, J.B. (1988). Dysfunctional attitudes are mood-state dependent. *Journal of Abnormal Psychology, 97*, 76–79.

Miranda, J., Persons, J.B., & Byers, C.N. (1990). Endorsement of dysfunctional beliefs depends on current mood state. *Journal of Abnormal Psychology, 99*, 237–241.

Morris, W.N. (1992). A functional analysis of the role of mood in affective systems. In M.S. Clark (Ed.), *Review of personality and social psychology: Vol. 13. Emotion* (pp. 256–293). Newbury Park, CA: Sage.

Morris, W.N., & Reilly, N.P. (1987). Toward the self-regulation of mood: Theory and research. *Motivation and Emotion, 11*, 215–249.

Myers, L.B. (1995). Onset vulnerability to depression. *Journal of Genetic Psychology, 156*, 503–504.

Nolen-Hoeksema, S. (1987). Sex differences in unipolar depression: Evidence and theory. *Psychological Bulletin, 101*, 259–282.

O'Hara, M.W., Neunaber, D.J., & Zekoski, E.M. (1984). Prospective study of postpartum depression: Prevalence, course, and predictive factors. *Journal of Abnormal Psychology, 93*, 158–171.

O'Hara, M.W., Schlechte, J.A., Lewis, D.A., & Varner, M.W. (1991). Controlled prospective study of postpartum mood disorders: Psychological, environmental, and hormonal variables. *Journal of Abnormal Psychology, 100,* 63–73.

Parrott, W.G., & Sabini, J. (1990). Mood and memory under natural conditions: Evidence for mood incongruent recall. *Journal of Personality and Social Psychology, 59,* 321–336.

Persons, J.B. (1993). Outcome of psychotherapy for unipolar depression. In T.R. Giles (Ed.), *Handbook of effective psychotherapy* (pp. 305–323). New York: Plenum.

Persons, J.B., & Miranda, J. (1992). Cognitive theories of vulnerability to depression: Reconciling negative evidence. *Cognitive Therapy and Research, 16,* 485–502.

Persons, J.B., & Rao, P.A. (1985). Longitudinal study of cognitions, life events, and depression in psychiatric inpatients. *Journal of Abnormal Psychology, 94,* 51–63.

Pyszczynski, T., & Greenberg, J. (1987). Self-regulatory perseveration and the depressive self-focusing style: A self-awareness theory of reactive depression. *Psychological Bulletin, 102,* 122–138.

Reda, M.A., Carpiniello, B., Secchiaroli, L., & Blanco, S.Y. (1985). Thinking, depression, and antidepressants: Modified and unmodified depressive beliefs during treatment with amitriptyline. *Cognitive Therapy and Research, 9,* 135–143.

Rippere, V. (1977). "What's the thing to do when you're feeling depressed?"—a pilot study. *Behavior Research and Therapy, 15,* 185–191.

Riskind, J.H., & Rholes, W.S. (1984). Cognitive accessibility and capacity of cognition to predict future depression: A theoretical note. *Cognitive Therapy and Research 8,* 1–12.

Roberts, J.E., & Kassel, J.D. (1996). Mood-state dependence in cognitive vulnerability to depression: The roles of positive and negative affect. *Cognitive Therapy and Research, 20,* 1–12.

Robins, L.H., Helzer, J.E., Croughan, J., & Ratcliff, K.S. (1981). National Institute of Mental Health Diagnostic Interview Schedule: Its history, characteristics, and validity. *Archives of General Psychiatry, 38,* 381–389.

Robinson, L.A., Berman, J.S., & Neimeyer, R.A. (1990). Psychotherapy for the treatment of depression: A comprehensive review of controlled outcome research. *Psychological Bulletin, 108,* 30–49.

Segal, Z.V., & Ingram, R.E. (1994). Mood priming and construct activation in tests of cognitive vulnerability to unipolar depression. *Clinical Psychology Review, 14,* 663–695.

Seligman, M.E.P. (1991). *Learned optimism.* New York: Knopf.

Shea, M.T., Elkin, I., Imber, S.D., Sotsky, S.M., Watkins, J.T., Collins, J.F., Pilkonis, P.A., Beckham, E., Glass, D., Dolan, R.T., & Parloff, M.B. (1992). Course of depressive symptoms over follow-up: Findings from the National Institute of Mental Health Treatment of Depression Collaborative Research Program. *Archives of General Psychiatry, 49,* 782–787.

Simons, A., Garfield, S., & Murphy, D. (1984). The process of change in cognitive therapy and pharmacotherapy for depression. *Archives of General Psychiatry, 41,* 45–51.

Smith, S.M., & Petty, R.E. (1995). Personality moderators of mood congruency effects on cognition: The role of self-esteem and negative mood regulation. *Journal of Personality and Social Psychology, 68,* 1097–1107.

Smith, T.W., Ingram, R.E., & Roth, D.L. (1985). Self-focused attention and depression: Self-evaluation, affect, and life-stress. *Motivation and Emotion, 9,* 381–389.

Snyder, M., & White, P. (1982). Moods and memories: Elation, depression and the remembering of the events of one's life. *Journal of Personality, 50,* 149–167.

Teasdale, J.D. (1983). Negative thinking in depression: Cause, effect, or reciprocal relationship? *Advances in Behaviour Research and Therapy, 5,* 3–25.

Teasdale, J.D. (1988). Cognitive vulnerability to persistent depression. *Cognition and Emotion, 2,* 247–274.

Teasdale, J.D., & Dent, J. (1987). Cognitive vulnerablity to depression: An investigation of two hypotheses. *British Journal of Clinical Psychology, 26,* 113–126.

Velten, E. (1968). A laboratory task for induction of mood states. *Behaviour Research and Therapy, 6,* 473–482.

Weissman, A. (1979). *The dysfunctional attitude scale: A validation study.* Unpublished doctoral dissertation, University of Pennsylvania, Philadelphia.

Wells, K.B., Stewart, A., Hays, R.D., Burnam, M.A., Rogers, W., Daniels, M., Berry, S., Greenfield, S., & Ware, J. (1989). The functioning and well-being of depressed patients: Results from the medical outcomes study. *Journal of the American Medical Association, 262,* 914–919.

COGNITION AND EMOTION, 1997, *11* (5/6), 607–618

Mania, Depression, and Mood Dependent Memory

Eric Eich, Dawn Macaulay, and Raymond W. Lam

University of British Columbia, Vancouver, Canada

Most of what is known about the conditions under which mood dependent memory (MDM) occurs, and the factors that enable its emergence, has come from cognitively oriented research involving experimentally engendered moods in normal subjects (typically university undergraduates). To date, little attention has been paid to the possibility of demonstrating MDM in people who experienced marked shifts in mood state as a consequence of a psychopathological condition. By studying patients with rapid-cycling bipolar illness, we sought to explore this possibility and to establish whether findings derived from cognitively oriented studies of MDM can be generalised to a clinically relevant context.

INTRODUCTION

The research reported here deals with mood dependent memory (MDM) in patients with rapid-cycling bipolar disorder, and it was designed to address two issues.

One is whether MDM occurs in conjunction with this disorder; that is, do bipolar patients retrieve more prior episodes or events when their mood at testing—manic or hypomanic as opposed to depressed—matches their mood at encoding than when there is a mismatch? Readers familiar with the MDM literature may wonder why we raise this issue, given the results of a well-known study by Weingartner, Miller, and Murphy (1977). Participants in this study were eight patients who cycled between states of mania and depression (or, occasionally, normal mood) over a span of several months. Periodically, the patients produced 20 word associations to each of two common nouns (such as *ship* and *street*) and were tested for their ability to recall all 40 associations four days later. Recall averaged

---

Requests for reprints should be sent to Eric Eich, Department of Psychology, University of British Columbia Vancouver, BC/Canada V6T 1Z4; e-mail via Internet: ee@cortex.psych.ubc.ca.

Preparation of this article was aided by grant MH48502 from the National Institute of Mental Health to the first author.

35% when the mood at testing (manic vs. normal or depressed) matched the mood at production, but only 18% when there was a mismatch. In an oft-cited essay, Bower (1981, p. 134) referred to these results as "the clearest early example of mood dependent memory".

Or is it? The question was posed in a review paper by Blaney (1986), who suggested that what Weingartner and his associates may have demonstrated was not mood *dependent* memory, but rather, mood *congruent* memory. As defined by Blaney (1986, p. 229), mood congruence "assumes that some material, by virtue of its affectively valenced content, is more likely to be stored and/or recalled when one is in a particular mood; concordance between mood at exposure and mood at recall is not required or relevant". In contrast, mood dependence (p. 229), "implies that what one remembers during a given mood is determined in part by what one learned (or focused on) when previously in that mood; the effective valence of the material is irrelevant". Although mood congruence and mood dependence are theoretically distinct phenomena, several studies—including that by Weingartner et al. (1977)—have provided results that can be interpreted as evidence for either. According to Blaney (1986, p. 237):

> Weingartner et al.'s (1977) results—indicating that subjects experiencing strong mood shifts were better able to regenerate associations first generated in same as opposed to different mood—could be seen as reflecting either mood congruence or (mood) state dependence. That is, the enhanced ability of subjects to recall what they had generated when last in a given mood was (a) because what was congruent with that mood at first exposure was still congruent with it at subsequent exposure, or (b) because return to that mood helped remind subjects of the material they were thinking about when last in that mood, irrespective of content.

This ambiguity in interpretation arises from an ambiguity in the test instructions that were given to the patients. Although it is clear from Weingartner et al.'s account that the patients were asked to recall their prior associations, it is unclear how the patients interpreted this request. One possibility is that understood "recall" to mean that they should restrict their search to episodic memory—in effect, saying to themselves: "What associations did I produce the last time I saw *ship*?"—in which case the results would seem to suggest mood dependence. Alternatively, they may have taken "recall" as a cue to search semantic memory—"What comes to mind now when I think of *street*, regardless of what I said four days ago?"—in which case the data may be more indicative of mood congruence.

Seeking to clarify the situation, we asked participants in the present study to produce 40 single-word associations while they were in a depressed or a (hypo)manic mood. Of these 40 associations, 20 were words beginning with (say) the letter E and 20 were words beginning with (say) S. Several days later, while the patients were in either the same or the opposing mood, retention of the associations was assessed in two ways. In one case, patients received *episodic memory instructions*, whereby they were asked to recall as many of their previously produced E words as possible, but to assiduously avoid making any intrusions; that is, they should respond with a given E word only if they were sure that they remembered having said that word during the preceding session. In the other case, patients received *semantic memory instructions*, whereby they were asked to name 20 words—any 20 words—starting with S; no specific intent to remember the original associations was required or even implied. We reasoned that if memory is truly mood dependent, such that returning to the orginal mood helps remind subjects of what they were thinking about when last in that mood, then performance in the episodic-memory task should show an advantage of matched over mismatched moods. In contrast, an analogous advantage in the semantic-memory task could be construed as evidence of mood congruence.

To date, most researchers have taken a purely cognitive approach to the study of MDM, their goal being to identify conditions that consistently produce mood dependence in normal subjects (typically university undergraduates) whose moods have been induced by some experimental means (e.g. hypnotic suggestions, guided imagery, or emotionally evocative music; see Martin, 1990). Whether MDM arises in association with abnormal and spontaneous shifts in mood state, such as between mania and depression, is a question that has seldom been addressed, much less answered. These observations point to the second issue of current concern; namely, whether findings derived from cognitively oriented studies of MDM can be generalised to a clinically relevant context.

Two findings are of especial interest in this regard. One is that robust and reliable evidence of mood dependence rarely emerges when retrieval is tested in the presence of specific, observable cues or reminders, such as the "copy cues" (Tulving, 1983) that are available in a test of recognition memory. Although several studies have sought, without success, to demonstrate mood dependent recognition (see Bower, 1981; Bower & Cohen, 1982; Eich, 1980; Eich & Metcalfe, 1989; but also see Beck & McBee, 1995; Leight & Ellis, 1981), most of these studies: (1) involved experimentally induced moods (typically happiness vs. sadness) in normal subjects; and (2) investigated recognition memory for materials (usually common, unrelated nouns) that are familiar, simple, meaningful, and unemotional.

Neither these moods, nor these materials, may be conducive to the occurrence of mood dependent recognition—the former because they are too mild to have much of an impact (see Bower, 1992; Eich, 1995); the latter because they allow little latitude for different encodings in different moods (see Bower & Cohen, 1982; Bower & Mayer, 1989). If so, then the present study may stand a better change than most at detecting mood dependent recognition, given that it: (1) involves moods (viz. mania or hypomania vs. depression) that can reasonably be considered strong; and (2) investigates recognition memory for novel, complex, and highly abstract stimuli (viz. Rorschach-like inkblots) that are likely to be subject to emotional biases at encoding.

The second finding of note stems from a recent study by Eich, Macaulay, and Ryan (1994, experiment 2). During the encoding session of this study, university undergraduates performed a task of autobiographical event generation while they were experiencing either a happy or a sad mood—affects that had been induced through a combination of affectively appropriate music and ideation. For purposes of this task, subjects were asked to recollect or generate as many as 16 real-life events, from any time in the personal past, when prompted with common-word probes. Subjects described every event in detail and rated it along several dimensions, including its original emotional valence (i.e. whether the event seemed positive, neutral, or negative when it occurred). During the retrieval session, held two days after encoding, subjects were asked to freely recall the gist of as many of their previously generated events as possible (preferably by recalling their precise corresponding probes). Mood at event recall matched the mood at event generation for a random half of the subjects and mismatched for the other half.

Replicating earlier experiments (see Blaney, 1986; Bower, 1981), results of the encoding session revealed mood *congruent* memory. Whereas happy mood subjects generated three times more positive than negative events, the corresponding ratio among sad subjects was 1:1.

More important for present concerns, results of the retrieval session demonstrated mood *dependent* memory. Relative to subjects whose encoding and retrieval moods matched, those whose moods mismatched recalled fewer events (26% vs. 35%), irrespective of emotional valence (i.e. positive, neutral, or negative). Similar results were obtained in two other studies (Eich et al., 1994, experiments 1 and 3), suggesting that the free recall of previously generated autobiographical events is a sensitive and reliable measure of MDM in normal subjects. Borrowing from the methods and materials developed by Eich et al. (1994), we sought to determine whether the same task would yield similar results in bipolar patients.

METHOD

Subjects and Design

Ten patients with rapid-cycling bipolar I or bipolar II disorder, diagnosed according to DSMIV criteria (APA, 1994), participated in the study.[1] The sample comprised 9 women and 1 man ranging in age from 21 to 47 years (mean = 33.7 years). All of the patients were recruited through either the UBC Mood Disorders Clinic or the Mood Disorders Association of British Columbia, and all were involved in long-term drug therapy for the disorder.

Every patient was seen on at least four separate occasions; the odd-numbered occasions serving as *encoding sessions* and the even-numbered occasions representing *retrieval sessions*. Although the interval separating successive encoding and retrieval sessions varied from 2 to 7 days between patients, the interval always remained constant within a given patient.

Superimposed on these sessions was a 2 × 2 design: mood at encoding—manic or hypomanic (M) versus depressed (D)—crossed with these same two moods at retrieval. Originally, we had planned to vary these factors within subjects, so that every patient would participate in all four combinations of encoding/retrieval moods (viz. M/M, M/D, D/M, and D/D). This plan proved unworkable, however, as several patients left the study prematurely for various reasons (e.g. they moved out of town, they started a new regimen of drug therapy, or they stopped cycling between moods). Of the 10 patients who took part in this study, 4 completed all four encoding/retrieval conditions, 3 completed three conditions, and 3 completed two; the order of completion varied unsystematically from one patient to the next, the determining factors being which mood a patient was in when testing began and on how rapidly the patient cycled from one state to the other. Thus, the 10 patients provided data on a total of 31 conditions, distributed as follows: M/M = 8; M/D = 7; D/M = 9; and D/D = 7. Owing to the many missing conditions, we decided to treat the data as if encoding and retrieval moods had been varied between rather than within subjects, and to analyse the results accordingly.

---

[1] Patients with rapid-cycling bipolar I disorder have a history of intermittent episodes of major depression and mania, the latter being sufficiently severe to: (1) cause marked impairment in occupational functioning or social relations; and/or (2) require hospitalisation on one or more occasions. Although patients with rapid-cycling bipolar II disorder have never experienced true mania (as just defined), their clinical course is characterised by recurrent episodes of depression and hypomania.

Encoding Session

At the outset of each encoding session, the patients' present mood was assessed by means of the Positive Affect-Negative Affect Schedule (PANAS).Developed and validated by Watson, Clark, and Tellegen (1988), the PANAS consists of 20 emotion-relevant adjectives such as *attentive* and *irritable*. Patients responded to each item with a number ranging from 1 (*very slightly or not at all*) to 5 (*extremely*) based on how they were feeling "right now".

The sum of ratings for 10 of the adjectives provided an index of Positive Affect (PA) and the sum of ratings for the other 10 items served as a measure of Negative Affect (NA); thus, the minimum and maximum values of both PA and NA are 10 and 50, respectively. According to Watson et al. (1988, p. 1063):

> Positive affect . . . reflects the extent to which a person feels enthusiastic, active, and alert. High PA is a state of high energy, full concentration, and pleasurable engagement, whereas low PA is characterised by sadness and lethargy. In contrast, Negative Affect . . . is a general dimension that subsumes a variety of aversive mood states, including anger, contempt, disgust, guilt, fear, and nervousness, with low NA being a state of calmness and serenity.

Given these definitions, we anticipated that the patients would report higher levels of PA, and possibly lower levels of NA, when they were experiencing a (hypo)manic as opposed to a depressed mood.

On completing the PANAS, the patients undertook a series of three tasks, summarised later. Although the tasks themselves remained constant from one encodng session to the next, the materials used in these tasks were systematically varied. The same applied to the tasks and materials involved in the retrieval sessions, which will be described in a later section.

Autobiographical Event Generation. Paralleling the procedures devised by Eich et al. (1994, experiment 2), the patients recollected a maximum of 10 specific experiences or events, from any time in the personal past, that were called to mind by neutral-noun probes. After recounting the gist of a given event (e.g. what happened, who was involved, etc.), patients categorised the experience in terms of its orginal emotional valence (i.e. whether it seemed positive, neutral, or negative when it occurred).

Inkblot Rating. The materials for this task consisted of four multi-colour inkblots, printed on large index cards. Patients viewed each card for

5 seconds, and rated the aesthetic appeal of the pattern on a 5-point numerical scale.

Letter Association Production.   Patients were asked to name aloud 20 words beginning with one letter of the alphabet (e.g. E) and 20 words beginning with a different letter (e.g. S); their responses were recorded in writing by the experimenter.

Retrieval Session

As was the case at encoding, patients began the retrieval session by rating their current mood on the PANAS. The patients then carried out the following tasks.

Inkblot Recognition.   Patients were shown four sets of six inkblots each. Within each set, one pattern was an inkblot that the patients had seen during the immediately preceding encoding session and the other five were perceptually similar lures. Patients were asked to select the old (previously viewed) pattern, and to rate their confidence in their recognition decision on a scale ranging from 0 (*guessing*) to 3 (*certain*).

Autobiographical Event Recall.   Patients were reminded that in the course of the most recent testing session, they had recollected and recounted 10 specific real-life events in response to neutral-noun probes. Patients were given 5 minutes in which to recall as many of these events as possible, preferably by recalling their precise corresponding probes. Patients were permitted to recall the events in any order they wished, but they were not provided with any specific, observable cues or reminders to assist them in their efforts.

Letter Association Retention.   The last task assessed retention of letter associations that had been produced in the immediately preceding encoding session. The task was divided into two phases, each entailing a different set of test instructions.

The first phase involved *episodic memory instructions*: After reminding the patients that they had previously produced 20 words beginning with a particular letter (e.g. E), we asked them to recall freely aloud as many of these words as possible. Patients were dissuaded from guessing and cautioned against making intrusions.

The second phase of testing involved *semantic memory instructions*: Patients were presented with the other letter to which they had previously responded (e.g. S) and were asked to name aloud 20 words—any 20 words—that began with that letter. Patients were encouraged explicitly to state the first responses that came to mind. To get them into the proper frame of mind, we had the patients produce 20 associations to each of two brand new letters before they responded to the critical semantic memory stimulus.

At the conclusion of the final retrieval session, patients received a thorough debriefing on the study's aims and methods, and were thanked for their participation.

RESULTS

Measures of Mood

Mean ratings of Positive and Negative Affect (PA and NA, respectively) are presented in Table 1 as a function of encoding/retrieval moods. As expected, patients reported higher levels of PA when they experienced a (hypo)manic as opposed to a depressed mood [means = 36.5 vs. 17.8; $t(60)$ = 11.40, $P < .01$]. Conversely, depression was associated with higher ratings of NA than was (hypo)mania [means = 24.2 vs. 16.3; $t(60)$ = 3.22, $P < .01$].

Autobiographical Event Generation

On average, positive events outnumbered negative events by a margin of 3.36 to 1 when patients generated autobiographical memories in a (hypo)manic mood, and by a margin of 1.51 to 1 when testing took place

Table 1
Ratings of Positive Affect (PA) and Negative Affect (NA) as a Function of Encoding/Retrieval Moods

Encoding/Retrieval Moods	n	Encoding Session		Retrieval Session	
		PA	NA	PA	NA
M/M	8	36.6	14.8	37.9	16.3
		(2.3)	(1.5)	(2.1)	(2.2)
M/D	7	35.6	20.7	19.0	20.0
		(2.0)	(3.1)	(3.1)	(3.0)
D/M	9	19.4	22.9	35.9	14.6
		(2.6)	(4.0)	(2.6)	(2.5)
D/D	7	16.6	27.9	15.7	26.6
		(2.2)	(3.9)	(1.7)	(4.0)

Note: M, manic or hypomanic mood; D, depressed mood. *n*, number of patients per mean rating; (standard errors are enclosed in parentheses). Maximum and minimum values of both PA and NA are 50 and 10, respectively.

in a depressed mood. Although the difference between these ratios is only marginally significant [$t(28) = 1.91$, $P < .10$], it is at least suggestive of mood congruence in autobiographical memory. To our knowledge, this is the first time any evidence of this phenomenon has been found in patients with bipolar mood disorder.

Autobiographical Event Recall

The white bars in Fig. 1 represent the mean percentage of previously generated autobiographical events that were freely recalled in each encoding/retrieval condition. Although the data are indicative of mood dependence—recall averaged 33% when encoding and retrieval moods matched (conditions M/M and D/D) but only 23% when they mismatched (conditions M/D and D/M)—the F-value for the interaction between encoding and retrieval moods was not reliable ($P > .10$) owing to marked variability in the M/M and D/M conditions. However, a significant advantage of matched over mismatched moods was secured when the recall data were analysed nonparametrically (z-score for the difference between two proportions = 2.16, $P < .05$). Similar to the pattern seen in earlier experiments (Eich et al., 1994), the advantage of matched over mismatched moods was apparent in the recall of both positive events (34% vs. 20%) and negative events (39% vs. 26%).

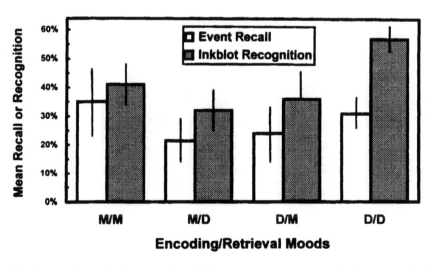

FIG. 1. Autobiographical event recall and inkblot recognition memory as a function of encoding/retrieval moods (M, manic or hypomanic; D, depressed). Thin vertical lines denote standard errors.

Inkblot Recognition

Results of the test of inkblot recognition were notable in two respects. First, as shown by the dark bars in Fig. 1, patients were better at discriminating old or previously presented inkblots from perceptually similar lures when tested under matched as opposed to mismatched mood conditions [mean correct recognition = 48% vs. 34%; $F(1/27)$ = 4.33, $P < .05$ for the encoding mood × retrieval mood interaction]. This is evidence of mood dependent recognition—an effect seldom seen in prior studies of MDM.

Second, patients expressed greater confidence in recognition decisions that proved to be correct (i.e. selecting the old inkblot from among the six alternatives; mean rating = 1.89) than those that were incorrect [i.e. falsely recognising one of the lures; mean rating = 1.12; $F(1/21)$ = 13.37, $P < .01$]. This difference in recognition confidence, which was found in every encoding/retrieval condition, implies that the test tapped explicit, recollective processes and that the patients did not respond to the recognition alternatives solely on the basis of an implicit feeling of familiarity.

Letter Association Retention

Performance in the test of letter association retention is depicted in Fig. 2 as a function of encoding mood, retrieval mood, and test instructions. Inspection of the figure reveals that, on average, the patients reproduced about 30% of their prior associations, regardless of whether or not they

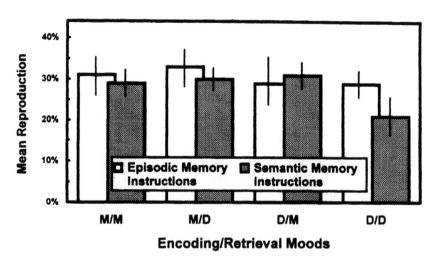

FIG. 2. Reproduction of associations to letter cues as a function of test instructions and encoding/retrieval moods (M, manic or hypomanic; D, depressed). Thin vertical lines denote standard errors.

intended to do so (i.e. episodic vs. semantic memory instructions) and regardless of whether they were tested under matched or mismatched mood conditions. Consistent with these observations, a 2 × 2 × 2 (encoding mood × retrieval mood × test instruction) mixed-design analysis disclosed no significant simple effects of interactions ($Ps > .10$). Thus, whereas Weingartner et al. (1977) found an effect in the reproduction of word associations that can be construed either as mood congruence or as mood dependence, we found no effect at all.

DISCUSSION

The results of the present study were disappointing in some respects, encouraging in others. Most disappointing were the data derived from the test of letter association retention. As was noted at the outset, a seminal study by Weingartner et al. (1977) had shown that word associations produced by patients who cycled between periods of mania and normality (or, occasionally, depression) were more apt to be reproduced when the patient's mood state remained constant than when it changed. We sought not only to replicate Weingartner et al.'s results, but also to resolve a long-standing ambiguity that surrounds their interpretation; specifically, whether the results reflect mood congruent memory or mood dependent memory (see Blaney, 1986). Neither of these aims was achieved, however, as we found no appreciable advantage in reproduction performance of constant over changed moods, even when the patients deliberately tried to remember their prior associations. Although the discrepancy between the present results and those reported by Weingartner et al. resists easy explanation, it is worth noting that whereas we used letters of the alphabet to prime the production of associative responses, Weingartner et al. used common words like *ship* and *street*—stimuli that bipolar patients may interpret in different ways, depending on their present mood state (see Henry, Weingartner, & Murphy, 1971).

Conceivably, associations made to letters may allow less room for state-specific interpretive processes to operate, and this in turn may lessen the likelihood of detecting either mood congruent or mood dependent effects (see Nissen, Ross, Willingham, MacKenzie, & Schacter, 1988). Whether there is any substance to these speculations remains to be seen.

On a more positive note, the bipolar patients who participated in the present study demonstrated mood congruence in the test of autobiographical event generation, and mood dependence in the test of autobiographical event recall. In both respects, their behaviour parallels the performance of normal subjects whose moods have been modified experimentally (Eich et al., 1994).

Interestingly, however, the patients also evinced an effect—mood dependent recognition—that normals seldom show, perhaps because the former subjects experience stronger, more intense moods than do the latter. Alternatively, it may be that the key to demonstrating mood dependent recognition is to use novel, complex, and highly abstract stimuli (like the inkblots used in the present study) that are apt to be encoded in an emotionally biased manner. These are but two of several possibilities that seem ripe for investigation, ideally through a programme of research that approaches mood dependence from a clinical as well as a cognitive point of view.

REFERENCES

APA (American Psychiatric Association) (1994). *Diagnostic and statistical manual of mental disorders* (4th ed.). Washington, DC: Author.

Beck, R.C., & McBee, W. (1995). Mood-dependent memory for generated and repeated words: Replication and extension. *Cognition and Emotion, 9*, 289–307.

Blaney, P.H. (1986). Affect and memory: A review. *Psychological Bulletin, 99*, 229–246.

Bower, G.H. (1981). Mood and memory. *American Psychologist, 36*, 129–148.

Bower, G.H. (1992). How might emotions affect learning? In S-A. Christianson (Ed.), *Handbook of emotion and memory* (pp. 3–31). Hillsdale, NJ: Lawrence Erlbaum Associates Inc.

Bower, G.H., & Cohen, P.R. (1982). Emotional influences in memory and thinking: Data and theory. In M.S. Clark & S.T. Fiske (Eds.), *Affect and cognition: The Seventeenth Annual Carnegie Symposium on Cognition* (pp. 291–331). Hillsdale, NJ: Lawrence Erlbaum Associates Inc.

Bower, G.H., & Mayer, J.D. (1989). In search of mood-dependent retrieval. *Journal of Social Behavior and Personality, 4*, 121–156.

Eich, E. (1980). The cue-dependent nature of state-dependent retrieval. *Memory and Cognition, 8*, 157–173.

Eich, E. (1995). Searching for mood dependent memory. *Psychological Science, 6*, 67–75.

Eich, E., Macaulay, D., & Ryan, L. (1994). Mood dependent memory for events of the personal past. *Journal of Experimental Psychology: General, 123*, 201–215.

Eich, E., & Metcalfe, J. (1989). Mood dependent memory for internal versus external events. *Journal of Experimental Psychology: Learning, Memory, and Cognition, 15*, 443–455.

Henry, G.M., Weingartner, H., & Murphy, D.L. (1971). Idiosyncratic patterns of verbal learning and word association during mania. *American Journal of Psychiatry, 128*, 564–573.

Leight, K.A., & Ellis, H.C. (1981). Emotional mood states, strategies, and state-dependency in memory. *Journal of Verbal Learning and Verbal Behavior, 20*, 251–266.

Martin, M. (1990). On the induction of mood. *Clinical Psychology Review, 10*, 669–697.

Nissen, M.J., Ross, J.L., Willingham, D.B., MacKenzie, T.B., & Schacter, D.L. (1988). Memory and awareness in a patient with multiple personality disorder. *Brain and Cognition, 8*, 21–38.

Tulving, E. (1983). *Elements of episodic memory*. Oxford: Oxford University Press.

Watson, D., Clark, L.A., & Tellegen, A. (1988). Development and validation of brief measures of positive and negative affect: The PANAS scales. *Journal of Personality and Social Psychology, 54*, 1063–1070.

Weingartner, H., Miller, H., & Murphy, D.L. (1977). Mood-state-dependent retrieval of verbal associations. *Journal of Abnormal Psychology, 86*, 276–284.

COGNITION AND EMOTION, 1997, *11* (5/6), 619–635

Cognitive Vulnerability in Children at Risk for Depression

Judy Garber and Nancy S. Robinson

Vanderbilt University, Nashville, USA

Cognitive vulnerability was studied in children (mean age = 11.87, SD = 0.57) who varied in their degree of risk for mood disorders as determined by their mothers' psychiatric histories. The "high-risk" group (*n* = 174) comprised offspring of mothers with histories of nonbipolar mood disorders, whereas the "low-risk" group (*n* = 55) included children whose parents were lifetime-free of psychopathology. Children completed a battery of questionnaires about deep level (i.e. attributions, self-worth, perceived competence, dysfunctional attitudes, self-criticism) and surface level cognitions (i.e. automatic negative thoughts, hopelessness). Children and mothers also were interviewed about the extent of the child's depressive symptoms during the previous two weeks. Results indicated that high-risk children, particularly offspring of mothers with a more chronic history of depression, reported a significantly more negative cognitive style than low-risk children. Even when children's current level of depressive symptoms was controlled, high- and low-risk children continued to differ with regard to their attributional style and perceived self-worth.

INTRODUCTION

According to cognitive models of depression, individuals who have a negative cognitive style regarding the causes of stressful life events (Abramson, Metalsky, & Alloy, 1989; Abramson, Seligman, & Teasdale, 1978) or about the self, world, and future (Beck, 1967, 1976) are particularly vulnerable to becoming depressed when important negative life

Requests for reprints should be sent to Judy Garber, Box 512 Peabody, Vanderbilt University, Nashville, TN 37203, USA; e-mail: GARBERJ0@ctrvax.Vanderbilt.Edu.

This research was supported in part by a FIRST Award from the National Institute of Mental Health (R29-MH4545801A1) and a Faculty Scholar Award (88–1214–88) and grant (95070390) from the W.T. Grant Foundation. Nancy Robinson was supported in part by a training grant from the National Institute of Mental Health (T32MH18921). We would like to acknowledge the co-operation of the Nashville Metropolitan School District, Dr Edward Binkley, and we thank the parents and children who participated in the project.

events occur. Both cross-sectional and prospective studies have found evidence consistent with this cognitive perspective. For example, depressed adults (Barnett & Gotlib, 1988; Haaga, Dyck, & Ernst, 1991) and children (Garber & Hilsman, 1992) report more negative cognitions than nondepressed individuals. In addition, among individuals who have experienced a negative life event, those who had reported negative cognitions prior to the event have been found to have more sustained depressive symptoms compared to individuals without such negative cognitions (e.g. Hilsman & Garber, 1995; Metalsky, Joiner, Hardin, & Abramson, 1993).

Cognitive vulnerability has also been studied by comparing the cognitions of currently depressed individuals with those of formerly depressed persons. The results of these studies have been more mixed. Whereas some studies have found that formerly depressed individuals continue to report negative cognitions even after their depression has remitted (e.g. Eaves & Rush, 1984), others have found that negative cognitions appear to be present only during the depressive episode (e.g. Hamilton & Abramson, 1983; Lewinsohn, Steinmetz, Larson, & Franklin, 1981). Several interpretations of these latter findings have been suggested. First, it is possible that the hypothesised negative cognitive style is latent and therefore difficult to access and assess until it is activated through exposure to a negative life event or a negative mood prime (Beck, Rush, Shaw, & Emery, 1979; Miranda, Persons, & Byers, 1990; Teasdale & Dent, 1987). Alternatively, it may be that negative cognitions are not stable, state-independent characteristics, but are only apparent in the presence of other depressive symptoms (Barnett & Gotlib, 1988).

Another strategy for studying cognitive vulnerability is to examine the cognitions of individuals who are known to be at risk for depression, such as children of depressed parents. There is clear evidence that offspring of depressed parents are at increased risk for developing mood disorders themselves (Downey & Coyne, 1990, Gelfand & Teti, 1990). If negative cognitions contribute to the development of such mood disorders, then one might hypothesise that these "high-risk" individuals would be more likely to exhibit cognitive vulnerability than children whose parents have not experienced mood disorders.

Only a few studies have explicitly tested this hypothesis. Jaenicke et al. (1987) compared children whose mothers had a history of unipolar depression, bipolar affective disorder, medical illness, and normal controls, and found that offspring of unipolar mothers reported significantly lower self-esteem and a more depressogenic attributional style than children of medically ill and control mothers. Goodman, Adamson, Riniti, and Cole (1994) similarly found that children of depressed mothers reported significantly lower perceived self-worth than children of well mothers.

The primary goal of the present study was to replicate and extend this earlier research by testing whether offspring of parents with a history of mood disorders ("high-risk") differ from offspring of parents who are lifetime-free of psychopathology ("low-risk") with regard to an even wider range of cognitions than have been studied previously. Several authors (e.g. Beck et al., 1979; Hollon & Bemis, 1981; Kwon & Oei, 1994) have suggested that there might be two types of cognitions: deep and surface level. Deep level cognitions are presumably traitlike and stable and include underlying assumptions, core beliefs, and dysfunctional attitudes, whereas surface level cognitions are presumably unstable and state-specific and are comprised of automatic thoughts and self-statements. The present study examined the extent to which deep level cognitions such as attributional style, perceived self-worth, perceived competence, self-criticism, and dysfunctional attitudes, and such surface level cognitions as automatic thoughts and hopelessness differentiated high- and low-risk children. If deep level cognitions reflect a stable vulnerability, then high-risk children should differ from low-risk children with regard to deep, but not necessarily surface, level cognitions.

The present study also extends earlier work by controlling for children's current depressive symptoms. It is possible that the cognitive differences between offspring of depressed and nondepressed parents found in the studies by Jaenicke et al. (1987) and Goodman et al. (1994) could have been due, in part, to the high-risk children themselves being more depressed. That is, their negative cognitions simply could have been part of their current depressive symptoms rather than reflecting a state-independent marker of cognitive vulnerability. To address this issue, the present study examined children's cognitions both with and without controlling for their current level of depressive symptoms.

Finally, one factor that might contribute to the development of a cognitive vulnerability is the amount of time children are exposed to a depressed parent. Keller et al. (1986), for example, revealed that more chronic depression in parents was associated with poorer adaptive functioning and greater psychopathology in their children. Campbell, Cohn, and Meyers (1995) found that mothers with more chronic depression had more negative interactions with their children than did mothers with more short-lived depressions. Campbell et al. (1995) suggested that the course of the parent's depression is important to consider when assessing the impact of this depresson on their children. Therefore, the present study explored whether children of more chronically depressed mothers would be more likely to report a negative cognitive style than offspring of mothers with shorter duration or no history of mood disorders. We reasoned that children who had had longer exposure to their mothers being depressed would be particularly at risk for the development of negative cognitions because they had more opportunity for the kinds of negative interactions that are likely to contribute to the development of the cognitive vulnerability.

METHOD

Participants

There were 240 children and their mothers. All children were assessed when they were in the sixth grade (mean age = 11.87, SD = 0.57). The sample of children was 54.2% girls; 82% were Caucasian, 14.7% were Afro-American, and 3.3% were other (Hispanic, Asian, Native American). Sixty-two percent of the mothers were currently married, 31% were currently divorced, 6% were never married, and 1% were widows. The sample was predominantly lower-middle to middle class with a mean socioeconomic status (SES) (Hollingshead, 1975) of 38.84 (SD = 13.27).

Procedure

Letters describing the study were sent to parents of children in the fifth grade at the Nashville metropolitan public schools during three consecutive years. Parents were asked to complete a brief health history questionnaire about whether they had ever had any of 24 different medical conditions, such as diabetes, cancer, heart disease, and depression, or if they had ever taken any of 34 different medications (e.g. Prozac, Elavil). Mothers who indicated either a history of depression or use of antidepressants or a history of no psychiatric problems were then interviewed further. Families were excluded if either parent had a history of schizophrenia, or if the mother had a psychiatric history that did not include a mood disorder. The "high-risk" group (HR) was comprised of offspring of mothers with a history of mood disorders (e.g. major depression, dysthymia, adjustment disorder with depressed mood) during the life of the child. The "low-risk" group (LR) included children whose parents were lifetime-free of psychopathology. The final sample consisted of 91 mothers (72 HR, 19 LR) from Cohort I, 69 (53 HR, 16 LR) from Cohort II, and 80 (60 HR, 20 LR) from Cohort III.[1]

When the children were in the sixth grade, which was several months after completion of the diagnostic interviews with the mothers, a different interviewer, blind to the mother's psychiatric history, interviewed the

---

[1] Eleven mothers who had a history of bipolar affective disorder were excluded from analyses in the present study. Demographic information provided in Table 1 describes this nonbipolar high-risk sample.

mother and child about the child and administered a battery of question-naires to the child. Only those measures relevant to the present study are described here.

Measures

The Structured Clinical Interview for DSMIII-R (SCID; Spitzer, Williams, Gibbon, & First, 1990).   This is a semistructured clinical interview that assesses history and current psychiatric disorders in adults according to DSMIII-R. Extensively trained graduate level interviewers administered the SCIDs to mothers several months before the children were assessed. All interviews were audiotaped and a subset were evaluated for inter-rater reliability using a second interviewer who was blind to the first interviewer's ratings. There was 94% agreement (kappa = .88) for SCID diagnoses of mood disorders. Percent agreement for other diagnoses was .88, kappa = .76.

The Children's Depression Rating Scale–Revised (CDRS; Poznanski, Mokros, Grossman, & Freeman, 1985).   This is a clinical interview used to assess the level of depressive symptoms in children. It is modelled after the Hamilton Rating Scale for Depression (Hamilton, 1960) used with adults. Mothers and children were interviewed separately about the extent of the children's depressive symptoms during the previous two weeks. Twelve depressive symptoms (e.g. anhedonia, insomnia, suicidal ideation) were rated on a 7-point severity scale. Total scores were based on combined information from both the mother and child and could range from 12 to 84.

Self-perception Profile for Children (Harter, 1982).   This assesses children's global perception of self-worth and perceived competence in four specific domains (scholastic, social, appearance, behaviour). The six items of the global self-worth subscale assess the extent to which children are satisfied with themselves, like the way they are leading their lives, like the kind of person they are, and think the way they do things is fine. Each item is presented in a structured alternative format (i.e. "Some kids are often unhappy with themselves BUT other kids are pretty pleased with themselves"). For each item, participants were read both statements and then were asked to decide if they were more like the kids described in the statement on the left side or on the right side. After choosing the statement that most accurately described them, they were asked to mark whether the chosen statement was "really true" or "sort of true" of them. The response was then scored on a 4-point scale. Lower scores indicate poorer global self-worth or lower perceived competence. Coefficient alpha for the global self-worth scale in this sample was .82. Internal consistency alphas for the other four subscales were .80 or higher.

The Children's Attributional Style Questionnaire (CASQ; Seligman et al., 1984). This measures attribution dimensions derived from the reformulated learned helplessness model (Abramson et al., 1978). The original CASQ included 48-item forced-choice items describing 24 positive and 24 negative events. Each item varies one causal dimension (locus, stability, globality) while holding the other two dimensions constant. Participants choose which of two alternative explanations they believe to be the reason the event happened. A revised CASQ (Gladstone & Kaslow, 1995) containing 12 positive and 12 negative items was used in this study.[2] A mean "positive composite" score was created by dividing the number of external, unstable, and specific responses to "good" events by the total number of positive events; a mean "negative composite" score was created by dividing the number of internal, stable, and global responses to all "bad" events by the total number of negative events. The difference score reported here was derived by subtracting the negative from the positive composite scores. Lower difference scores reflect a more depressogenic attributional style.

Scores on the CASQ have been found to be relatively stable over a six-month period (Nolen-Hoeksema, Girgus, & Seligman, 1986; Seligman et al., 1984) and to correlate with self-reported depressive symptoms (Gladstone & Kaslow, 1995). In this sample, coefficient alpha for the difference score was .65, which is consistent with what has been found elsewhere in the literature (Robins & Hinkley, 1989; Seligman & Peterson, 1986).

The Dysfunctional Attitudes Scale (DAS; Weissman & Beck, 1978). This assesses depressogenic attitudes and beliefs. The 40-item DAS was used in this study. Garber, Weiss, and Shanley (1993) had redefined or simplified some of the wording to increase comprehensibility for young adolescents. Items are rated on a 7-point scale, from "totally agree" to "totally disagree". Total scores can range from 40 to 280, with higher scores indicating greater endorsement of maladaptive beliefs. The DAS has high test-retest reliability and good internal consistency ranging from .79 to .93 (Dobson & Brieter, 1981; Oliver & Baumgart, 1985), and discriminates significantly between depressed and nondepressed subjects

---

[2] The CASQ given to Cohorts II and III had an additional 12 negative items from the original CASQ. For these subjects, their mean negative composite scores were created by dividing the total number of internal, stable, and global responses by the total number of negative items (i.e. 24).

(Eaves & Rush, 1984; Hamilton & Abramson, 1983; Silverman, Silverman & Eardley, 1984). Coefficient alpha for the DAS in this sample was .86.

The Depressive Experiences Questionnaire (DEQ; Blatt, D'Afflitti, & Quinlan, 1976). This consists of 66 items reflecting feelings about the self and social relationships. The DEQ has two subscales that measure self-criticism and interpersonal dependency. The DEQ had been found to have good test-retest reliability, internal consistency, and concurrent validity (Blatt, Quinlan, Chevron, McDonald, & Zuroff, 1982; Zuroff, Moskowitz, Wieglus, Powers, & Franko, 1983). In the present sample, coefficient alpha was .78 for the self-criticism scale and .79 for the dependency scale.

The Automatic Thoughts Questionnaire (ATQ; Hollon & Kendall, 1980). This is a 30-item self-report measure of surface level depressotypic cognitions. Subjects rate each statement on a 5-point scale indicating how frequently they have the particular negative automatic thought, from 1 = never to 5 = always. Total scores can range from 30 to 155, with higher scores indicating a greater frequency of negative cognitions. The ATQ has good internal consistency, correlates significantly with severity of depression (Dobson & Breiter, 1981; Harrell & Ryan, 1983; Hollon & Kendall, 1980), and differentiates significantly between depressed and nondepressed patients and normal controls (Eaves & Rush, 1984; Hollon, Kendall, & Lumry, 1986). Garber et al. (1993) modified the ATQ to make it more age-appropriate for young adolescents. Internal consistency for the ATQ in this sample was .96.

The Children's Hopelessness Scale (ATQ; Kazdin, Rodgers, & Colbus, 1986). This is a modification of the adult Hopelessness Scale (Beck, Weissman, Lester, & Trexler, 1974), measures the extent to which children are pessimistic about their future. It contains 17 True-False items scored either as a *0* for the optimistic direction of a *1* for the pessimistic direction. The CHS has been found to have adequate reliability and construct validity (Kazdin, French, Unis, Esveldt-Dawson, & Sherick, 1983; Kazdin et al., 1986). Internal consistency alpha for the CHS in this sample was .73.[3]

---

[3] Two items were not included in the final calculation of the total scores for the CHS because they decreased the internal consistency of the scale; coefficient alpha was .68 when they were included compared to .73 when they were excluded. These items were: "I want to grow up because I think things will be better"; and "when I grow up, I think I will be happier than I am now".

RESULTS

Demographic Characteristics of the Sample

Table 1 shows the demographic characteristics of the high- and low-risk groups. The groups did not differ significantly with regard to children's age, sex, or ethnic origin. The high-risk group had a lower SES (Hollingshead, 1975) and more divorces than the low-risk group. Other studies have similarly found a significant association between divorce and mood disorders in women (Weissman & Paykel, 1974).[4]

Do High-risk Children Report more Negative Cognitions than Low-risk Children?

Table 2 shows the means and standard deviations for the high- and low-risk groups on each cognitive measure. Offspring of mothers with a history of nonbipolar mood disorders reported a significantly more depressogenic attributional style, lower perceived self-worth, lower perceived academic and behavioural competence, greater self-criticism, and more frequent automatic negative thoughts than did children of mothers who were life-time-free of psychopathology.

However, the high- ($M = 16.41$, SD = 3.16) and low-risk ($M = 15.56$, SD = 3.00) groups also were marginally significantly different with regard to their current level of depressive symptoms on the Children's Depression Rating Scale (CDRS), [$F(1,225) = -1.75$, $P < .08$]. Reanalysis of these data, controlling for their CDRS score, revealed that high-risk offspring had significantly lower perceived self-worth [$F(1,224) = 6.49$, $P < .01$], lower perceived academic [$F(1,224) = 5.06$, $P < .03$], and behavioural competence [$F(1,224) = 4.61$, $P < .03$], and greater self-criticism [$F(1,224) = 4.26$, $P < .04$] than low-risk offspring.

Chronicity of Mothers' Depression and Children's Cognitions

High-risk children were divided into two groups based on the chronicity of their mother's depression. Mothers in the chronic high-risk (CHR) group had had depressive disorders for four or more years or had had four or more depressive episodes during the child's lifetime ($n = 45$). The remaining high-risk children ($n = 129$) had mothers who had been depressed for less than four years and had had less than four depressive episodes in the child's

---

[4] Although we tried to match on this variable, it was difficult to find divorced women who had not at least had a mild adjustment disorder.

TABLE 1
TABLE 1
Demographic Characteristics of High- and Low-risk Offspring

	High-risk Offspring (n = 174)	Low-risk Offspring (n = 55)
Mean age of target child	11.85 (0.57)	11.93 (0.58)
Mean SES	37.89 (12.73)	43.95 (13.28)
Female (%)	56.9	49.1
Ethnic origin (%)		
Caucasian	83.9	74.0
Afro-American	13.8	18.5
Other	2.3	7.5
Mother's marital status (%)		
Married	53.3	87.2
Separated or divorced	39.6	5.5
Never married	5.9	7.3
Widow	1.2	–

TABLE 2
Cognitions of High- and Low-risk Offspring

	High-risk Offspring (n = 174)		Low-risk Offspring (n = 55)		
	Mean	SD	Mean	SD	t
Attributional Style (CASQ)	.44	(0.26)	.52	(0.26)	2.00*
Global self-worth	3.31	(0.58)	3.58	(0.50)	3.05**
Perceived competence					
Academic	3.06	(0.70)	3.36	(0.67)	2.77**
Behavioural	3.05	(0.66)	3.30	(0.59)	2.52*
Social	3.21	(0.63)	3.37	(0.61)	1.74[a]
Appearance	2.83	(0.71)	3.03	(0.74)	1.85[a]
Depressive experiences (DEQ)					
Self-criticism	2.62	(0.58)	2.40	(0.60)	−2.43*
Dependency	3.35	(0.55)	3.36	(0.59)	.14
Hopelessness scale (CHS)	1.76	(1.87)	1.26	(1.69)	−1.77[a]
Automatic thoughts (ATQ)	46.01	(17.14)	40.84	(12.22)	−2.46*
Dysfunctional attitudes (DAS)	92.00	(19.48)	91.09	(19.42)	−.30

[a] $P < .10$; * $P < .05$; ** $P < .01$.

life. Analyses of variance comparing the cognitions of offspring in the two high-risk groups and the low-risk group indicated that children of chronically depressed mothers reported significantly lower self-worth, lower perceived academic competence, worse perceived appearance, greater self-criticism, greater hopelessness, and more frequent automatic negative thoughts than low-risk children. Offspring of the chronically depressed mothers also had a significantly more depressogenic attributional style and lower perceived behavioural competence than offspring of both the less chronically depressed and never-depressed mothers (see Table 3).

Analyses of covariance (CDRS scores as the covariate), conducted to control for current level of depressive symptoms, revealed that offspring of the chronically depressed mothers still had a more depressogenic attributional style ($F(2,223) = 5.98$, $P < .01$], lower perceived self-worth [$F(2,223) = 5.62$, $P < .01$], lower perceived academic [$F(2,223) = 5.27$, $P < .01$], and behavioural competence, [$F(2,223) = 6.59$, $P < .01$], and greater hopelessness [$F(2,223) = 3.11$, $P < .05$], than offspring of both the less chronically depressed and never-depressed mothers.[5] There also was a marginally significant trend for the groups to differ with regard to self-criticism [$F(2,223) = 2.69$, $P < .07$]. The groups did not differ significantly, however, with regard to perceived social competence, perceived appearance, dysfunctional attitudes, dependence, or automatic thoughts.

DISCUSSION

Consistent with other studies (Goodman et al., 1994; Jaenicke et al., 1987), the present investigation found that offspring of mothers with a history of nonbipolar affective disorders reported significantly lower perceived self-worth, lower perceived academic and behavioural competence, a more depressogenic attributional style, greater self-criticism, and more frequent automatic negative thoughts than offspring of mothers who were lifetime-free of psychopathology. Because it is possible that the observed differences between the high- and low-risk children's cognitions could have been partially the result of their current level of depression, further analyses

---

[5] To address the possibility that the observed differences between the high- and low-risk offspring could have been due to there being more children in the high-risk group with a history of mood disorders, we reanalysed all the data eliminating such children. Psychiatric histories were obtained using the Schedule for Affective Disorders and Schizophrenia epidemiological version (K-SADS-E) (Orvaschel, Puig-Antich, Chamber, Tabrizi, & Johnson, 1982), at the same time the CDRS and questionnaires were administered. Eight high-risk children were identified as having had a history of a mood disorder diagnosis (i.e. major depression, dysthymia, or depression not otherwise specified). Reanalysis of all comparisons between the high- and low-risk groups indicated that the findings were essentially unchanged when these eight children were removed.

TABLE 3
Cognitions of Offspring of Chronically Depressed, Depressed,
and Never-depressed Mothers

	Chronic High-risk Offspring (n = 45)		High-risk Offspring (n = 129)		Low-risk Offspring (n = 55)		
	Mean	SD	Mean	SD	Mean	SD	F
Attributional style (CASQ)	33[a]	(.25)	.48[b]	(.25)	.52[b]	(.26)	7.28***
Global self-worth	3.15[a]	(.61)	3.37	(.56)	3.58[b]	(.51)	7.29***
Perceived competence							
Academic	2.85[a]	(.69)	3.13	(.69)	3.36[b]	(.67)	6.65**
Behavioural	2.81[a]	(.63)	3.13	(.65)[b]	3.30[b]	(.59)	7.73***
Social	3.08	(.57)	3.25	(.65)	3.37	(.61)	2.74
Appearance	2.64[a]	(.71)	2.90	(.70)	3.03[b]	(.73)	3.90*
Depressive experiences (DEQ)							
Self-criticism	2.70[a]	(.62)	2.59	(.56)	2.40[b]	(.60)	3.62*
Dependency	3.40	(.46)	3.33	(.58)	3.36	(.59)	.29
Hopelessness scale (HS)	2.29	(2.11)	1.57	(1.76)	1.26	(1.69)	4.19*
Automatic thoughts (ATQ)	49.26[a]	(17.02)	44.87	(17.10)	40.84[b]	(12.22)	3.42*
Dysfunctional attitudes (DAS)	96.76	(19.86)	90.34	(19.15)	91.09	(19.42)	1.88

* $P < .05$; ** $P < .01$; *** $P < .001$.
[a,b] Means with different letters are significantly different.

were conducted to address this issue. Results indicated that even when controlling for current depression, high-risk children still reported lower perceived self-worth, lower perceived academic and behavioural competence, and greater self-criticism. Moreover, these differences between the high- and low-risk groups remained even when children with a history of mood disorders were removed. This suggests that the negative cognitions reported by high-risk children were not simply due to their current mood or scarring from a prior depressive episode (Lewinsohn et al., 1981). Thus, perceptions of low self-worth and lack of competence might be state-independent markers of a cognitive vulnerability among offspring of mothers with a history of mood disorders.

This cognitive vulnerability was most apparent among offspring of the more chronically depressed mothers. Results indicated that, even after controlling for their current level of depressive symptoms, children whose mothers had been depressed during four or more years of the child's lifetime were significantly more likely to report a depressogenic attributional style, low self-worth, low perceived academic and behavioural competence, and greater hopelessness than offspring of mothers with a less chronic or no history of depression. The fact that negative cognitions characterised the children of the chronically depressed mothers and not all offspring of mothers with a history of depression highlights the heterogeneity of such "high-risk" samples. These findings are interesting because of their possible implications regarding the development of a negative cognitive style. Several potential mechanisms might underlie the transmission of increased cognitive risk among offspring of chronically depressed mothers.

First, it is possible that children acquire negative views of themselves and the causes of events in the context of interactions with their depressed mothers. There is increasing evidence that the interactions of depressed mothers and their children are characterised by hostility, rejection, criticism, and overcontrol (e.g. Garber, Braafladt, & Zeman, 1991; Gordon et al., 1989; Keitner & Miller, 1990). We speculate that children who are more frequently exposed to such negative interactions are more likely to develop a negative cognitive style (Garber, 1992). Thus, if depressed mothers engage in negative patterns of interactions with their children and these interactions contribute to the development of depressogenic thinking, then it makes sense that children of more chronically depressed mothers will have more opportunity for the development of negative cognitions than will offspring of less chronically depressed and never-depressed mothers. Longitudinal studies are needed to examine the extent to which negative family interactions occur both during and after an episode of maternal depression. Experimental laboratory studies also are needed to identify the specific processes by which children develop depressogenic cognitions during negative parent-child interactions.

Second, it also is possible that more chronically depressed mothers have a greater genetic vulnerability that is inherited by their children. One phenotypic manifestation of such a genetic vulnerability could be a negative cognitive style. That is, the cognitive vulnerability observed among offspring of the more chronically depressed mothers could be a reflection of a genetic diathesis.

A third possibility is that some common and chronic life experience (e.g. poverty, abuse) leads to both mothers becoming depressed and children developing negative cognitions about themselves and their world. All three explanations of the relation between the chronicity of the mother's depression and children's cognitive style are possible and are not mutually exclusive. Future studies need to examine the links among genetic, environmental, and interpersonal factors in the development of negative cognitions and depression.

The present findings also were generally consistent with the view that there may be two different levels of cognitions (Beck et al., 1979; Kwon & Oei, 1994). Whereas surface cognitions (i.e. automatic negative thoughts) did not characterise the high-risk children when their level of depressive symptoms were controlled, deep cognitions (i.e. depressogenic attributions, low perceived self-worth) did differentiate high- and low-risk children, particularly among offspring of more chronically depressed mothers. Thus, these results provide further support of the existence of a state-independent marker of cognitive vulnerability that can be identified among children at risk for developing depression. Longitudinal studies need to examine the stability of these cognitions and test the role of negative cognitive style in the prediction of the onset of depressive disorders.

The high- and low-risk groups did not differ, however, on the Dysfunctional Attitudes Scale (DAS), which presumably measures deep level beliefs (Beck et al., 1979). This could have been the result of several factors. First, it might be that 11- and 12-year-old children have not yet developed the kinds of global attitudes and beliefs that are measured by the DAS, although such dysfunctional attitudes might still develop as the children become more cognitively mature. Continued assessments of the cognitions of these high- and low-risk children are needed to address this possibility.

It also might be that the dysfunctional attitudes measured by the DAS need to be activated by life events or primed by a mood induction (Miranda et al., 1990; Riskind & Rholes, 1984). According to Beck and colleagues (Beck, 1984; Beck, Brown, Steer, & Weissman, 1991), the DAS was intended to identify rigid and inappropriate beliefs that would be activated by and would interact with a congruent stressor to produce depressive symptoms. Therefore, high- and low-risk children might not differ with regard to dysfunctional attitudes unless they complete the DAS under such activating conditions.

Finally, it is possible that dysfunctional attitudes, as measured by the DAS, simply are not a cognitive vulnerability for depression (Barnett & Gotlib, 1988; Haaga et al., 1991). Rather, the DAS might measure surface level, state-dependent beliefs that are present during a depressive episode, but are not a traitlike risk factor. Other cognitions measured in the present study, however, such as attributions about the causes of events and beliefs about one's self-worth, may be indicators of a vulnerability to depression even if dysfunctional attitudes as measured by the DAS are not.

One caution should be noted with regard to the findings about perceived competence. It is possible that for some children in the high-risk group their perceptions of lower academic and behavioural competence might have accurately reflected their reality. That is, as a group, offspring of depressed mothers have been found to have more school and behavioural problems than low-risk children (Lee & Gotlib, 1989). The relation between perceived and objective competence among the children in this and other samples is unclear, however. It may very well be that depressogenic cognitions about the self and world are based, in part, on actual negative life experiences (Garber, 1992). Problems develop, however, when these "reality-based" negative cognitions overgeneralise to inappropriate situations or are unresponsive to new and conflicting information (Beck, 1967, 1976). Future studies are needed to identify the processes underlying the development of these cognitive distortions as well as the development of other depressogenic cognitions such as those that were found to differentiate the high- and low-risk children in this study (e.g. attributions, self-worth, hopelessness).

In sum, the present study found that offspring of mothers with a history of depressive disorders reported more negative cognitions about the causes of events and about their self-worth than did children whose mothers were lifetime-free of psychopathology. These results are consistent with the view that some cognitions might be state-independent markers of a vulnerability to depression. Such negative cognitions might be particularly likely to develop among children who have had a more prolonged exposure to negative patterns of interactions with their depressed mother.

REFERENCES

Abramson, L.Y., Metalsky, G.I., & Alloy, L.B. (1989). Hopelessness depression: A theory-based subtype of depression. *Psychological Review, 96*, 358–372.

Abramson, L.Y., Seligman, M.E.P., & Teasdale, J. (1978). Learned helplessness in humans: Critique and reformulation. *Journal of Abnormal Psychology, 87*, 49–74.

Barnett, P.A., & Gotlib, I.H. (1988). Psychosocial functioning and depression: Distinguishing among antecedents, concomitant, and consequences. *Psychological Bulletin, 104*, 97–126.

Beck, A.T. (1967). *Depression: Clinical, experiential, and theoretical aspects.* New York: Harper & Row.

Beck, A.T. (1976). *Cognitive therapy and the emotional disorders.* New York: International Universities Press.

Beck, A.T. (1984). Cognition and therapy. *Archives of General Psychiatry, 41*, 1112–1114.

Beck, A.T., Brown, G., Steer, R.A., & Weissman, A.N. (1991). Factor analysis of the dysfunctional attitude scale in a clinical population. *Psychological Assessment, 3*, 478–483.

Beck, A.T., Rush, A.J., Shaw, B.F., & Emery, G. (1979). *Cognitive therapy of depression.* New York: Guilford Press.

Beck, A.T., Weissman, A., Lester, D., & Trexler, L. (1974). The measurement of pessimism: The Hopelessness Scale. *Journal of Consulting and Clinical Psychology, 42*, 56–571.

Blatt, S.J., D'Afflitti, J.P., & Quinlan, D.M. (1976). Experiences of depression in normal young adults. *Journal of Abnormal Psychology, 85*, 383–389.

Blatt, S.J., Quinlan, D.M., Chevron, E.S., McDonald, C., & Zuroff, D. (1982). Dependency and self-criticism: Psychological dimensions of depression. *Journal of Consulting and Clinical Psychology, 150,* 113–124.

Campbell, S.B., Cohn, J.F., & Meyers, T. (1995). Depression in first-time mothers: Mother-infant interaction and depression chronicity. *Developmental Psychology, 31,* 349–357.

Dobson, K.S., & Breiter, H.J. (1981). Cognitive assessment of depression: Reliability and validity of three measures. *Journal of Abnormal Psychology, 92,* 107–109.

Downey, G., & Coyne, J.C. (1990). Children of depressed parents: An integrative review. *Psychological Bulletin, 108,* 50–76.

Eaves, G., & Rush, A.J. (1984). Cognitive patterns in symptomatic and remitted unipolar major depression. *Journal of Abnormal Psychology, 93,* 31–40.

Garber, J. (1992). Cognitive models of depression: A developmental perspective. *Psychological Inquiry, 3,* 235–240.

Garber, J., Braafladt, N., & Zeman, J. (1991). The regulation of sad affect: An information processing perspective. In J. Garber & K.A. Dodge (Eds.), *The development of affect regulation and dysregulation* (pp. 208–240). New York: Cambridge University Press.

Garber, J., & Hilsman, R. (1992). Cognitions, stress, and depression in children and adolescents. *Child and Adolescent Psychiatric Clinics of North America, 1,* 129–167.

Garber, J., Weiss, B., & Shanley, N. (1993). Cognitions, depressive symptoms, and development in adolescents. *Journal of Abnormal Psychology, 102,* 47–57.

Gelfand, D.M., & Teti, D.M. (1990). The effects of maternal depression on children. *Clinical Psychology Review, 10,* 329–353.

Gladstone, T.R.G., & Kaslow, N.J. (1995). Depression and attributions in children and adolescents: A meta-analytic review. *Journal of Abnormal Child Psychology, 23,* 597–606.

Goodman, S.H., Adamson, L.B., Riniti, J., & Cole, S. (1994). Mothers' expressed attitudes: Associations with maternal depression and children's self-esteem and psychopathology. *Journal of the American Academy of Child and Adolescent Psychiatry, 33,* 1265–1274.

Gordon, D., Burge, D., Hammen, C., Adrian, C., Jaenicke, C., & Hiroto, D. (1989). Observations of interactions of depressed women with their children. *American Journal of Psychiatry, 146,* 50–55.

Haaga, D., Dyck, M., & Ernst, D. (1991). Empirical status of cognitive theory of depression. *Psychological Bulletin, 110,* 215–236.

Hamilton, E.W., & Abramson, L.Y. (1983). Cognitive patterns in major depressive disorder: A longitudinal study in a hospital setting. *Journal of Abnormal Psychology, 92,* 173–184.

Hamilton, M. (1960). A rating scale for depression. *Journal of Neurology, Neurosurgery, and Psychiatry, 23,* 56–62.

Harrell, T.H., & Ryan, N.B. (1983). Cognitive behavioral assessment of depression: Clinical validation of the Automatic Thoughts Questionnaire. *Journal of Consulting and Clinical Psychology, 51,* 721–725.

Harter, S. (1982). The perceived competence scale for children. *Child Development, 53,* 87–97.

Hilsman, R., & Garber, J. (1995). A test of the cognitive diathesis-stress model in children: Academic stressors, attributional style, perceived competence and control. *Journal of Personality and Social Psychology, 69,* 370–380.

Hollingshead, A.B. (1975). *Four factor index of social status.* Working paper. New Haven, CT: Department of Sociology, Yale University.

Hollon, S.D., & Bemis, K.M. (1981). Self-report and the assessment of cognitive functions. In M. Hersen & A.S. Bellack (Eds.), *Behavioral assessment: A practical handbook* (2nd ed.) (pp. 125–174). New York: Pergamon.

Hollon, S.D., & Kendall, P.C. (1980). Cognitive self-statements in depression: Development of an automatic thoughts questionnaire. *Cognitive Therapy and Research, 4,* 383–395.

Hollon, S.D., Kendall, P.C., & Lumry, A. (1986). Specificity of depressotypic cognitions in clinical depression. *Journal of Abnormal Psychology, 95*, 52–59.

Jaenicke, C., Hammen, C., Zupan, B., Hiroto, D., Gordon, D., Adrian, C., & Burge, D. (1987). Cognitive vulnerability in children at risk for depression. *Journal of Abnormal Child Psychology, 15*, 559–572.

Kazdin, A.E., French, N.H., Unis, A.S., Esveldt-Dawson, K., & Sherick, R.B. (1983). Hopelessness, depression, and suicidal intent among psychiatrically disturbed inpatient children. *Journal of Consulting and Clinical Psychology, 51*, 504–510.

Kazdin, A.E., Rodgers, A., & Colbus, D. (1986). The Hopelessness Scale for Children: Psychometric characteristics and concurrent validity. *Journal of Consulting and Clinical Psychology, 54*, 241–245.

Keitner, G.I., & Miller, I.W. (1990). Family functioning and major depression. *American Journal of Psychiatry, 147*, 1128–1137.

Keller, M.B., Beardslee, W.R., Dorer, D.J., Lavori, P.W., Samuelson, H., & Klerman, G.R. (1986). Impact of severity and chronicity of parental affective illness on adaptive functioning and psychopathology in children. *Archives of General Psychiatry, 43*, 930–937.

Kwon, S.M., & Oei, T.P. (1994). The roles of two levels of cognitions in the development, maintenance, and treatment of depression. *Clinical Psychology Review, 14*, 331–358.

Lee, C.M., & Gotlib, I.H. (1989). Clinical status and emotional adjustment of children of depressed Mothers. *American Journal of Psychiatry, 146*, (4), 478–483.

Lewinsohn, P., Steinmetz, J., Larson, D., & Franklin, J. (1981). Depression-related cognitions: Antecedent or consequence? *Journal of Abnormal Psychology, 90*, 213–219.

Metalsky, G.I., Joiner, T.E., Hardin, T.S., & Abramson, L.Y. (1993). Depressive reactions to failure in a naturalistic setting: A test of the hopelessness and self-esteem theories of depression. *Journal of Abnormal Psychology, 102*, 101–109.

Miranda, J., Persons, J.B., & Byers, C.N. (1990). Endorsement of dysfunctional beliefs depends on current mood state. *Journal of Abnormal Psychology, 99*, 237–241.

Nolen-Hoeksema, S., Girgus, J.S., & Seligman, M.E.P. (1986). Learned helplessness in children: A longitudinal study of depression, achievement, and explanatory style. *Journal of Personality and Social Psychology, 51*, 435–442.

Oliver, J.M., & Baumgart, E.P. (1985). The Dysfunctional Attitudes Scale: Psychometric properties and relation to depression in an unselected adult population. *Cognitive Therapy and Research, 9*, 161–167.

Orvaschel, H., Puig-Antich, J., Chambers, W.J., Tabrizi, M.A., & Johnson, R. (1982). Retrospective assessment of prepubertal major depression with the Kiddie-SADS-E. *Journal of the American Academy of Child Psychiatry, 21*, 392–397.

Poznanski, E., Mokros, H.B., Grossman, J., & Freeman, L.N. (1985). Diagnostic criteria in childhood depression. *American Journal of Psychiatry, 142*, 1168–1173.

Riskind, J.H., & Rholes, W.S. (1984). Cognitive accessibility and the capacity of cognitions to predict future depression: A theoretical note. *Cognitive Therapy and Research, 8*, 1–12.

Robins, C.J., & Hinkley, K. (1989). Social-cognitive processing and depressive symptoms in children: A comparison of measures. *Journal of Abnormal Child Psychology, 17*, 29–36.

Seligman, M.E.P., & Peterson, C.A. (1986). A learned helplessness perspective on childhood depression: Theory and research. In M. Rutter, C.E. Izard, & P.B. Read (Eds.), *Depression in young people: Clinical and developmental perspectives* (pp. 223–249), New York: Guilford Press.

Seligman, M.E.P., Peterson, C.A., Kaslow, N.J., Tanenbaum, R.L., Alloy, L.B., & Abramson, L.Y. (1984). Attributional style and depressive symptoms among children. *Journal of Abnormal Psychology, 93*, 235–238.

Silverman, J.S., Silverman, J.A., & Eardley, D.A. (1984). Do maladaptive attitudes cause depression? *Archives of General Psychiatry, 41,* 28–30.

Spitzer, R.L., Williams, J.B.W., Gibbon, M., & First, M.B. (1990). *User's guide for the structured clinical interview for DSM-III-R.* Washington, DC: American Psychiatric Press.

Teasdale, J.D., & Dent, J. (1987). Cognitive vulnerability to depression: An investigation of two hypotheses. *British Journal of Clinical Psychology, 26,* 113–126.

Weissman, A.N., & Beck, A.T. (1978). *Development and validation of the Dysfunctional Attitude Scale.* Paper presented at the American Educational Research Association Annual Convention, Toronto, Canada.

Weissman, M.M., & Paykel, E.S. (1974). *The depressed woman: A study of social relationships.* Chicago: University of Chicago Press.

Zuroff, D.C., Moskowitz, D.S., Wieglus, M.S., Powers, T.A., & Franko, D.L. (1983). Construct validation of the dependency and self-criticism scales of the Depressive Experiences Questionnaire. *Journal of Research in Personality, 17,* 226–241.

Regional Brain Activity in Emotion: A Framework for Understanding Cognition in Depression

Wendy Heller and Jack B. Nitschke

University of Illinois at Urbana-Champaign, USA

A variety of cognitive characteristics have been shown to be associated with depressed moods. We propose that these tendencies are directly related to activity in specific regions of the brain. Using a comprehensive model of brain activity in emotion as a guide, we review the literature on cognitive function in depression and induced sad mood to provide evidence that depressed people are characterised by deficits and biases in performance on cognitive tasks that depend on regions of the brain that are more or less active in depression.

INTRODUCTION

The current *Diagnostic and Statistical Manual of Mental Disorders* (DSMIV; APA, 1994) identifies cognitive factors (e.g. indecisiveness, difficulties in thinking and concentrating) as fundamental components of depressive episodes and dysthymia. Numerous studies have also identified a variety of other cognitive characteristics associated with depressed moods. These findings have given rise to models of depression that have focused on cognitive factors as important in the aetiology and maintenance of the disorder (e.g. Beck, 1967, 1976; Bower, 1981, 1987; Teasdale, 1988). For the most part, these models have not considered physiological or neuropsychological concomitants of depression.

In a separate literature, converging evidence from a variety of paradigms in neuroscience has shown that depression is characterised by unique

---

Requests for reprints should be sent to Wendy Heller, Department of Psychology, University of Illinois at Urbana-Champaign, 603 E. Daniel Street, Champaign, IL 61820, USA; e-mail: wheller@s.psych.uiuc.edu.

Wendy Heller was supported by NIMH grant MH52079 and by a grant from the University of Illinois Research Board. Jack B. Nitschke was supported by NIMH training grant MH14257 to the University of Illinois. The authors gratefully acknowledge the comments of Marie T. Banich and Gerald L. Clore on an earlier draft of this paper.

---

patterns of brain activity and function. Despite the fact that the same brain regions involved in depression are also fundamental for various aspects of cognition, the implications of these neuropsychological findings for cognitive processing in depression have rarely been explored (cf. George et al., 1994; Rubinow & Post, 1992).

Various brain regions are known to be specialised for particular kinds of cognitive processes. The extent to which a brain region is engaged in or recruited for the performance of a particular task, however, is reflected in the degree to which that region is active. Whereas we tend to think of specialised processes as relatively "hard-wired", the activity of a brain region is a dynamic process that can fluctuate and change. Thus, although a particular region might be specialised for a particular cognitive process, the extent to which it is active can vary (e.g. Levy, Heller, Banich, & Burton, 1983a; Levy & Trevarthen, 1976).

Activity of a brain region has been shown to correlate with performance on cognitive tasks for which that region is specialised. Performance advantages are typically accompanied by relative increases in activity of the specialised region during task performance, as measured by electroencephalographic (EEG) activity in the alpha band (Davidson, Chapman, Chapman, & Henriques, 1990; Doyle, Ornstein, & Galin, 1974; Galin & Ellis, 1975; Galin, Ornstein, Herron, & Johnstone, 1982; Green, Morris, Epstein, West, & Engler, 1992; McKee, Humphrey, & McAdams, 1973; Morgan, MacDonald, & Hilgard, 1974; Ornstein, Johnstone, Herron, & Swencionis, 1980), event-related brain potentials (ERPs; Deecke, Uhl, Spieth, Lang, & Lang, 1987; Galin & Ellis, 1975; Lang, Lang, Goldenberg, Podreka, & Deecke, 1987; Rasmussen, Allen, & Tate, 1977), and blood flow (George et al., 1993; Gur & Reivich, 1980; Lang et al., 1987). These results imply that at one extreme, an information-processing deficit could result if a brain region is inadequately activated during performance of a cognitive task for which that region is specialised. At the other extreme, an information-processing superiority could result for a particular task if the brain region specialised for that task is highly active. Moreover, relative activity or inactivity of a particular brain region could be associated with a tendency or bias to process or to avoid processing information in a particular way.

It should be noted that measures of brain activity do not always reflect cognitive performance in this linear fashion. When examined in the context of task difficulty or repeated practice, better performance on same tasks has been associated with decreased brain activity (for a review, see Galin, Johnstone, & Herron, 1978; see also Haier et al., 1992). These effects have been attributed to various factors, including decreases in the use of nonessential brain areas, changes in cognitive strategies, and changes in task demands. In general, however, relatively greater activity for specialised brain regions has been found to reflect better performance on the majority of tasks examined.

For the most part, researchers examining the neuropsychology of depression have focused on the relationship of regional brain activity to emotion, not to cognition. Although a few studies have been conducted examining brain activity and a very select subset of cognitive functions, such as attributional style (Davidson, in press), visuospatial abilities (Davidson, Chapman, & Chapman, 1987; George et al., 1994), and facial processing (Deldin, Keller, Gergen, & Miller, submitted), research examining cognition and brain activity in depression is clearly in its infancy. A somewhat larger literature on neuropsychological functioning in affective disorders has floundered in inconsistencies (for a review, see Silberman & Weingartner, 1986). Furthermore, a theoretical formulation explicating the relationship betwen various brain regions and cognition in depression has been lacking.

Models of brain activity in depression have the capacity to provide an explicit framework for the investigation of cognitive function in this disorder. In previous research, we have proposed and researched such a model of brain function during different emotional states (for reviews, see Heller, 1990, 1993a, b; Heller & Nitschke, in press). The model is based on factor analytical studies depicting the psychological structure of emotions as represented along two dimensions—valence (pleasant/unpleasant) and arousal (high/low) (see Fig. 1). Briefly, valence is associated with activity of the anterior regions, such that pleasant valence is linked to greater left than right anterior activity and unpleasant valence to greater right than left anterior activity. The posterior regions are associated with the arousal dimension, with increased right parietotemporal activity associated with high arousal and decreased right parietotemporal activity with low arousal.

As discussed at length elsewhere, subsequent research has both supported and refined this model (Heller & Nitschke, in press). Numerous studies using a variety of research paradigms have consistently found the anterior regions to be asymmetrically active during valenced states, in the direction predicted (for a review, see Heller, 1990). Other studies have shown that the right parietotemporal region is uniquely involved in various aspects of arousal, including global cortical activity, autonomic activity, anxious arousal, and behavioural arousal (Heller, 1990, 1993b; Heller, Nitschke, Etienne, & Miller, in press; Heller, Nitschke, & Lindsay, 1997).

The value of this model is that it provides a useful framework for predicting how specific patterns of brain activity should be associated with both emotional and cognitive functions. Because brain activity in particular regions should be reflected in performance for the cognitive

VALENCE DIMENSION
(Frontal)

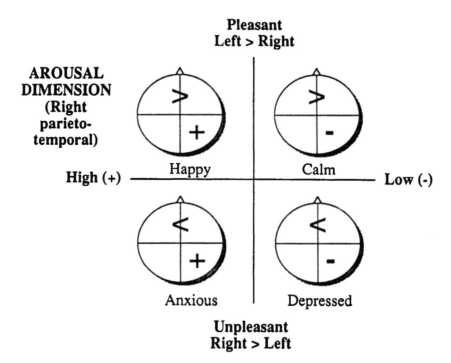

Pleasant
Left > Right

AROUSAL
DIMENSION
(Right
parieto-
temporal)

High (+) ———— Happy | Calm ———— **Low (-)**

Anxious | Depressed

Unpleasant
Right > Left

FIG. 1. A neuropsychological model of emotion hypothesising patterns of brain activity during different emotions dependent on relative activity of right posterior and anterior regions. The right posterior region is differentially involved in the arousal dimension (depicted here as the x-axis), whereas the anterior regions are involved in the valence dimension (depicted here as the y-axis). Higher activity of the right posterior region is associated with higher levels of arousal (+), whereas lower activity of this region is associated with lower levels of arousal (−). Higher left compared to right anterior activity is associated with pleasant valence, whereas higher right compared to left anterior activity is associated with unpleasant valence. The circles symbolise the brain, with the top two quadrants representing the left and right anterior regions and the bottom two quadrants representing the left and right posterior regions. Each circle portrays the pattern of brain activity that would be expected to accompany the emotion stipulated beneath. (Adapted from Heller, 1993b.)

functions specialised to those regions, the model allows us to make explicit predictions about the nature of a wide variety of cognitive functions in depression. The model also allows us to modulate our predictions about cognition when depression is coincident with other emotional states, such as anxiety.

A primary goal of this article is, therefore, to argue that the patterns of brain activity associated with depression are intrinsically related to many of the cognitive characteristics that have been described in depression. Using our model as a guide, we will review the findings for brain activity in depression. Then, we will draw from the literature on cognitive function in depression to provide evidence that depressed people are characterised by deficits in performance on tasks that depend on regions of the brain that are less active in depression. Ultimately, we hope to construct a more comprehensive account of the neuropsychological foundations of cognition in depression than has previously been accomplished. By necessity, many of these associations will be inferential, as there is a limited amount of empirical research linking neurophysiological and cognitive processes. Nonetheless, the time is ripe for the interface of these two areas in depression, especially with the advancing technologies in the field of cognitive neuroscience that make it more feasible to examine brain activity during the performance of relevant cognitive tasks.

BRAIN ACTIVITY IN DEPRESSION

Various methodologies have been used to examine brain activity and function in depression, including neurodynamic techniques, electrocortical measures (EEG, ERPs), and behavioural measures, such as dichotic listening, tachistoscopic presentation, and the Chimeric Faces Test (CFT; Levy, Heller, Banich, & Burton, 1983b) that are believed to index lateralised cognitive processes and biases. Populations have included people with regional brain damage (see Depression and Regional Specialisation of Cognitive Functions section below), people classified as depressed in various ways, and people who have been induced into sad moods. Although studies of clinical depression, psychometrically defined depression, and sad mood will all be reviewed here, it remains to be seen whether they are addressing the same phenomenon. The number of consistent findings across these populations suggests some commonality; on the other hand, some inconsistencies in this literature could be in part due to the heterogeneity of the samples studied.

For the anterior regions, a prominent finding has been asymmetric activity during depressed mood states. In studies of EEG alpha, depression has been associated with less left than right anterior activity (Allen, Iacono, Depue, & Arbisi, 1993; Henriques & Davidson, 1990, 1991; Schaffer, Davidson, & Saron, 1983). Consistent with the EEG findings, numerous positron emission tomography (PET) studies have reported deficiencies in left anterior activity (Baxter et al., 1985, 1989; Bench, Friston, Brown, Frackowiak, & Dolan, 1993; Bench et al., 1992; George et al., 1994; Martinot et al., 1990). However, blood flow studies have also reported significant (e.g. Baxter et al., 1989) or marginally significant (e.g. Bench et al., 1992) reductions in right anterior brain activity for depressed patients. Taken together, these results suggest that regional asymmetries in anterior activity may be superimposed upon or co-occur with bilateral anterior or global decreases in activity (see Sackeim et al., 1990).

For the posterior regions, we have argued that depression is characterised by deficient activity in the parietotemporal area of the right hemisphere, except when anxiety is comorbid (Heller, Etienne, & Miller, 1995; Heller et al., in press; Heller & Nitschke, in press). In EEG, ERP, and blood flow studies that report positive findings, depression is typically associated with less right posterior activity (Deldin et al., submitted; Flor-Henry, 1979; Henriques & Davidson, 1990; Post et al., 1987; Uytdenhoef et al., 1983). Studies that have directed information to one or the other hemisphere using lateralised paradigms, such as dichotic listening or tachistoscopic presentation, have also found specific deficits for the right hemisphere in depressed people and in induced sad mood (for a review, see Bruder, 1995; see also Banich, Stolar, Heller, & Goldman, 1992; Ladavas, Nicoletti, Umilta, & Rizzolatti, 1984). On the CFT, a free-vision task of face-processing that typically elicits a left hemispatial bias suggesting greater right hemisphere activation, studies have reported smaller left-hemispatial biases for depressed than nondepressed participants for clinical depression (Jaeger, Borod, & Peselow, 1987) and for psychometrically defined depression (Heller et al., 1995; Keller et al., submitted).

In this brief review, we have ignored some of the inconsistencies that have been reported in this literature; for example, the findings reviewed earlier have not always been replicated for depression (e.g. Baxter et al., 1985; Drevets et al., 1992; Nitschke, Heller, Etienne, & Miller, 1995; Tomarken & Davidson, 1994) or sad mood (e.g. George et al., 1995), and other regions of the brain have also been reported as either hyper- or hypoactive in depression (e.g. Sackeim et al., 1990). Elsewhere, we have argued for the importance of comorbidity with anxiety and of subtypes of depression in explaining the reported discrepancies (Heller et al., 1995; Heller & Nitschke, in press). It is also not clear whether the patterns of anterior brain activity associated with depression disappear on remission. Henriques and Davidson (1990) found evidence of similar patterns of brain activity in remitted depressives; however, Baxter et al. (1989) reported an increase of left (but not right) anterior activity following successful treatment. Despite these complicating factors, there is nonetheless compelling evidence that in many cases depression is associated with reductions or deficiencies in left anterior and right posterior activity. It now remains to examine the cognitive specialisations of the areas implicated in depression.

DEPRESSION AND REGIONAL SPECIALISATION OF COGNITIVE FUNCTIONS

Anterior Regions

Emotional Valence. There is a preponderance of evidence from a variety of research paradigms that anterior asymmetries are associated with valence (for a review, see Heller, 1990). More left than right anterior activity has been consistently associated with pleasant affect and happy mood states, whereas the converse has been found for unpleasant affect and sad mood states. This pattern has emerged in studies of brain-damaged populations (Gainotti, 1972; Robinson, Kubos, Starr, Rao, & Price, 1984; Sackeim et al., 1982), patients undergoing the WADA test (Ahern et al., 1994; Lee, Loring, Meador, Flanigin, & Brooks, 1988; Lee, Loring, Meador, & Brooks, 1990), right versus left hemisphere ECT (Cohen, Penick, & Tarter, 1974; Decina, Sackeim, Prohovnik, Portnoy, & Malitz, 1985), EEG studies following mood induction (Davidson, Schwartz, Saron, Bennett, & Goleman, 1979; Davidson, Schaffer, & Saron, 1985), and EEG research on facial expressions of emotion (Davidson, Ekman, Saron, Senulis, & Friesen, 1990; Ekman, Davidson, & Friesen, 1990). Moreover, the same pattern of anterior EEG asymmetries has been associated with pleasant and unpleasant affect (Tomarken, Davidson, Wheeler, & Doss, 1992) as well as with pleasant and unpleasant affect in response to emotion elicitors such as film clips (Tomarken, Davidson, & Henriques, 1990; Wheeler, Davidson, & Tomarken, 1993).

The extensive literature on cognitive biases in depression is very pertinent to this relationship between anterior asymmetries and emotional valence. Attention, memory, and judgement biases in depression have been reported by numerous researchers (for reviews, see Gotlib & MacLeod, in press; Gotlib, Gilboa, & Kaplan, in press). Gotlib and colleagues concluded that depressed people attend more strongly to unpleasant than to pleasant stimuli, fail to avoid unpleasant stimuli (whereas nondepressed people avoid such stimuli), show better recall of unpleasant than pleasant information, and make more negative judgements about hypothetical and actual life events. Several studies have also shown that cognitive biases are not present in remitted depressives (e.g. Gotlib & Cane, 1987; McCabe & Gotlib, 1993), consistent with the PET findings of increased left anterior activity following successful treatment of depression (Baxter et al., 1989).

The findings are perhaps most salient for memory biases, especially on explicit memory tasks (for reviews, see Gotlib et al., in press; Mineka & Sutton, 1992). Although studies on implicit memory tasks that depend primarily on perceptual features have found no evidence for a memory bias (Denny & Hunt, 1992; Watkins, Mathews, Williamson, & Fuller, 1992), a recent study using a conceptually driven implicit memory task did find a memory bias for depression despite finding no implicit memory deficit (Watkins, Vache, Verney, Mathews, & Muller, 1996). This set of cognitive biases ties in neatly with the association of less left than right anterior activity for unpleasant emotional valence as indicated by our model.

Executive Functions.   The anterior regions of the brain have also been shown to be specialised for a class of behaviours that have, rather loosely, been referred to as "executive functions". These behaviours include judgement, planning, abstract thinking, metacognition (i.e. "thinking about thinking"), cognitive flexibility (i.e. flexibility in strategy use), ability to generate alternate strategies, verbal fluency, initiative, and motivation. Damage to this area of the brain does not affect the knowledge base of the person; rather, it affects the degree to which that stored information can be accessed, strategically deployed, and adaptively applied to routine or novel situations (e.g. Stuss & Benson, 1986). Deficits are observed in sequencing tasks (Petridies & Milner, 1982), in the ability to shift response set and modify strategies in task performance (e.g. Cicerone, Lazar, & Shapiro, 1983), in the evaluation of a situation and the use of cues and extra information in the environment to guide behaviour (Alivisatos & Milner, 1989), and in the ability to monitor behaviour or performance accurately (e.g. Luria, 1966). Furthermore, the frontal lobes have been described as selectively involved in effortful (i.e. controlled) but not automatic processing (Banich, 1997).

In addition, there are differences between the left and right anterior regions. For example, the left is more involved in verbal fluency and sequencing, whereas the right is more involved in design fluency and recency judgements (for a review, see Banich, 1997). However, Banich also reviews evidence that many of the deficits observed for executive functions occur after damage to either side of the brain.

A selected review of the literature suggests that depressed people display deficits in many of the cognitive activities we have described as dependent on anterior functions. Various studies have indicated that depressed people are poor problem-solvers (for reviews, see Hartlage, Alloy, Vazquez, & Dykman, 1993; see also Klein, Fencil-Morse, & Seligman, 1976; Klein & Seligman, 1976; Price, Tryon, & Raps, 1978). There is also substantial evidence of deficits for other types of effortful processing, such as explicit memory, general learning, and reading (for a review, see Hartlage et al., 1993). In contrast, Hartlage and colleagues reviewed the evidence indicating that depression is not associated with tasks reliant on automatic processing. The distinction between effortful and automatic processing has received the most focus in studies of memory, for which depressed people have predominantly been found to have explicit but not implicit memory deficits (for reviews, see Johnson & Magaro, 1987; Roediger & McDermott, 1992; see also Watkins et al., 1996). Similarly, depressed children performed more poorly than nondepressed children on an effortful memory task (the Children's Auditory Verbal Learning Test), but not on an automatic memory task (Lauer et al., 1994).

Other types of anterior brain function have also been found to be compromised in depression. On the Halstead–Reitan Categories Test, typically considered to measure anterior brain functioning, depressed patients performed more poorly than controls, a deficit which improved on remission (Savard, Rey, & Post, 1980). Roth and Rehm (1980) found that depressed patients were less accurate than nondepressed patients in their estimation of the amount of positive and negative feedback received, a deficit that was not due to memory differences for personally relevant adjectives. As pointed out by Slife and Weaver (1992), these findings indicate that although their knowledge and memories were unaffected, their metacognitive skills were deficient. Using a mathematical estimation task, Slife and Weaver showed that both induced depression and psychometrically defined depression were associated with inaccurate predictions about problem-solving abilities in relation to the task, as well as with inaccurate ratings of performance. Furthermore, this rating inaccuracy increased with severity of depression. Importantly, there was no evidence that the rating inaccuracy was due to a negative response bias or lower expectations for success on the part of the depressives. Similarly, depressed children were less accurate than nondepressed children on a metamemory task, particularly for judgements of memory capacity (Lauer et al., 1994).

Other studies have indicated that depressed patients show deficits in the use of organising strategies that would help them in task performance. For category learning, Smith, Tracy, and Murray (1993) found that depressed participants were impaired in performance when the task required a flexible analytical strategy. Similarly, Weingartner, Cohen, Murphy, Martello, and Gerdt (1981) found that depressed people failed to use spontaneously encoding operations that would facilitate later recall. However, when the task provided them with organising information, they were able to make use of it to improve their performance.

Based on a series of studies yielding similar results to those reported by Weingartner et al. (1981), Hertel (1994) argued that impaired memory in depressed people is not due to a lack of effort or to a limited capacity to attend to or process information. Rather, she posited that cognitive resources are sufficient, whereas the initiative to deploy them is lacking. For example, nondepressed participants, whose performance was superior to that of the depressed patients, appeared to make use of an implicit strategy for recognising words they had previously seen (Hertel & Hardin, 1990). When depressed patients were explicitly directed to use such a strategy, their performance improved to the level of the nondepressed group. In another study, Hertel and Rude (1991) found that depressed people in an unfocused condition performed more poorly than nondepressed people on an unintentional learning task. However, when part of the task imposed a focus on the critical information, the deficit disappeared.

Other research has found that providing depressed individuals with problem-solving strategies leads to improved performance (Abramson, Alloy, & Rosoff, 1981; Silberman, Weingartner, & Post, 1983). However, when such strategies are not provided, research on decision making has found that depressed individuals use a smaller amount of available relevant information (Conway & Giannopoulos, 1993). In sum, evidence that depressed people perform at normal levels when given explicit strategies suggests that the fundamental deficit is in initiative and in strategic use of information, cognitive functions that are strongly dependent on the frontal lobes.

One area of anterior function not highlighted in the cognitive literature on depression is working memory, which is integrally tied to executive functions, including those compromised in depression. Working memory is the portion of memory that temporarily holds information used in the performance of a task. Several studies have localised working memory in the prefrontal cortex (Funahashi, Bruce, & Goldman-Rakic, 1989; Goldman-Rakic, 1987; Jonides et al., 1993); however, other regions have also been identified (for a review, see Raichle, 1993; see also Jonides et al., 1993). Although speculative, if difficulties in working memory interfere with a depressed individual's abilities to keep information about and objectives of a task in mind, deficits in initiative, strategy generation, and cognitive flexibility should ensue. Future research on the neuropsychology of cognitive processing in depression is needed to address whether working memory is impaired in depressed individuals.

Studies that have examined the cognitive characteristics associated with induced pleasant and unpleasant affect also suggest that unpleasant affect is associated with a decrease in the cognitive processes associated with frontal lobe function (for a review, see Isen, 1990). In both adults and children, pleasant affect facilitates creative problem-solving, more flexible thinking, and a more integrated organisation of cognitive material. These findings for pleasant affect are consistent with the reports of compromised cognitive flexibility, problem-solving skills, and organising strategies in depression reviewed earlier. Clore, Schwarz, and Conway (1994) reviewed other evidence on cognitive processing and mood that are highly consistent with the findings for depression and again implicate anterior regions of the brain. They argued that pleasant affect is associated with a focus on heuristic processing (generalisations, information integration, global or top-down processing), more cognitive flexibility, and more novel responses. In contrast, they asserted that sad affect is associated with a reduction in abstract thinking, less cognitive flexibility, and fewer novel responses.

In summary, evidence from a variety of sources suggests that depressed people show biases or deficits on cognitive tasks that involve functions of the anterior brain regions. Given the present state of research, the relative contribution of the left versus the right hemisphere to the executive functions altered in depression is not known. Thus, definitive statements pertaining to the anterior asymmetries hypothesised by our model are not warranted at this time. Compromised executive functions in depression may be related to decreases in bilateral anterior activity, decreased left anterior activity alone, or less left than right asymmetric activity.

Posterior Regions

Depressed people have also been shown to display deficits on tasks associated with cognitive functions of the right posterior regions of the brain. This has been suggested by a rather extensive literature in which neuropsychological research has been carried out with depressed patients. These studies typically administered full or partial neuropsychological batteries and were therefore able to examine relative right- versus left-side differences (e.g. performance of the nondominant compared to the dominant hand on the Tactual Performance Test), which serves as a way to evaluate relative function of the contralateral hemisphere. Such neuropsychological batteries also assess performance on right hemisphere tasks (e.g. judgement of line orientation, three-dimensional constructional praxis, spatial association learning, subtests of the WAIS-R Performance scale) compared to left hemisphere tasks (e.g. vocabulary, verbal learning, subtests of the WAIS-R Verbal scale). Often, indices of abnormality were computed based on multiple tests comparing right versus left hemisphere performance. In general, despite criticisms of limitations in some studies (e.g. Miller, Fujioka, Chapman, & Chapman, 1995), depression has been rather consistently associated with impairments on right but not left hemisphere tasks (Berndt & Berndt, 1980; Flor-Henry, 1976; Flor-Henry, Fromm-Auch, & Schopflocher, 1983; Fromm & Schopflocher, 1984; Goldstein, Filskov, Weaver, & Ives, 1977; Gruzelier, Seymour, Wilson, Jolley, & Hirsch, 1988; Kronfol, Hamsher, Digre, & Waziri, 1978; Miller et al., 1995; Rubinow & Post, 1992; Sapin, Berrettini, Nurnberger, & Rothblat, 1987; Silberman & Weingartner, 1986; Silberman et al., 1983).

Confusions and conflicts arose in this literature in part because authors were attempting to argue that depression was uniquely associated with pathology of one hemisphere or the other. As pointed out by Silberman and Weingartner (1986), evidence was inconclusive regarding relatively greater right hemisphere dysfunction in affective illness, because some neuropsychological studies also found impairments on traditional left hemisphere tasks as well. These concerns can be resolved by considering a caudal distinction as well as a lateral one. Our model predicts that deficits would be present for both hemispheres, but that for the left they would primarily reflect anterior functions, and for the right, primarily posterior functions. Although it is difficult to evaluate comprehensively the caudality of all tasks that have been used in this literature, our model provides a framework for integrating these apparently conflicting findings.

A separate line of research examining depressed children using various neuropsychological tasks has also supplied evidence for posterior right hemisphere dysfunction (for a review, see Brumback, 1988). Brumback and colleagues described a hemisyndrome of right cerebral dysfunction that they argue is commonly associated with depression in children. The description of this syndrome is essentially the same as that described in the literature on nonverbal learning disabilities (Rourke, 1988). Characteristics include left-sided pathognomonic signs indicating right hemisphere dysfunction, large discrepancies between Verbal and Performance IQ in favour of the former, and deficits in visuospatial skills. In addition, children with nonverbal learning disabilities have been shown to have significant difficulties in social functioning and social/emotional adjustment (Rourke, 1988). Many of these problems have been attributed to deficits in the ability to interpret nonverbal information, such as facial expression, voice prosody, and gesture, which is strongly associated with right posterior functioning (e.g. Ahern et al., 1991; Etcoff, 1984a, b; Heilman, Bowers, Speedie, & Coslett, 1984).

Deficits in social functioning have also been extensively described in right brain-damaged patients (see Lezak, 1995). In addition, there is a large literature describing deficits in the ability to express and interpret emotional information after damage to the right hemisphere (for reviews, see Borod, 1993; Bowers, Bauer, & Heilman, 1993), suggesting that the processing of emotional material is an aspect of cognition modulated by posterior right hemisphere regions. Although we are not aware of studies directly linking deficits in emotional information processing with subsequent impairments in social functioning, case studies and clinical observation strongly suggest such a connection (Lezak, 1995).

Few studies have examined emotional information processing in depressed patients from a neuropsychological perspective. However, a number of studies have found depressed patients to display impaired recognition of affect in facial expression (Feinberg, Rifkin, Schaffer, & Walker, 1986; Persad & Polivy, 1993; Rubinow & Post, 1992). These results are consistent with other evidence of right hemisphere deficits in specialised cognitive domains. Clearly, much more research is needed, but it may be that such deficits contribute to the social difficulties exhibited by depressed people.

Although social functioning in depression has not been examined from a neuropsychological perspective, there is a substantial literature demonstrating that depressed people have significant difficulties in relationships, including marital, family, and community interactions (for a review, see Barnett & Gotlib, 1988). Problematic interpersonal behaviours, such as slow and monotonous speaking, poor eye contact, poor timing in verbal interchanges, and use of awkward gestures, are all phenomena of depression (Barnett & Gotlib, 1988) that have been described in patients with right hemisphere damage (Lezak, 1995) and in people diagnosed with nonverbal learning disabilities (Rourke, 1988).

A number of additional aspects of information processing in depressed people and people induced into sad moods may be related to right hemisphere functions, although a great deal of further research is needed. Several authors have argued that the right hemisphere (particularly posterior regions) plays an important role in locating information in a larger social, environmental, and ecological context (for a review, see Heller, 1994; see also Gardner, Brownell, Wapner, & Michelow, 1983; Grossman, 1988). This concept is illustrated in the tendency for patients with right hemisphere damage to attribute specific features of categories in an indiscriminate or inappropriate manner (e.g. drawing a picture of a "potato bush"; Grossman, 1988). Based on findings that right brain-damaged patients tend to violate the overall reality of a verbal narrative in favour of irrelevant or nonsensical details, Gardner et al. argued that the right hemisphere has a unique ability to assess "plausibility", or the likelihood that a particular event is appropriate with reference to a particular context. Remarkably similar to Gardner and colleagues' description of the behaviour of right brain-damaged patients, depressed patients failed to recall the central aspects of a story they were asked to memorise, but recalled more specific items than did controls (Leight & Ellis, 1981). Similarly, Basso, Schefft, Ris, and Dember (1996) found questionnaire-defined depression to be directly associated with a local (i.e. detail) bias and inversely related with a global (i.e configural) bias on a perceptual judgement task of visual processing.

Along these lines, Clore et al. (1994) reviewed evidence that individuals in pleasant mood states are more likely to rely on heuristic processing strategies that simplify information configurations and intuitive decision strategies (more typical of right hemisphere information processing). In contrast, they argued that depressed mood is associated with greater attention to details and more systematic information processing (more typical of left hemisphere information processing), which is consistent with the focus on specific items or details observed in depressed patients (e.g. Basso et al., 1996; Leight & Ellis, 1981).

In other research, Isen, Means, Patrick, and Nowicky (1982) showed that happy people were more likely to rely on simplistic response strategies in that they produced judgements biased by the ease to which exemplars came to mind (e.g. the "availability heuristic"; Tversky & Kahneman, 1973). Happy people were also less attentive to the substance of arguments in persuasion situations, responding more to relatively superficial heuristic cues (Bless, Bohner, Schwarz, & Strack, 1990; Mackie & Worth, 1989; Worth & Mackie, 1987). Consistent with a heuristic as opposed to a systematic strategy, people in a pleasant mood following a success experience responded more quickly and efficiently on a decision-making task (Isen & Means, 1983). Similarly, other researchers have reported that sad individuals were more systematic in information-processing strategies on a visual attention task (Gotlib, McLachlan, & Katz, 1988) and in processing a persuasive message (Bless et al., 1990). Because the posterior right hemisphere is uniquely suited for processing contextual, relational, and global information, whereas the posterior left hemisphere for systematic processing of details, this set of findings is consistent with other evidence that sad or depressed mood is associated with reduced right hemisphere activity.

A number of studies have also examined the tendency to resort to stereotypes in decision making (for a review, see Bodenhausen, in press). These findings suggest that happy people are more likely to engage in this type of information processing than sad or depressed people, which is consistent with the tendency of happy people to resort more to superficial heuristic cues and to attend less to the specific details of a situation than depressed people do. Although few studies have examined this particular information-processing style from a neuropsychological perspective, the available evidence suggests that it is likely to reflect right as opposed to left hemisphere processing (e.g. Zaidel & Kasher, 1989).

The cognitive-processing strategies outlined here correspond rather well with distinctions that have been made between right hemisphere (heuristic) and left hemisphere (detail-oriented) information-processing styles (for a review, see Heller, 1994). Indeed, Clore et al. (1994) presented evidence that depression and sad affect are associated with better performance on some detail-oriented tasks than is pleasant affect, consistent with earlier suggestions that relative activity of a certain brain region could be reflected in superior or inferior performance for tasks specialised to that region or in a bias to process information in a particular way. More specifically, the reduced right posterior activity in depression might result in the tendency to utilise left hemisphere information-processing strategies.

Also addressed in the literature is the possibility that the posterior right hemisphere plays a special role in aspects of arousal (for reviews, see Heller, 1993b; Heller et al., 1997; Wittling, 1995). Furthermore, the right hemisphere may be involved in modulating the responses of the hypothalamic-pituitary-adrenal axis (HPA; Heller, 1993b). Given that abnormalities of the HPA axis are well established in depression, it will be important in future studies of depression to consider further the role of the right hemisphere in various arousal systems (e.g. behavioural arousal, cortisol secretion, autonomic functions; see Heller et al., in press) and potential indirect effects on aspects of cognition such as speed and efficiency of information processing.

In summary, a large number of cognitive findings reported in the literature on depression and pleasant/unpleasant mood states implicate posterior regions of the brain. Furthermore, these findings are highly consistent with the reduced levels of right posterior activity reported for depression in neurodynamic, EEG, dichotic listening, tachistoscopic, and CFT studies.

QUESTIONS FOR FUTURE RESEARCH

In general, it will be important to consider that most tasks depend on more than one brain region for efficient performance. Furthermore, there are often multiple strategies that the brain can call on to carry out a task. Therefore, we will need to disentangle carefully the various cognitive demands imposed by any one task and then examine the relationship between the task components and the patterns of brain activity exhibited by depressed and nondepressed people. For example, the literature on information processing in affective states tends to lump together the concepts of top-down processing, flexible thinking, and capacity for novel responses (see Clore et al., 1994). Our neuropsychological perspective suggests that these concepts are distinguishable. For example, some aspects of top-down processing may rely on specialisation of right posterior regions for processing relational information (i.e. "seeing the forest instead of the trees"), whereas flexible thinking may be more dependent on functions of the anterior regions.

It is also likely that a consideration of the neuropsychological findings will lead us to investigate novel ways in which cognition may be affected in depression. For example, the right parietotemporal region has been found to be specialised for the pragmatic aspects of language (e.g. Hough, 1990; Kaplan, Brownell, Jacobs, & Gardner, 1990). Included among these are the perception of intonation, language contours, conversational conventions, and complex narrative comprehension. One might argue that these aspects of language are critical for successful treatment in conventional forms of therapy, and hence, important to investigate as possibly impaired in depression.

It will also be crucial to deal with the issue of comorbidity. The evidence that patterns of brain activity in left anterior and right posterior regions are discrepant for depression and certain types of anxiety, such as anxious apprehension (e.g. worry) and anxious arousal (e.g. panic) (Heller et al., in press; Heller & Nitschke, in press; Keller et al., submitted), suggests that cognitive concomitants of depression and anxiety may be similarly confounded. Anxiety has been shown to promote less systematic thinking in the processing of persuasive appeals (Baron, Burgess, Kao, & Logan, 1990; Jepson & Chaiken, 1991). This is in direct contrast to the evidence that sad moods are associated with more systematic information-processing and consistent with predictions based on our model that anxious arousal would be associated with increased, as opposed to decreased, right posterior activity (Heller & Nitschke, in press). Similarly, Bodenhausen (in press) reviews evidence that stereotyping is seen more often in anxiety, happiness, and states of heightened arousal, and less often in sadness. If stereotyping, as suggested earlier, is more characteristic of a right hemisphere cognitive style, these data are consistent with the notion that right posterior regions are relatively more active in anxious arousal and happiness, and less active in sadness and depression. Given the high rates of comorbidity reported for depression and anxiety (Akiskal, 1990; Alloy, Kelly, Mineka, & Clements, 1990; Heller et al., 1995; Hiller, Zaudig, & Rose, 1989), it appears imperative that future studies examining the neuropsychology and cognition of depression attend to the possible effects of anxiety.

Finally, it remains unclear as to whether the patterns of brain activity and cognitive function described here as characteristic of depression are present regardless of mood state. As noted earlier, Henriques and Davidson (1990) reported findings consistent with a trait view, whereas other studies find that patterns of brain activity (e.g. Baxter et al., 1989) and performance on cognitive tasks (e.g. Barnett & Gotlib, 1988; Gotlib & Cane, 1987; Kronfol et al., 1978; McCabe & Gotlib, 1993) normalise with remission of depression. The work by Miranda and Persons on dysfunctional attitudes in depression (e.g. Miranda & Persons, 1988; Miranda, Persons, & Byers, 1990) may inform future research in this area. They argued that dysfunctional attitudes are traits (i.e. vulnerability factors) that are mood-state dependent. Specifically, previously depressed people showed more dysfunctional beliefs than never-depressed people when in an induced or naturally occurring unpleasant mood, but not when in a pleasant mood. Similarly, Teasdale and Dent (1987) found that after a negative mood induction, remitted depressives exhibited a memory bias for unpleasant words, whereas subjects with no history of depression did not; without the negative mood induction, no group differences emerged. Following this pattern, previously depressed people might show less left anterior and right posterior activity than never-depressed people only when in an unpleasant mood. It will thus be crucial to measure current mood, as well as depression, in future research examining remitted depression.

In summary, we have made an attempt to formulate a more comprehensive account of cognition in depression from a neuropsychological perspective than has previously been attempted. Although it was not possible to review the entire literature on aspects of cognition in depression, we were able to draw on a variety of sources to suggest that there are clear parallels between the predictions that would be made on the basis of brain activity data and the cognitive characteristics that have been identified in depression. The conceptual integration of the neuropsychological and cognitive concomitants of depression attempted here suggests the need for greater interdisciplinary collaboration between researchers in cognitive neuroscience, clinical psychology, cognitive psychology, and emotion.

REFERENCES

Abramson, L.Y., Alloy, L.B., & Rosoff, R. (1981). Depression and the generation of complex hypotheses in the judgment of contingency. *Behavior Research and Therapy*, *19*, 35–45.

Ahern, G.L., Schumer, D., Kleefield, J., Blume, H., Cosgrove, G., Weintraub, S., & Mesulam, M. (1991). Right hemisphere advantage for evaluating emotional facial expressions. *Cortex*, *27*, 193–202.

Ahern, G.L., Herring, A.M., Tackenburg, J.N., Schwartz, G.E., Seeger, J.F., Labiner, D.M., Weinand, M.E., & Oommen, K.J. (1994). Affective self-report during the intracarotid sodium amobarbital test. *Journal of Clinical and Experimental Neuropsychology*, *16*, 372–376.

Akiskal, H.S. (1990). Toward a clinical understanding of the relationship of anxiety and depressive disorders. In J. Maser & R. Cloninger (Eds.), *Comorbidity in anxiety and mood disorders* (pp. 597–607). Washington, DC: American Psychiatric Press.

Alivisatos, B., & Milner, B. (1989). Effects of frontal or temporal lobectomy on the use of advance information in a choice reaction time task. *Neuropsychologia*, *27*, 495–503.

Allen, J.J., Iacono, W.G., Depue, R.A., & Arbisi, X. (1993). Regional EEG asymmetries in bipolar seasonal affective disorder before and after phototherapy. *Biological Psychiatry*, *33*, 642–646.

Alloy, L.B., Kelly, K.A., Mineka, S., & Clements, C.M. (1990). Comorbidity of anxiety and depressive disorders: A helplessness-hopelessness perspective. In J.D. Maser & C.R. Cloninger (Eds.), *Comorbidity of mood and anxiety disorders* (pp. 499–543). Washington, DC: American Psychiatric Press.

APA (American Psychiatric Association) (1994). *Diagnostic and statistical manual of mental disorders* (4th ed.). Washington, DC: Author.

Banich, M.T. (1997). *Neuropsychology: The neural bases of mental function*. Boston: Houghton Mifflin.

Banich, M.T., Stolar, N., Heller, W., & Goldman, R. (1992). A deficit in right-hemisphere performance after induction of a depressed mood. *Neuropsychiatry, Neuropsychology, and Behavioral Neurology, 5,* 20–27.

Barnett, P.A., & Gotlib, I.H. (1988). Psychosocial functioning and depression: Distinguishing among antecedents, concomitants, and consequences. *Psychological Bulletin, 104,* 97–126.

Baron, R.S., Burgess, M.L., Kao, C.F., & Logan, H. (1990, May). *Fear and superficial social processing: Evidence of stereotyping and simplistic persuasion.* Paper presented at the annual convention of the Midwestern Psychological Association, Chicago, IL.

Basso, M.R., Schefft, B.K., Ris, M.D., & Dember, W.N. (1996). Mood and global-local visual processing. *Journal of the International Neuropsychological Society, 2,* 249–255.

Baxter, L.R., Phelps, M.E., Mazziotta, J.C., Schwartz, J.M., Gerner, R.H., Selin, C.E., & Sumida, R.M. (1985). Cerebral metabolic rates for glucose in mood disorders: Studies with positron emission tomography and fluorodeoxyglucose F 18. *Archives of General Psychiatry, 42,* 441-447.

Baxter, L.R., Schwartz, J.M., Phelps, M.E., Mazziotta, J.C., Guze, B.H., Selin, C.E., Gerner, R.H., & Sumida, R.M. (1989). Reduction of prefrontal cortex glucose metabolism common to three types of depression. *Archives of General Psychiatry, 46,* 243–250.

Beck, A.T. (1967). *Depression.* New York: Hober Medical.

Beck, A.T. (1976). *Cognitive therapy and the emotional disorders.* New York: International Universities Press.

Bench, C.J., Friston, K.J.,Brown, R.G., Frackowiak, R.S.J., & Dolan, R.J. (1993). Regional cerebral blood flow in depression measured by positron emission tomography: The relationship with clinical dimensions. *Psychological Medicine, 23,* 579–590.

Bench, C.J., Friston, K.J., Brown, R.G., Scott, L.C., Frackowiak, R.S.J., & Dolan, R.J. (1992). The anatomy of melancholia: Focal abnormalities of cerebral blood flow in major depression. *Psychological Medicine, 22,* 607–615.

Berndt, D.J., & Berndt, S.M. (1980). Relationship of mild depression to psychological deficit in college students. *Journal of Clinical Psychology, 36,* 868–874.

Bless, H., Bohner, G., Schwarz, N., & Strack, F. (1990). Mood and persuasion: A cognitive response analysis. *Personality and Social Psychology Bulletin, 16,* 331–345.

Bodenhausen, G.V. (in press). Emotions, arousal, and stereotypic judgments: A heuristic model of affect and stereotyping. In D.M. Mackie & D.L. Hamilton (Eds.), *Affect, cognition, and stereotyping: Interactive processes in group perception.* San Diego, CA: Academic Press.

Borod, J.C. (1993). Cerebral mechanisms underlying facial, prosodic, and lexical emotional expression: A review of neuropsychological studies and methodological issues. *Neuropsychology, 7,* 445–463.

Bower, G.H. (1981). Mood and memory. *American Psychologist, 36,* 129–148.

Bower, G.H. (1987). Commentary on mood and memory. *Behavior Research and Therapy, 25,* 443–455.

Bowers, D., Bauer, R.M., & Heilman, K.M. (1993).The nonverbal affect lexicon: Theoretical perspectives from neuropsychological studies of affect perception. *Neuropsychology, 7,* 433–444.

Bruder, G.E. (1995). Cerebral laterality and psychopathology: Perceptual and event-related potential asymmetries in affective and schizophrenic disorder. In R.J. Davidson & K. Hugdahl (Eds.) *Brain asymmetry* (pp. 661–691). Cambridge, MA: MIT Press.

Brumback, R.A. (1988). Childhood depression and medically treatable learning disability. In D.L. Molfese & S.J. Segalowitz (Ed.), *Brain lateralization in children: Developmental implications* (pp. 463–505). New York: Guilford Press.

Cicerone, K., Lazar, R., & Shapiro, W. (1983). Effects of frontal lobe lesions on hypothesis sampling during concept formation. *Neuropsychologia, 21,* 513–524.

Clore, G.L., Schwarz, N., & Conway, M. (1994). Affective causes and consequences of social information processing. In R.S. Wyer & T. Srull (Eds.), *The handbook of social cognition* (2nd ed.) (pp. 323–417). Hillsdale, NJ: Lawrence Erlbaum Associates Inc.

Cohen, B.D., Penick, S.B., & Tarter, R.E. (1974). Antidepressant effects of unilateral electric convulsive shock therapy. *Archives of General Psychiatry, 31,* 673–675.

Conway, M., & Giannopoulos, C. (1993). Dysphoria and decision making: Limited information use in the evaluation of multiattribute targets. *Journal of Personality and Social Psychology, 64,* 613–623.

Davidson, R.J. (Ed.) (in press). *Wisconsin symposium on emotion* (Vol. 1). New York: Oxford University Press.

Davidson, R.J., Chapman, J.P., & Chapman, L.J. (1987). Task-dependent EEG asymmetry discriminates between depressed and non-depressed subjects. *Psychophysiology, 24,* 585.

Davidson, R.J., Chapman, J.P., Chapman, L.J., & Henriques, J.B. (1990). Asymmetrical brain electrical activity discriminates between psychometrically-matched verbal and spatial cognitive tasks. *Psychophysiology, 27,* 528–543.

Davidson, R.J., Ekman, P., Saron, C.D., Senulis, J.A., & Friesen, W.V. (1990). Approach-withdrawal and cerebral asymmetry: Emotional expression and brain physiology: I. *Journal of Personality and Social Psychology, 58,* 330–341.

Davidson, R.J., Schaffer, C.E., & Saron, C. (1985). Effects of lateralized presentations of faces on self-reports of emotion and EEG asymmetry in depressed and non-depressed subjects. *Psychophysiology, 22,* 353–364.

Davidson, R.J., Schwartz, G.E., Saron, C., Bennett, J., & Goleman, D.J. (1979). Frontal versus parietal EEG asymmetry during positive and negative affect. *Psychophysiology, 16,* 202–203.

Decina, P., Sackeim, H.A., Prohovnik, I., Portnoy, S., & Malitz, S. (1985). Case report of lateralized affective states immediately after ECT. *American Journal of Psychiatry, 142,* 129–131.

Deecke, L., Uhl, F., Spieth, F., Lang, W., & Lang, M. (1987). Cerebral potential preceding and accompanying verbal and spatial tasks. In R. Johnson Jr., J.W. Rohrbaugh, & R. Parasuraman (Eds.), *Current trends in event-related potential research (EEG Suppl. 40)* (pp. 17–23). New York: Elsevier.

Deldin, P.J., Keller, J., Gergen, J.A., & Miller, G.A. (submitted). *Right-posterior N200 anomaly in depression.*

Denny, E.R., & Hunt, R.R. (1992). Affective valence and memory in depression: Dissociation of recall and fragment completion. *Journal of Abnormal Psychology, 101,* 575–580.

Doyle, J.C., Ornstein, R., & Galin, D. (1974). Lateral specialization of cognitive mode: II. EEG frequency analysis. *Psychophysiology, 11,* 567–578.

Drevets, W.C., Videen, T.O., Preskorn, S.H., Price, J.L., Carmichael, S.T., & Raichle, M.E. (1992). A functional anatomical study of unipolar depression. *Journal of Neuroscience, 12,* 3628–3641.

Ekman, P., Davidson, R.J., & Friesen, W.V. (1990). The Duchenne smile: Emotional expression and brain physiology: II. *Journal of Personality and Social Psychology, 58,* 342–353.

Etcoff, N.L. (1984a). Perceptual and conceptual organization of facial emotions: Hemispheric differences. *Brain and Cognition, 3,* 385–412.

Etcoff, N.L. (1984b). Selective attention to facial identity and facial emotion. *Neuropsychologia, 22,* 281–295.

Feinberg, T.E., Rifkin, A., Schaffer, C., & Walker, E. (1986). Facial discrimination and emotional recognition in schizophrenia and affective disorders. *Archives of General Psychiatry, 43,* 276–279.

Flor-Henry, P. (1976). Lateralized temporal-limbic dysfunction and psychopathology. *Annals of the New York Academy of Science, 280,* 777–795.

Flor-Henry, P. (1979). On certain aspects of the localization of the cerebral systems regulating and determining emotion. *Biological Psychiatry, 14,* 677–698.

Flor-Henry, P., Fromm-Auch, D., & Schopflocher, D. (1983). Neuropsychological dimensions in psychopathology. In P. Flor-Henry & J. Gruzelier (Eds.), *Laterality and psychopathology* (pp. 59–82). Amsterdam: Elsevier.

Fromm, D., & Schopflocher, D. (1984). Neuropsychological test performance in depressed patients before and after drug therapy. *Biological Psychiatry, 19,* 55–71.

Funahashi, S., Bruce, C.J., & Goldman-Rakic, P.S. (1989). Mnemonic coding of visual space in the monkey's dorsolateral prefrontal cortex. *Journal of Neurophysiology, 61,* 331–349.

Galin, D., & Ellis, R.R. (1975). Asymmetry in evoked potentials as an index of lateralized cognitive processes: Relation to EEG alpha asymmetry. *Neuropsychologia, 13,* 45–50.

Galin, D., Johnstone, J., & Herron, J. (1978). Effects of task difficulty on EEG measures of cerebral engagement. *Neuropsychologia, 16,* 461–472.

Galin, D., Ornstein, R., Herron, J., & Johnstone, J. (1982). Sex and handedness differences in EEG measures of hemispheric specialization. *Brain and Language, 16,* 19–55.

Gardner, H., Brownell, H.H., Wapner, W., & Michelow, D. (1983). Missing the point: The role of the right hemisphere in the processing of complex linguistic materials. In E. Perecman (Ed.), *Cognitive processing in the right hemisphere* (pp. 169–191). New York: Academic Press.

George, M.S., Ketter, T.A., Gill, D.S., Haxby, J.V., Ungerleider, L., Herscovitch, P., & Post, R.M. (1993). Brain regions involved in recognizing facial emotion or identity: An O_{15} PET study. *Journal of Neuropsychiatry and Clinical Neuroscience 5,* 384–394.

George, M.S., Ketter, T.A., Perekh, P., Gill, D.S., Huggins, T., Marangell, L., Pazzaglia, P.J., & Post, R.M. (1994). Spatial ability in affective illness: Differences in regional brain activation during a spatial matching task. *Neuropsychiatry, Neuropsychology, and Behavioral Neurology, 7,* 143–153.

George, M.S., Ketter, T.A., Perekh, P.I., Horowitz, B., Herscovitch, P., & Post, R.M. (1995). Brain activity during transient sadness and happiness in healthy women. *American Journal of Psychiatry, 152,* 341–351.

Gianotti, G. (1972). Emotional behavior and hemisphere side of lesion. *Cortex, 8,* 41–55.

Goldman-Rakic, P.S. (1987). Circuitry of the prefrontal cortex and the regulation of behavior by representation knowledge. In F. Plum & V. Mountcastle (Eds.), *Handbook of physiology* (Vol. 5). Bethesda, MD: American Physiological Society.

Goldstein, S.G., Filskov, S.B., Weaver, L.A., & Ives, J.O. (1977). Neuropsychological effects of electroconvulsive therapy. *Journal of Clinical Psychology, 37,* 187–197.

Gotlib, I.H., & Cane, D.B. (1987). Self-report assessment of depression and anxiety. In P.C. Kendall & D. Watson (Eds.), *Anxiety and depression: Distinctive and overlapping features* (pp. 131–169). Orlando, FL: Academic Press.

Gotlib, I.H., Gilboa, E., & Kaplan, B.L. (in press). Cognitive functioning in depression: Nature and origins. In R.J. Davidson (Ed.), *Wisconsin symposium on emotion* (Vol. 1). New York: Oxford University Press.

Gotlib, I.H., & MacLeod, C. (in press). Information processing in anxiety and depression: A cognitive developmental perspective. In J. Burach & J. Enns (Eds.), *Attention, development, and psychopathology.* New York: Guilford Press.

Gotlib, I.H., McLachlan, A.L., & Katz, A.N. (1988). Biases in visual attention in depressed and non-depressed individuals. *Cognition and Emotion, 2,* 185–200.

Green, J., Morris, R.D., Epstein, C.M., West, P.D., & Engler, H.F.J. (1992). Assessment of the relationship of cerebral hemisphere arousal asymmetry to perceptual asymmetry. *Brain and Cognition, 20,* 264–279.

Grossman, M. (1988). Drawing deficits in brain-damaged patients' freehand pictures. *Brain and Cognition, 8,* 192–213.

Gruzelier, J., Seymour, K., Wilson, L., Jolley, A., & Hirsch, S. (1988). Impairments on neuropsychologic tests of temporohippocampal and frontohippocampal functions and word fluency in remitting schizophrenia and affective disorders. *Archives of General Psychiatry, 45,* 623–629.

Gur, R.C., & Reivich, M. (1980). Cognitive task effects on hemispheric blood flow in humans: Evidence for individual differences in hemispheric activation. *Brain and Language, 9,* 78–92.

Haier, R.J., Siegel, B.V., Jr., MacLachlan, A., Soderling, E., Lottenberg, S., & Buchsbaum, M.S. (1992). Regional glucose metabolic changes after learning a complex visuospatial/motor task: A positron emission tomographic study. *Brain Research, 570,* 134–143.

Hartlage, S., Alloy, L.B., Vazquez, C., & Dykman, B. (1993). Automatic and effortful processing in depression. *Psychological Bulletin, 113,* 247–278.

Heilman, K.M., Bowers, D., Speedie, L., & Coslett, H.B. (1984). Comprehension of affective and nonaffective prosody. *Neurology, 34,* 917–930.

Heller, W. (1990). The neuropsychology of emotion: Developmental patterns and implications for psychopathology. In N. Stein, B.L. Leventhal, & T. Trabasso (Eds.), *Psychological and biological approaches to emotion* (pp. 167–211). Hillsdale, NJ: Lawrence Erlbaum Associates Inc.

Heller, W. (1993a). Gender differences in depression: Perspectives from neuropsychology. *Journal of Affective Disorders, 29,* 129–143.

Heller, W. (1993b). Neuropsychological mechanisms of individual differences in emotion, personality, and arousal. *Neuropsychology, 7,* 1–14.

Heller, W. (1994). Cognitive and emotional organization of the brain: Influences on the creation and perception of art. In D. Zaidel (Ed.), *Neuropsychology* (pp. 271–292). San Diego, CA: Academic Press.

Heller, W., Etienne, M.A., & Miller, G.A. (1995). Patterns of perceptual asymmetry in depression and anxiety: Implications for neuropsychological models of emotion and psychopathology. *Journal of Abnormal Psychology, 104,* 327–333.

Heller, W., & Nitschke, J.B. (in press). The puzzle of regional brain activity in depression and anxiety: The importance of subtypes and comorbidity. *Cognition and Emotion.*

Heller, W., Nitschke, J.B., Etienne, M.A., & Miller, G. A. (in press). Patterns of regional brain activity differentiate types of anxiety.

Heller, W., Nitschke, J.B., & Lindsay, D.L. (1997). Neuropsychological correlates of arousal in self-reported emotion. *Cognition and Emotion, 11,* 383–402.

Henriques, J.B., & Davidson, R.J. (1990). Regional brain electrical asymmetries discriminate between previously depressed and healthy control subjects. *Journal of Abnormal Psychology, 99,* 22–31.

Henriques, J.B., & Davidson, R.J. (1991). Left frontal hypoactivation in depression. *Journal of Abnormal Psychology, 100,* 535–545.

Hertel, P.T. (1994). Depression and memory: Are impairments remediable through attentional control? *Current Directions in Psychological Science, 3,* 190–193.

Hertel, P.T., & Hardin, T.S. (1990). Remembering with and without awareness in a depressed mood: Evidence of deficits in initiative. *Journal of Experimental Psychology: General, 119,* 45–59.

Hertel, P.T., & Rude, S.S. (1991). Depressive deficits in memory: Focusing attention improves subsequent recall. *Journal of Experimental Psychology: General, 120,* 301–309.

Hiller, W., Zaudig, M., & Rose, M. (1989). The overlap between depression and anxiety on different levels of psychopathology. *Journal of Affective Disorders, 16,* 223–231.

Hough, M.S. (1990). Narrative comprehension in adults with right and left hemisphere brain-damage: Theme organization. *Brain and Language, 38,* 253–277.

Isen, A.M. (1990). The influence of positive and negative affect on cognitive organization: Some implications for development. In N.L. Stein, B. Leventhal, & T. Trabasso (Eds.), *Psychological and biological approaches to emotion* (pp. 75–94). Hillsdale, NJ: Lawrence Erlbaum Associates Inc.

Isen, A.M., & Means, B. (1983). The influence of positive affect on decision-making strategy. *Social Cognition, 2,* 18–31.

Isen, A.M., Means, B., Patrick, R., & Nowicky, G. (1982). Some factors influencing decision-making strategy and risk taking. In M.S. Clark & S.J. Fiske (Eds.), *Affect and cognition: The Seventeenth Annual Carnegie Symposium on Cognition* (pp. 243–261). Hillsdale, NJ: Lawrence Erlbaum Associates Inc.

Jaeger, J., Borod, J.C., & Peselow, E.D. (1987). Depressed patients have atypical hemispace biases in the perception of emotional chimeric faces. *Journal of Abnormal Psychology, 96,* 321–324.

Jepson, C., & Chaiken, S. (1991). Chronic issue-specific fear inhibits systematic processing of persuasive communications. *Journal of Social Behavior and Personality, 5,* 61–84.

Johnson, M.H., & Magaro, P.A. (1987). Effects of mood and severity on memory processes in depression and mania. *Psychological Bulletin, 101,* 28–40.

Jonides, J., Smith, E.E., Koeppe, R.A., Awh, E., Minoshima, S., & Mintun, M.A. (1993). Spatial working memory in humans as revealed by PET. *Nature, 363,* 623–625.

Kaplan, J.A., Brownell, H.H., Jacobs, J.R., & Gardner, H. (1990). The effects of right hemisphere damage on the pragmatic interpretation of conversational remarks. *Brain and Language, 38,* 315–333.

Keller, J., Nitschke, J.B., Bhargava, T., Deldin, P.J., Gergen, J.A., Miller, G.A., & Heller, W. (submitted). Neuropsychological differentiation of depression and anxiety.

Klein, D.C., Fencil-Morse, E., & Seligman, M.E.P. (1976). Learned helplessness, depression and the attribution of failure. *Journal of Personality and Social Psychology, 33,* 447–454.

Klein, D.C., & Seligman, M.E.P. (1976). Reversal of performance deficits in learned helplessness and depression. *Journal of Abnormal Psychology, 85,* 11–26.

Kronfol, Z., Hamsher, K.D., Digre, K., & Waziri, R. (1978). Depression and hemispheric functions: Changes associated with unilateral ECT. *British Journal of Psychiatry, 132,* 560–567.

Ladavas, E., Nicoletti, R., Umilta, C., & Rizzolatti, G. (1984). Right hemisphere interference during negative affect: A reaction time study. *Neuropsychologia, 22,* 479–85.

Lang, W., Lang, M., Goldenberg, G., Podreka, I., & Deecke, L (1987). Cerebral potentials preceding and accompanying verbal and spatial tasks. In R. Johnson Jr., J.W. Rohrbaugh, & R. Parasuraman (Eds.), *Current trends in event-related potential research (EEG Suppl. 40)* (pp. 328–334.) New York: Elsevier.

Lauer, R.E., Giordani, B., Boivin, M.J., Halle, N., Glasgow, B., Alessi, N.E., & Berent, S. (1994). Effects of depression on memory performance and metamemory in children. *Journal of the American Academy of Child and Adolescent Psychiatry, 33,* 679–685.

Lee, G.P., Loring, D.W., Meador, K.J., & Brooks, B.B. (1990). Hemispheric specialization for emotional expression: A reexamination of results from intracarotid administration of sodium amobarbital. *Brain and Cognition, 12,* 267–280.

Lee, G.P., Loring, D.W., Meador, K.J., Flanigin, H.F., & Brooks, B.S. (1988). Severe behavioral complications following intracarotid sodium amobarbital injection: Implications for hemispheric asymmetry of emotion. *Neurology, 38,* 1233–6.

Leight, K.A., & Ellis, H.C. (1981). Emotional mood states, strategies, and state-dependency in memory. *Journal of Verbal Learning and Verbal Behaviour, 20,* 251–266.

Levy, J., Heller, W., Banich, M.T., & Burton, L.A. (1983a). Are variations among right-handed individuals in perceptual asymmetries caused by characteristic arousal differences between hemispheres? *Journal of Experimental Psychology: Human Perception and Performance, 9*, 329–359.

Levy, J., Heller, W., Banich, M.T., & Burton, L.A. (1983b). Asymmetry of perception in free viewing of chimeric faces. *Brain and Cognition, 2*, 404–419.

Levy, J., & Trevarthen, C. (1976). Metacontrol of hemispheric function in human split-brain patients. *Journal of Experimental Psychology: Human Perception and Performance, 2*, 299–312.

Lezak, M.D. (1995). *Neuropsychological assessment* (3rd ed.). New York: Oxford University Press.

Luria, A.R. (1966). *Higher cortical functions in man*. New York: Basic Books.

Mackie, D.M., & Worth, L.T. (1989). Processing deficits and the mediation of positive affect in persuasion. *Journal of Personality and Social Psychology, 57*, 27–40.

Martinot, J.L., Hardy, P., Feline, A., Huret, J.D., Mazoyer, B., Attar-Levy, D., Pappata, S., & Syrota, A. (1990). Left prefrontal glucose hypometabolism in the depressed state: A confirmation. *American Journal of Psychiatry, 147*, 1313–1317.

McCabe, S.B., & Gotlib, I.H. (1993). Attentional processing in clinically depressed subjects: A longitudinal investigation. *Cognitive Therapy and Research, 17*, 1–19.

McKee, G., Humphrey, B., & McAdams, D. (1973). Scaled lateralization of alpha activity during linguistic and musical tasks. *Psychophysiology, 10*, 441–443.

Miller, E.N., Fujioka, T.A., Chapman, L.J., & Chapman, J.P. (1995). Hemispheric asymmetries of function in patients with major affective disorders. *Journal of Psychiatric Research, 29*, 173–183.

Mineka, S., & Sutton, S.K. (1992). Cognitive biases and the emotional disorders. *Psychological Science, 3*, 65–69.

Miranda, J., & Persons, J.B. (1988). Dysfunctional attitudes are mood-state dependent. *Journal of Abnormal Psychology, 97*, 76–79.

Miranda, J., Persons, J.B., & Byers, C.N. (1990). Endorsement of dysfunctional beliefs depends on current mood state. *Journal of Abnormal Psychology, 99*, 237–241.

Morgan, A.H., MacDonald, H., & Hilgard, E.R. (1974). EEG alpha: Lateral asymmetry related to task and hypnotizability. *Psychophysiology, 11*, 275–282.

Nitschke, J.B., Heller, W., Etienne, M.A., & Miller, G.A. (1995). Specificity of frontal EEG asymmetry in anxiety and depression during emotion processing (Abstract). *Psychophysiology, 32*, S56.

Ornstein, R., Johnstone, J., Herron, J., & Swencionis, C. (1980). Differential right hemisphere engagement in visuospatial tasks. *Neuropsychologia, 18*, 49–64.

Persad, S.M., & Polivy, J. (1993). Differences between depressed and nondepressed individuals in the recognition of and response to facial emotional cues. *Journal of Abnormal Psychology, 102*, 358–368.

Petridies, M., & Milner, B. (1982). Deficits on subject-ordered tasks after frontal- and temporal-lobe lesions in man. *Neuropsychologia, 20*, 249–262.

Post, R.M., DeLisi, L.E., Holcomb, H.H., Uhde, T.W., Cohen, R., & Buchsbaum, M. (1987). Glucose utilization in the temporal cortex of affectively ill patients: Positron emission tomography. *Biological Psychiatry, 22*, 545–553.

Price, K.P., Tryon, W.W., & Raps, C.S. (1978). Learned helplessness and depression in a clinical population: A test of two behavioural hypotheses. *Journal of Abnormal Psychology, 87*, 113–121.

Raichle, M.E. (1993). The scratchpad of the mind. *Nature, 363*, 583–584.

Rasmussen, C.T., Allen, R., & Tate, R.D. (1977). Hemispheric asymmetries in the cortical evoked potential as a function of arithmetical computations. *Bulletin of the Psychonomic Society, 10*, 419–421.

Robinson, R.G., Kubos, K.L., Starr, L.B., Rao, K., & Price, T.R. (1984). Mood disorders in stroke patients. Importance of location of lesion. *Brain, 107,* 81–93.

Roediger, H.L., III, & McDermott, K.B. (1992). Depression and implicit memory: A commentary. *Journal of Abnormal Psychology, 101,* 587–591.

Roth, D., & Rehm, L.P. (1980). Relationships among self-monitoring processes, memory, and depression. *Cognitive Therapy and Research, 4,* 149–157.

Rourke, B.P. (1988). The syndrome of Nonverbal Learning Disabilities: Developmental manifestation in neurological disease, disorder, and dysfunction. *Clinical Neuropsychologist, 2,* 293–330.

Rubinow, D.R., & Post, R.M. (1992). Impaired recognition of affect in facial expression in depressed patients. *Biological Psychiatry, 31,* 947–953.

Sackeim, H.A., Greenberg, M.S., Weiman, A.L., Gur, R.C., Hungerbuhler, J.P., & Geschwind, N. (1982). Hemispheric asymmetry in the expression of positive and negative emotions: Neurological evidence. *Archives of Neurology, 39,* 210–218.

Sackeim, H.A., Prohovnik, I., Moeller, J.R., Brown, R.P., Apter, S., Prudic, J., Devanand, D.P., & Mukherjee, S. (1990). Regional cerebral blood flow in mood disorders. *Archives of General Psychiatry, 47,* 60–70.

Sapin, L.R., Berrettini, W.H., Nurnberger, J.J., & Rothblat, L.A. (1987). Mediational factors underlying cognitive changes and laterality in affective illness. *Biological Psychiatry, 22,* 979–986.

Savard, R.J., Rey, A.C., & Post, R.M. (1980). Halstead–Reitan category test in bipolar and unipolar affective disorders: Relationship to age and phase of illness. *Journal of Nervous and Mental Disease, 168,* 297–304.

Schaffer, C.E., Davidson, R.J., & Saron, C. (1983). Frontal and parietal electroencephalogram asymmetry in depressed and nondepressed subjects. *Biological Psychiatry, 18,* 753–762.

Silberman, E.K., & Weingartner, H. (1986). Hemispheric lateralization of functions related to emotion. *Brain and Cognition, 5,* 322–353.

Silberman, E.K., Weingartner, H., & Post, R.M. (1983). Thinking disorder in depression: Logic and strategy in an abstract reasoning task. *Archives of General Psychiatry, 40,* 775–780.

Slife, B.D., & Weaver, C.A. (1992). Depression, cognitive skill, and metacognitive skill in problem solving. *Cognition and Emotion, 6,* 1–22.

Smith, J.D., Tracy, J.I., & Murray, MJ. (1993). Depression and category learning. *Journal of Experimental Psychology: General, 122,* 331–346.

Stuss, D.T., & Benson, D.F. (1986). *The frontal lobes.* New York: Raven.

Teasdale, J.D. (1988). Cognitive vulnerability to persistent depression. *Cognition and Emotion, 2,* 247–274.

Teasdale, J.D., & Dent, J. (1987). Cognitive vulnerability to depression: An investigation of two hypotheses. *British Journal of Clinical Psychology, 26,* 113–126.

Tomarken, A.J., & Davidson, R.J. (1994). Frontal brain activation in repressors and non-repressors. *Journal of Abnormal Psychology, 103,* 339–349.

Tomarken, A.J., Davidson, R.J., & Henriques, J.B. (1990). Resting frontal brain asymmetry predicts affective responses to films. *Journal of Personality and Social Psychology, 59,* 791–801.

Tomarken, A.J., Davidson, R.J., Wheeler, R.E., & Doss, R.C. (1992). Individual differences in anterior brain asymmetry and fundamental dimensions of emotion. *Journal of Personality and Social Psychology, 62,* 676–687.

Tversky, A., & Kahneman, D. (1973). Availability: A heuristic for judging frequency and probabilities. *Cognitive Psychology, 5,* 207–232.

Uytdenhoef, P., Portelange, P., Jacquy, J., Charles, G., Linkowski, P., & Mendlewicz, J.

(1983). Regional cerebral blood flow and lateralized hemispheric dysfunction in depression. *British Journal of Psychiatry, 143,* 128–132.

Watkins, P.C., Mathews, A., Williamson, D.A., & Fuller, R.D. (1992). Mood-congruent memory in depression: Emotional priming or elaboration? *Journal of Abnormal Psychology, 101,* 581–586.

Watkins, P.C., Vache, K., Verney, S.P., Mathews, A., & Muller, S. (1996). Unconscious mood-congruent memory bias in depression. *Journal of Abnormal Psychology, 105,* 34–41.

Weingartner, H., Cohen, R., Murphy, D., Martello, J., & Gerdt, C. (1981). Cognitive processes in depression. *Archives of General Psychiatry, 38,* 42–47.

Wheeler, R.E., Davidson, R.J., & Tomarken, A.J. (1993). Frontal brain asymmetry and emotional reactivity: A biological substrate of affective style. *Psychophysiology, 30,* 82–89.

Wittling, W. (1995). Brain asymmetry in the control of autonomic-physiologic activity. In R.J. Davidson & K. Hugdahl (Eds.), *Brain asymmetry* (pp. 305–357). Cambridge: MIT Press.

Worth, L.T., & Mackie, D.M. (1987). Cognitive mediation of positive mood in persuasion. *Social Cognition, 5,* 76–94.

Zaidel, D.W., & Kasher, A. (1989). Hemispheric memory for surrealistic versus realistic paintings. *Cortex, 25,* 617–641.

COGNITION AND EMOTION, 1997, *11* (5/6), 663–673

Cognition and Depression: Issues and Future Directions

Ian H. Gotlib

Stanford University, Stanford, CA, USA

Howard S. Kurtzman and Mary C. Blehar

National Institute of Mental Health, Rockville, MD, USA

As we noted in the Introduction, the papers in this Special Issue represent a wide range of approaches to examining the relation between cognition and depression. They also raise a number of important specific issues. In this epilogue, we will identify and discuss two major issues in some detail that were touched on by almost all of the papers in this Special Issue: the assessment of cognition in depression and the definition and assessment of vulnerability to depression. We will then offer some concluding comments concerning fruitful directions for future research and the need to integrate cognitive paradigms with more biological approaches to the study of depression.

ASSESSMENT OF COGNITION IN DEPRESSION

The examination of cognitive aspects of depression arguably began in earnest almost three decades ago, spurred by the publication of Beck's seminal book on depression in 1967. Beck theorised that depression was associated with a variety of biases in cognitive functioning. More specifically, Beck hypothesised that depressed individuals demonstrate cognitive distortions, manifested as systematic biases or errors in thinking, such as arbitrary inference, selective abstraction, and overgeneralisation. Beck also postulated the existence of a negative "cognitive triad" in depressed individuals: a negative view of themselves, their environments, and the future.

Requests for reprints should be sent to Ian H. Gotlib, Department of Psychology, Bldg. 420, Jordan Hall, Stanford University, Stanford, CA 94305, USA; e-mail: gotlib@psych. stanford. edu.

Neither this paper nor any other in this issue of Cognition and Emotion reflects the official policies or positions of the National Institute of Mental Health or of any other component of the United States Government.

Finally, and perhaps most importantly, Beck hypothesised that depressed persons are characterised by negative schemata, "chronically atypical" cognitive processes that represent "a stable characteristic of (the depressive's) personality" (Kovacs & Beck, 1978, p. 530). Beck posited further that these schemata play a causal role in depression by influencing the selection, encoding, categorisation, and evaluation of stimuli in the environment, which leads subsequently to depressive affect or, in more severe cases, to clinically significant episodes of depression.

Numerous studies have now been conducted examining the cognitive functioning of depressed persons. Much of the early work in this area relied on self-report methodologies to assess the negativity of the content of depressed persons' thoughts, beliefs, and recollections. It is clear from this body of work that depressed individuals report experiencing more negative cognitions than do nondepressed persons (e.g. Dobson & Breiter, 1983; Gotlib, 1984), although it is not clear either that depressed persons are unique in having negative cognitions, or that the content of the negative cognitions of depressed individuals is specifically concerned with depression-relevant themes (e.g. Blackburn, Jones, & Lewin, 1987; Gotlib, Lewinsohn, Seeley, Rohde, & Redner, 1993). The results of investigations examining the putative causal role played by negative cognitions in depression have been less consistent. Indeed, in contrast to these findings demonstrating the concurrent association of negative cognitions and depression, investigators have not been uniformly successful in predicting subsequent levels of depression from the presence of self-reported dysfunctional attitudes. For example, Lewinsohn, Steinmetz, Larson, and Franklin (1981); O'Hara, Rehm, and Campbell (1982); and Rush, Weissenburger, and Eaves (1986) were all unable consistently to predict subsequent depression from earlier scores on the self-report Dysfunctional Attitude Scale (DAS; Weissman & Beck, 1978). Barnett and Gotlib (1988, 1990) found that whereas the interaction dysfunctional attitudes, as measured by the DAS, with social support predicted the severity of future depressive symptoms among women, the interaction of dysfunctional attitudes with negative life events did not. Moreover, the DAS, either alone or in interaction with social support or negative life events, did not predict subsequent depressive symptoms among men. Finally, a number of studies have reported that the elevated level of negative cognitions found in depressed persons decreases following symptomatic recovery, so that remitted depressives do not differ from nondepressed controls (e.g. Hamilton & Abramson, 1983; Hollon, Kendall, & Lumry, 1986; Reda, Carpiniello, Secchiarole, & Blanco, 1985; Silverman, Silverman, & Eardley, 1984).

It appears, therefore, that although researchers have typically found currently depressed persons to be characterised by an elevated level of negative or dysfunctional cognitions, the evidence that these negative thoughts either predict subsequent levels of depression or remain elevated following recovery from a depressive episode is less consistent. There is a critical difficulty with this body of literature, however, which concerns the extent to which an examination of individuals' responses to self-report measures of cognitions actually assess the existence and functioning of the negative cognitive biases and schemata described by cognitive theorists. One aspect of this difficulty, as Gotlib and McCabe (1992) have noted, is that self-report data are clearly subject to the whims and diverse motivations of study participants. This point is particularly important when the participants are depressed subjects, who are often selected initially by their willingness to endorse negative statements on such questionnaires as the Beck Depression Inventory and the Center for Epidemiologic Studies Depression Scale, and are then assessed with respect to their willingness to endorse other negative statements on self-report measures of cognitions. The tautology here is clear.

A more important aspect of this difficulty, however, involves the ability of self-report paper-and-pencil measures to assess schematic functioning. Questionnaires, such as the DAS or the Attributional Style Questionnaire, require subjects to make conscious and deliberate responses to relatively structured and unambiguous stimuli. In contrast, schemata (which these questionnaires were developed to measure) are hypothesised to be structures that operate automatically, largely out of conscious awareness, and that are often activated by ambiguous stimuli. Thus, it is unlikely that responses to self-report questionnaires accurately reflect the operation of "schemata" that are so central to cognitive theories of depression. Given this critical shortcoming of self-report methodologies, researchers have recently begun to use paradigms derived from research in cognitive psychology to assess the information-processing of depressed persons. Indeed, this important trend is reflected in the contribution of several of the papers in this issue.

Segal and Gemar; Gilboa and Gotlib; and Alloy and her colleagues all used tasks that are based in part on paradigms developed in experimental cognitive laboratories. Segal and Gemar were interested in examining the cognitive organisation of self-relevant material in a sample of depressed patients. To do this, they used a cognitive priming procedure in a modified version of the emotion Stroop task. Moreover, to examine the effects of treatment for depression on cognitive organisation, Segal and Gemar assessed depressed patients on this primed Stroop task both before and after the patients' participation in a 20-week course of cognitive behaviour therapy. Gilboa and Gotlib also utilised an emotion Stroop task in their study, but rather than focusing on cognitive organisation, Gilboa and Gotlib assessed attentional biases for positive and negative stimuli in previously depressed individuals following a negative mood-induction procedure. Finally, Alloy and colleagues utilised various judgement and memory tasks to examine the differential processing of positive and negative information by individuals who were classified a priori as cognitively vulnerable or not cognitively vulnerable to depression.

The use of information-processing tasks in these studies permits a much more fine-grained analysis of cognitive functioning in depression than is possible with self-report questionnaires. These tasks, for example, can be used to examine the automaticity of cognitive functioning in depressed persons, as well as the structure and organisation of their cognitive-processing. In contrast to self-report measures, these tasks also allow us to decompose "cognition" into specific processes or stages and relate them more confidently to depression. And, extending Alloy and colleagues' focus on "hopelessness depression", these tasks might also be used to identify and examine various cognitive "subtypes" of depressed individuals. Nevertheless, despite these potential advantages over self-report methodologies, it is important at this relatively early stage of research in this area to recognise that these procedures also have shortcomings. As but one example, there is now reasonable consensus that the emotion Stroop procedure confounds input and output processes, such that it is not clear to what specific cognitive processes biases on this task should be attributed (cf. Gotlib, McLachlan, & Katz, 1988). Thus, it is critical at this juncture that investigators grapple thoughtfully with issues involving exactly what is being assessed on these information-processing tasks and precisely what cognitive processes and mechanisms are being activated and utilised by participants in these studies.

We would like to make two final points concerning the use of information-processing paradigms in studies of depression. First, we believe that these paradigms have considerable potential to make important contributions not only to our understanding of depression, but to our understanding of the nature of the association between cognition and affect more generally. For example, Bower (1981, 1992) has developed and expanded an associative network model of emotion and cognition. Essentially, Bower posits that cognitions (and, in particular, memories) that are repeatedly associated with specific emotions become more accessible when an individual is experiencing that emotion. Teasdale (1988) has hypothesised more specifically that the dysfunctional cognitive processes of persons who are at risk for experiencing depression are activated in part by negative mood. In testing this more specific theory of the nature of the association between cognition and emotion, manipulations such as those described in this issue by Miranda and Gross, by Hertel, and by Eich and his colleagues, have been designed to examine mood-based activation of negative schemata. Moreover, this work, as well as that described by Hertel and by Gilboa and Gotlib, is conceptually rooted in research on nondepressed people. Results of these studies, which suggest that the relation between cognition and mood may have certain distinctive features in individuals with a history of depressive episodes, raise questions about how cognitions and mood are encoded and represented more generally, and clearly have implications for formulations of the association between affect and cognitive functioning. Thus, the domain of cognition and depression can serve as a "testbed" for the development of new theoretical and empirical approaches to study in this complex area.

Second, it is noteworthy that, although the tasks employed in these investigations differ in a number of important respects, they are all used in these studies to examine the processing or organisation explicitly of self-referential material, either by depressed persons or by individuals at risk for becoming depressed. This focus on the self parallels current work in social cognition with "normal" subjects that also examines the functioning of schemata concerning the self. The studies reported in this Special Issue, therefore, should inform this recent work in social cognition. Nevertheless, we should remember that Beck (1967, 1976) postulated the existence of a negative "cognitive triad" in depression: a negative view of the self, the world, and the future. Although this current focus on the self is laudable, it is also important to design and conduct studies examining systematically the generality of this negative cognitive functioning beyond the self, to depressed persons' conceptions of the environment and the future. Moreover, it will also be important to try to understand more generally how particular self-schemata affect daily cognitive and social functioning. In this context, Hertel (this issue) also discusses how biases in the processing of negative self-relevant information may be related to depression-associated difficulties in attentional control for neutral information.

VULNERABILITY TO DEPRESSION

Both clinicians and researchers have long known that depression is a recurrent disorder; over 80% of depressed patients have more than one depressive episode (Clayton, 1983), and over 50% of depressed patients relapse within two years of recovery (cf. Keller, 1985; Keller & Shapiro, 1981). On the basis of these and other similar data, theorists have reasoned that particular individuals are at elevated risk for experiencing depression, and further, that these individuals are characterised by stable factors that increase their vulnerability for experiencing repeated episodes of this disorder. The identification of these factors has been the focus of a number of research programmes. Indeed, the concept of individuals at risk for depression, with "risk" defined in a variety of ways, is also central to several of the papers in this issue.

Perhaps most explicitly, Alloy and her colleagues attempt to classify currently nondepressed individuals as being at elevated risk for depression.

In Alloy's study, risk for depression was defined as evidencing depression-relevant dysfunctional cognitions in the absence of depressed mood. Alloy et al. found that these "cognitively vulnerable" individuals demonstrated biased information-processing similar to that exhibited in other studies by currently depressed persons. This is an important finding that suggests that performance on information-processing tasks might be used to identify individuals at increased risk for becoming depressed. Indeed, a number of investigations have now demonstrated that negative cognitive functioning, as evidenced by biased performance on an information-processing task, is a significant predictor of subsequent emotional distress (e.g. Bellew & Hill, 1991; Brittlebank, Scott, Williams, & Perrier, 1993; MacLeod & Hagan, 1992). It will be important to follow the "high cognitive vulnerability" participants in Alloy and coworkers' study to track rates of depression in order to determine whether this cognitive style places individuals at increased risk for the development of depressive episodes and, equally important, whether the phenomenology of the depression experienced by these cognitively vulnerable individuals differs in significant ways from that reported by other individuals.

Other contributors to this Special Issue have defined risk for depression in different ways. For example, Gilboa and Gotlib examined attentional and memory biases in individuals who were previously depressed. Given that these individuals have had a depressive episode in the past, they are at increased risk as a group for experiencing depression again. Indeed, Miranda and Gross eloquently articulate how these individuals might be vulnerable to experiencing further episodes of depression. Unfortunately, it is unclear whether these biases are risk factors for subsequent depressive episodes or scars of having had an earlier episode of depression. One way that these alternative explanations can be teased apart is for investigators to examine factors that differentially predict first-onset depressive episodes versus remissions: Factors that predict first onsets of depression cannot be scars of a previous episode. Although it is possible that the same factors are involved in both first onsets and remissions, it is also possible that these two types of depression onset are due to different processes. This is an important area for researchers to examine.

Garber and Robinson also describe a study of individuals at elevated risk for developing depression. In this investigation, Gaber and Robinson defined risk as being an offspring of a depressed mother. This definition of high risk as having a parent with major psychopathology has a long tradition, beginning 30 years ago with studies of offspring of schizophrenic parents (e.g. Mednick & Schulsinger, 1968; Sameroff & Zax, 1973). These high-risk studies later began to include control groups composed of children of parents suffering from affective disorders (e.g. Cohler, Gallant, Grunebaum, & Kauffman, 1983; Sameroff, Seifer, & Zax, 1982; Weintraub,

Prinz, & Neale, 1975). Contrary to predictions, the results of these large-scale projects indicated that not only do children of depressed parents demonstrate cognitive and social deficits similar to those exhibited by children of schizophrenic parents, but that the impairment is often greater with depressed parents (see Gotlib & Lee, 1996 for a more detailed review of this literature).

The results of these studies provided the impetus for investigations of children of depressed mothers that examined more systematically children's functioning on variables more explicitly related to depression than schizophrenia (e.g. Hammen et al., 1987: Lee & Gotlib, 1989, 1991). Garber and Robinson's study similarly assesses children of depressed mothers on variables that have been linked theoretically with depression. Indeed, a noteworthy aspect of Garber and Robinson's investigation involves the assessment not only of psychopathology in the children of depressed mothers, but also of the presence of constructs, such as negative cognitions, that are theorised to *lead to* depression in adults. Garber and Robinson found that offspring of depressed mothers, and particularly of more chronically depressed mothers, were characterised by the negative cognitive style that has been found to be characteristic of adult depressives. It is intriguing to consider that the individuals with a negative cognitive style that Alloy and her colleagues identified as being at risk for depression may have a family history of this disorder, in which case a significant proportion of them would have earlier in their lives been the type of children that were studied by Garber and Robinson. Clearly, this is a tentative link that awaits further research, but it does appear to be a promising and integrative direction for study.

CONCLUDING COMMENTS

The papers in this Special Issue of *Cognition and Emotion* on The Cognitive Psychology of Depression represent state-of-the-art theory and research in the area of cognitive functioning and the affective disorders. Although we have focused in this epilogue on the two issues involving the assessment of cognition in depression and the nature of vulnerability to this disorder, these papers clearly raise other issues and highlight important directions for future research. For example, further work is necessary to examine reasons for the discrepancies across studies concerning the existence and nature of depression-related biases in attention and in both implicit and explicit memory (cf. McCabe & Gotlib, 1993; Watkins, Vache, Verney, Mathews, & Muller, 1996; Williams, Watts, MacLeod, & Mathews, 1988). It is likely that this work will involve a systematic assessment of the effects of different mood states, and of comorbidity with anxiety, on information-processing performance. Similarly, Garber and

Robinson delineated the presence of negative cognitions in the offspring of depressed mothers. It will be important to now examine the mechanism of transmission of these cognitions, and to explicate the roles of parent-child interactions, shared environments, and genetics in this transmission of risk (cf. Gotlib & Goodman, in press).

It will also be important now to begin to address the relevance of these cognitive studies for treatment of affective disorders. A key issue in this regard concerns the centrality of cognitive vulnerability to the mood disorders, and its clinical significance in efforts aimed at both treatment and prevention. As yet, there is no systematic, isomorphic, association between the kinds of information-processing biases obtained in these studies and cognitive therapeutic procedures. Certainly, this will be an important focus for future research.

Especially relevant to clinical work, future research might also profitably examine the relation of personality factors to vulnerability to depression. Some investigators are focusing on neuroticism as a risk factor for the onset of depression, a factor that might contribute to the cognitive profile of a subset of depressed individuals (e.g. Nolan, Roberts, & Gotlib, in press), although it is clear that much more work needs to be done in this area. Furthermore, just as comorbidity of depression with anxiety disorders will be of increasing interest, researchers are advised to consider seriously the role of comorbid personality disorders in the onset and maintenance of depression.

Finally, it is clear from Heller and Nitschke's (this issue) paper that there is considerable potential to integrate findings from studies of the cognitive functioning of depressed persons with results of investigations of biological aspects of depression. In particular, recent studies in neuroscience have examined similar issues to those raised in the present set of papers, including memory biases in depressed patients (cf. Heller and Nitschke, this issue) and physiological aspects of affective functioning in depressed persons (e.g. Gotlib, Ranganath, & Rosenfeld, in press; Wheeler, Davidson, & Tomarken, 1993). Earlier, Gotlib and Hammen (1992) called for investigators in the area of depression to begin to integrate cognitive and interpersonal aspects of this disorder; it is now also time that researchers examine intersections of cognitive and biological approaches to the study of depression.

REFERENCES

Barnett, P.A., & Gotlib, I.H. (1988). Dysfunctional attitudes and psychosocial stress: The differential prediction of future psychological symptomatology. *Motivation and Emotion, 12*, 251–270

Barnett, P.A., & Gotlib, I.H. (1990). Cognitive vulnerability to depressive symptoms among men and women. *Cognitive Therapy and Research, 14* 47–61.

Beck, A.T. (1967). *Depression.* New York: Hober Medical.

Beck, A.T. (1976). *Cognitive therapy and the emotional disorders.* New York: International Universities Press.

Bellew, M., & Hill, B. (1991). Schematic processing and the prediction of depression following childbirth. *Personality and Individual Differences, 12,* 943–949,

Blackburn, I.M., Jones, S., & Lewin, R.J.P. (1987). Cognitive style in depression. *British Journal of Clinical Psychology, 25,* 241–251.

Bower, G.H. (1981). Mood and memory. *American Psychologist, 36,* 129–148.

Bower, G.H. (1992). How might emotions affect learning? In S.A. Christianson (Ed.), *Handbook of emotion and memory* (pp. 3–31). Hillsdale, NJ: Lawrence Erlbaum, Associates Inc.

Brittlebank, A.D., Scott, J., Williams, J.M., & Perrier, I.N. (1993). Autobiographical memory in depression: State or trait marker? *British Journal of Psychiatry, 162,* 118–121.

Clayton, P.J. (1983). The prevalence and course of the affective disorders. In J.M. Davis & J.W. Maas (Eds.), *The affective disorders.* Washington, DC: American Psychiatric Press.

Cohler, B.J., Gallant, D.H., Grunebaum, H.U., & Kaufman, C. (1983). Social adjustment among schizophrenic, depressed, and well mothers and their school-aged children. In H.L. Morrison (Ed.), *Children of depressed parents: Risk, identification, and intervention* (pp. 65–98). New York: Grune & Stratton.

Dobson, K.S., & Breiter, H.J. (1983). Cognitive assessment of depression: Reliability and validity of three measures. *Journal of Abnormal Psychology, 92,* 107–109.

Gotlib, I.H. (1984). Depression and general psychopathology in university students. *Journal of Abnormal Psychology, 93,* 19–30.

Gotlib, I.H., & Goodman, S.H. (in press). Children of parents with depression. In W.K. Silverman & T.H. Ollendick (Eds.), *Developmental issues in the clinical treatment of children and adolescents.* New York: Allyn & Bacon.

Gotlib, I.H., & Hammen, C.L. (1992). *Psychological aspects of depression: Toward a cognitive-interpersonal integration.* Chichester: Wiley.

Gotlib, I.H., & Lee, C.M. (1996). Impact of parental depression on young children and infants. In C. Mundt, M.J. Goldstein, K. Hahlweg, & P. Fiedler (Eds.), *Interpersonal factors in the origin and course of affective disorders* (pp. 218–239). London: Royal College of Psychiatrists.

Gotlib, I.H., Lewinsohn, P.M., Seeley, J.R., Rohde, P., & Redner, J.E. (1993). Negative cognitions and attributional style in depressed adolescents: An examination of stability and specificity. *Journal of Abnormal Psychology, 102,* 607–615.

Gotlib, I.H., & McCabe, S.B. (1992). An information-processing approach to the study of cognitive functioning in depression. In E.F. Walker, B.A. Cornblatt, & R.H. Dworkin (Eds.), *Progress in experimental personality and psychopathology research,* (Vol. 15, pp. 131–161). New York: Springer.

Gotlib, I.H., McLachlan, A.L., & Katz, A.N. (1988). Biases in visual attention in depressed and nondepressed individuals. *Cognition and Emotion, 2,* 185–200.

Gotlib, I.H., Ranganath, C., & Rosenfeld, J.P. (in press). Frontal EEG alpha asymmetry depression, and cognitive functioning. *Cognition and Emotion.*

Hamilton, E.W., & Abramson, L.Y. (1983). Cognitive patterns and major depressive disorder: A longitudinal study in a hospital setting. *Journal of Abnormal Psychology, 92,* 173–184.

Hammen, C., Gordon, D., Burge, D., Adrian, C., Jaenicke, C., & Hiroto, D. (1987). Maternal affective disorders, illness, and stress: Risk for children's psychopathology. *American Journal of Psychiatry, 144,* 736–741.

Hollon, S.D., Kendall, P.C., & Lumry, A. (1986). Specificity of depressotypic cognitions in clinical depression. *Journal of Abnormal Psychology, 95,* 52–59.

Keller, M.B. (1985). Chronic and recurrent affective disorders: Incidence, course and influencing factors. In D. Kemali & G. Recagni (Eds.), *Chronic treatments in neuropsychiatry*. New York: Raven.

Keller, M.B., & Shapiro, R.W. (1981). Major depressive disorder: Initial results from a one-year prospective naturalistic follow-up study. *Journal of Nervous and Mental Disease, 169*, 761–768.

Kovacs, M., & Beck, A.T. (1978). Maladaptive cognitive structures in depression. *American journal of Psychiatry, 135*, 525-533.

Lee, C.M., & Gotlib, I.H. (1989). Clinical status and emotional adjustment of children of depressed mothers. *American Journal of Psychiatry, 146*, 478–483.

Lee, C.M., & Gotlib, I.H. (1991). Adjustment of children of depressed mothers: A ten-month follow-up. *Journal of Abnormal Psychology, 100*, 473–477.

Lewinsohn, P.M., Steinmetz, J.L., Larson, D.W., & Franklin, J. (1981). Depression related cognitions: Antecedent or consequence? *Journal of Abnormal Psychology, 91*, 213–219.

Macleod, C., & Hagan, R. (1992). Individual differences in selective processing of threatening information, and emotional responses to a stressful life event. *Behaviour Research and Therapy, 30*, 151–161.

McCabe, S.B., & Gotlib, I.H. (1993). Attentional processing in clinically depressed subjects: A longitudinal investigation. *Cognitive Therapy and Research, 17*, 359–377.

Mednick, S.A., & Schulsinger, F. (1968). Some premorbid characteristics related to breakdown in children with schizophrenic mothers. In D. Rosenthal & S.S. Kety (Eds.), *The transmission of schizophrenia*. Oxford: Pergamon.

Nolan, S.A., Roberts, J.E., & Gotlib, I.H. (in press). Neuroticism and ruminative response style as predictors of change in depressive symptomatology. *Cognitive Therapy and Research*.

O'Hara, M.W., Rehm, L.P., & Campbell, S.B. (1982). Predicting depressive symptomatology: Cognitive-behavioural models and postpartum depression. *Journal of Abnormal Psychology, 91*, 457–461.

Reda, M.A., Carpiniello, B., Secchiaroli, L., & Blanco, S. (1985). Thinking, depression, and antidepressants: Modified and unmodified beliefs during treatment with amitryptiline. *Cognitive Therapy and Research, 9*, 135–143.

Rush, A.J., Weissenburger, J., & Eaves, G. (1986). Do thinking patterns predict depressive symptoms? *Cognitive Therapy and Research, 10*, 225–236.

Sameroff, A.J., Seifer, R., & Zax, M. (1982). Early development of children at risk for emotional disorder. *Monographs of the Society for Research in Child Development, 47* (7), Serial No. 199.

Sameroff, A.J., & Zax, M. (1973). Perinatal charteristics of the offspring of schizophrenic women. *Journal of Nervous and Mental Disease, 157*, 191–199.

Silverman, J.S., Silverman, J.A., & Eardley, D.A. (1984). Do maladaptive attitudes cause depression? *Archives of General Psychiatry, 41*, 28–30.

Teasdale, J.D., (1988). Cognitive vulnerability to persistent depression. *Cognition and Emotion, 2*, 247–274.

Watkins, P.C., Vache, K., Verney, S.P., Mathews, A., & Muller, S. (1996). Unconscious mood-congruent memory bias in depression. *Journal of Abnormal Psychology, 105*, 34–41.

Weintraub, S., Prinz, R., & Neale, J.M. (1975). Peer evaluations of the competence of children vulnerable to psychopathology. *Journal of Abnormal Child Psychology, 6*, 461–473.

Weissman, A.N., & Beck, A.T., (1978). *Development and validation of the dysfunctional attitude scale: A preliminary investigation*. Paper presented at the annual meeting of the American Educational Research Association, Toronto, Ontario, Canada.

Wheeler, R.E., Davidson, R.J., & Tomarken, A.J. (1993). Frontal brain asymmetry and emotional reactivity: a biological substrate of affective style. *Psychophysiology, 30,* 82–89.

Williams, J.M.G., Watts, F.N., MacLeod, C., & Mathews, A. (1988). *Cognitive psychology and emotional disorders.* Chichester: Wiley.

Subject Index

www.ingramcontent.com/pod-product-compliance
Ingram Content Group UK Ltd.
Pitfield, Milton Keynes, MK11 3LW, UK
UKHW020351010325
455677UK00021B/393